MARKETS, UNCERTAINTY A

A History of the Introduction of Uncertainty into Economics

Markets, Uncertainty and Decision-making

A History of the Introduction of Uncertainty into Economics

(Markten, Onzekerheid en Besluitvorming:
Een geschiedschrijving over de introductie van
onzekerheid in de economische wetenschappen)

PROEFSCHRIFT

ter verkrijging van de graad van doctor
aan de Erasmus Universiteit te Rotterdam
op gezag van de Rector Magnificus
Prof.dr. P.W.C. Akkermans M.Lit
en volgens het besluit van het College van Dekanen.

De openbare verdediging zal plaatsvinden op
donderdag 7 oktober om 13.30 uur.

door

Engelbertus Franciscus Maria Wubben
geboren te 's-Gravenzande

promotiecommissie

promotor: Prof. dr. J.H.P. Paelinck
co-promotor: Dr. A. Vandevelde
overige leden: Prof. dr. J. Koerts
                  Prof. dr. N.B. de Marchi

Ter nagedachtenis aan mijn vader

In memory of my father

The book is no. 55 of the Tinbergen Institute Research Series. This series is established through cooperation between Thesis Publishers and the Tinbergen Institute. A list of books which already appeared in the series can be found in the back.

ACKNOWLEDGEMENTS

If it is true that one gains a better understanding of visions and techniques by adopting different perspectives with regard to the same subject matter, then the structure of my research has provided me with ample opportunity for becoming acquainted with the idiosyncrasies of a number of economic standpoints. When writing a thesis which involves a number of schools of economic thought, one enjoys the additional pleasure of discussing a number of subjects with a variety of persons who together present a spectrum of implicit and explicit opinions. Both pleasures were mine in the course of this research. The result was a continuous learning process in an intellectual alchemy which may not have produced the philosopher's stone vis-à-vis uncertainty, but hopefully paved the way towards it.

This book could not have been written if it was not for the faith, time and attention which Toon Vandevelde invested in me ever since we discussed the subject at an embryonic level some five years ago. He took upon himself the task of, on the one hand, preventing me from taking too much hay on my rack, while, on the other, regularly directing me back to the wider themes within science.

Furthermore, I would like to thank Professor J.H.P. Paelinck for his contribution as supervisor during this research. In view of our faculty's failure to fill the chair in the history of economic thought, his willingness to jump into the breach has been most appreciated. Professor N.B. de Marchi was always ready to supply critical observations and stimulating remarks.

I am indebted to H. van den Berg, J. van Daal, R. Dullaart, B. Elzas, R. Emmett, S. Frowen, G. Hodgson, B. Hamminga, G. Harcourt, H. Keizer, T. Lawson, A. Leen, A. Miller, H. de Swart, J. Runde, S. Tijs, J. Vromen, R. van Zijp, and those others who should have been mentioned here, for their valuable comments, suggestions and advice. I alone am responsible for the end result.

Finally I must mention my cherished memories of lively discussions with fellow-researchers and staff at the Tinbergen Institute.

I do not know how to thank friends and family for their enduring support during my research. The fact that I could rely on them in both good and bad periods was a great help to me.

TABLE OF CONTENTS

1: UNCERTAINTY AND ECONOMICS: INTRODUCTION

'Uncertainty is one of the fundamental facts of life.'

(Knight 1921, 347)

'Uncertainty is an intimate dimension of our daily lives.
For some, it is the zest of life. ... Yet, for others,
uncertainty is the curse of life.'

(Drèze 1985, 322)

1.1 Introduction

The credit for being the first economist to distinguish between risk and uncertainty commonly goes to Frank Hyneman Knight (1885-1972). His *Risk, Uncertainty, and Profit*, published in 1921, was soon acknowledged as a major contribution to economic theory, especially for introducing the concept of uncertainty into economics (Mitchell 1922, 274). However, notwithstanding the warnings contained in Knight's work, which have fundamental implications for economics, many economists have nevertheless acted as if they could theorize without considering uncertainty and/or were able to deal with uncertainty. Most of the attempts to pay lip service to Knightian uncertainty have hitherto been unsatisfactory: uncertainty was either not taken seriously enough, was pressed into a probabilistic straightjacket, or it was plainly neglected. To conflate uncertainty with risk and represent them by means of probabilities is evidence of a fundamental misunderstanding of uncertainty tantamount to an illusion of knowledge, resulting in false self-confidence among the economists concerned. Economists who tried seriously to understand uncertainty and introduce it into economics may be found in various schools of economic thought.

It is not surprising that recent economic thought has seen various, and in fact often conflicting, opinions about how to analyse and appraise uncertainty: (1) New Classical economists bluntly exclude uncertainty from economics: 'In cases of uncertainty, economic reasoning will be of no value.' (Lucas 1981, 224); (2) Microeconomists have developed several techniques to fit uncertainty functionally into a variety of models: 'This may be an appropriate moment to point out that many authors -myself included- have come to use the term "uncertainty" rather loosely as a blanket term meaning "the lack of certainty".' (Hey 1979, 41). (3) In contrast to these rather insubstantial opinions, the theorists of important groups of economists, such as Austrian, Post-Keynesian and Game-theory economists, take Knight's position seriously and appreciate uncertainty as an important fact of (economic) life and of crucial importance for scientific research.

In order to support our position that uncertainty cannot be ignored, we can first examine the view of uncertainty often alluded to: Knight's understanding of uncertainty. Knight defines uncertainty as '... the fact of ignorance and necessity of acting upon opinion rather than knowledge.' (Knight 1921, 268). The decisive factor separating risk and uncertainty is thought to be measurability. The term uncertainty must be restricted '...to cases of the non-quantitative type' (ibid., 20), that is when there '...is *no valid basis of any kind* for classifying instances.' (ibid., 225). Risk is defined as the presence of an *a priori* or an empirically-based probability distribution. According to Knight, economic situations in which calculations can be based on general principles, that is on *a priori* probabilities, rarely exist in the real economic world (ibid., 215). Furthermore, in situations of uncertainty, the uniqueness of the situation in question precludes the possibility of a distribution of outcomes (ibid., 226, 233). No sufficiently homogeneous groups can be formed in such cases to make possible an empirical determination of the occurrences of alternatives: 'The conception of an objectively measurable probability or chance is simply inapplicable.' (ibid., 231). In situations of uncertainty there are neither *a priori* probabilities nor empirically-based probabilities.

This understanding of the term uncertainty underpins our research. The profitability of producing and selling cans of onion soup is at most risky, as is the waiting time at traffic-lights. But the profitability of an investment in a new generation of micro-processors is highly uncertain, as is the price of Brent-oil ten years hence. To repeat the point in other terms, with uncertainty we neither have general principles about the results at our disposal and nor has relevant experience yet been acquired.

That uncertainty is generic in economic life is most evident when we exclude uncertainty from analysis. When uncertainty is ignored, men will act like automatons, without personal motivation or surprises, and with a blurred view of the distinction between the future, the present and the past. Knight argues that in such situations there are no deliberate decisions being made or profits being realized. In an efficiently operating economy there will be no profits in an environment of certainty. Any risks which may be present can be insured against and merely result in extra costs. All inputs are being paid for according to their productive capacity. In the absence of uncertainty, the rate of return must be uniform in all directions. The introduction of time will, in principle, not result in imperfect competition and profits. Predictable future changes in supply and demand by themselves will not result in profits, losses or managerial problems (Knight 1921, 268). Such results are conditional upon the presence of uncertainty.

Above and beyond the importance of uncertainty in economic endeavours, there is a fundamental point to be made in relation to any economic scientific research. For even when monopoly conditions are absent uncertainty appears to underlie the differences between '... the conditions which theory is compelled to assume and those which exist in fact.' (ibid., 51). To what extent can a social scientist actually understand human life and endeavours? The forward-looking character of the economic process is at the bottom of this uncertainty problem in economics (ibid., 237-238). Because uncertainty relates to the troublesome business of foreseeing the future, it seems to escape scientists time and time again; '... the existence of a problem of knowledge depends on the future being different from the past, while the possibility of the solution of the problem depends on the future being like the past.' (ibid., 313). It may, accordingly, appear impossible to encompass the existence of uncertainty itself in a theory. Our powers of dealing with our total environment through knowledge are highly inadequate, making perfect knowledge of, and anticipation for, future developments impossible. Therefore, it is to be concluded that when scientists approach changes simply by regarding them as following known laws, they explain uncertainty by explaining it away (ibid., 313).

One of the main objects of the present work is to reveal that the specific interpretation of uncertainty carries significant implications for scientists' claims about discussing reality in theoretical terms. To recognize the importance of uncertainty is to recognize an important boundary in the social sciences. Knight, and other eminent economists such as L. von Mises (hereafter called Mises), Hayek, J.M. Keynes (hereafter called Keynes), Lachmann, Shackle, and Morgenstern, try to discuss uncertainty while remaining painfully aware of the tensions between fostering science and applying theories to singular situations. Economists may be able to outline some critical relations and underlying structures, build coherent theories and closed models, but in the final analysis human beings go their own way irrespective of, or learning from, the models they are supposed to follow.

This insight, which will surface time and time again in this study, is epitomized in the following speculation by Knight: 'Given the inescapable fact that it took several millennia to teach man that inanimate objects have no choice and behave according to the simple principles of Newtonian mechanics, how long will it take to teach man that he does have choice and does not behave according to any such simple sets of principles.' (Perlman 1990, 14). The fact that Newtonian mechanics is now shaking on its pedestal only adds to the importance of Knight's remark.

The ensuing research question to be addressed in this thesis is: how has uncertainty been introduced into economics and what are the consequences for decision-making? To facilitate the writing of an overview, we intend to delineate various economic schools of thought. We will pursue an historical approach highlighting the literature assessing the consequences of uncertainty for individual economic decision-making in a market economy.

1.2 Putting uncertainty back onto the agenda

We intend to show, largely by means of historical overviews, that uncertainty has been a hot issue among a large number of frank and broad-minded economists in various schools of economic thought. Knight (1921) serves as a suitable starting point, because uncertainty seems to become manifest in economic research during that interwar period. Our account on mainstream economics in general, and in particular the chapters two and three, reflects the scientists' urge to find optimal structures and mechanisms in the economy, to build closed theories, and to present single-valued results. The inevitable conclusion is that, if economics is to become more realistic, regardless of any detriment to technocratic precision, and if economic analyses are meant to delineate economic developments and human choices, then uncertainty should be an integral element of the economist's outlook on the economy. In this respect, this study examines the need to put uncertainty back onto the economist's agenda.

In order to construct an argument which highlights the importance of uncertainty for economic research, we will review how uncertainty has hitherto been discussed in economics. We do not intend to speculate about which introduction of uncertainty was more or less successful, because dissimilar problems may require dissimilar concepts of uncertainty theories.

Suffice it to say that in our view the Austrian and Post-Keynesian views on uncertainty are the most appealing among the viewpoints to be discussed, if only because these positions are more open with respect to uncertainty and most willing to acknowledge the related boundary on theorizing. It will argued that discarding or downgrading uncertainty is to the detriment of economics.

The concept of uncertainty may be qualified by the adjective external when uncertainty can be attributed to one's environment. Similarly, internal uncertainty refers to uncertainty which may be attributed to one's state of mind (Tversky and Kahneman, 1982). Furthermore, there is also a distinction to be made between endogenous uncertainty and exogenous uncertainty. Uncertainty is an inherent characteristic of the situation in the case of endogenous uncertainty, and not in the case of exogenous uncertainty. Coincidences, for example, may be classified as exogenous, external uncertainty, while ignorance is an example of exogenous, internal uncertainty. The purchasing of a house changes both the purchaser's relation to the situation and the situation itself. This is called an example of endogenous, internal uncertainty.

Uncertainty creates decision-making problems, and necessitates the use of, for example, non-conventional, customary or habitual practices. It is partly due to the existence of uncertainties that one cannot always simply optimise at the margin and identify some single best outcome. The future is uncertain, if only because of unknown technical and political developments. Although one may use logical or mathematical tools to grasp some features of the future, human beings create the future and can also frustrate analysis with their often capricious and sometimes automaton-like behaviour. Agents often apply heuristics to scrutinise information, somehow identify a general pattern, form expectations and come to a resolution. Examples of such related heuristics would be: concentrating attention on the information gathered in the form of hard statistics, converting price-information into a monthly average, extrapolating the trend of price changes affecting inputs, and using a rule of thumb for acceptable maximum prices, before acting according to the result of the calculation. The presence of uncertainty will thus provide a reason for following social usages, or, broadly speaking, create an institution. By providing stable patterns of behaviour, institutions serve to ameliorate the unboundedness of the economic system (O'Driscoll and Rizzo 1985, 6).

An institution is '... a verbal symbol which .. describes a cluster of social usages. It connotes a way of thought or action of some prevalence and permanence, which is embedded in the habits of a group or the customs of a people. .. Institutions fix the confines of and impose form upon the activities of human beings. .. The function of each [institution; EW] is to set a pattern of behaviour and to fix a zone of tolerance for an activity or a complement of activities.' (Hamilton 1932, 84). Thus, an institution can be identified by three characteristics: (1) a group of persons; (2) common behaviour patterns; (3) explanations or justifications of activities or rules (Neale 1987, 1182; Gordon 1984; Frey 1989).

When studying institutions we can find certain patterns, but not laws, of behaviour. The essence of an institution may lie in an accidental, an arbitrary or a conscious action (Hamilton 1932). But, '...as more or less stabilized forms of behaviour they tend to assume an autonomy of their own and mould human conduct.' (Kapp 1968, 3).

Our research is focused on the discussions about uncertainty within economics and the consequences of uncertainty for decision-making. The study should provide the reader with an historical overview of ideas, concepts and theories, including methodological questions, concerning economic uncertainty and its influence on decision-making as such ideas are dealt with, or ignored as the case may be, in major schools of economic thought. Attention is concentrated on those writings within economics in which uncertainty and its consequences are discussed. Furthermore, just as there is no need for a wine-taster to swallow the wine to discover the critical differences in taste, we need no great degree of exhaustiveness when presenting the most important positions and the shifts in them.

Methodological themes will frequently command attention, if only because of the troublesome relation between the conditions of theory and facts of economic practices. Therefore, whenever they arise, relevant questions relating our subject of research to such concepts as time, rationality, stability, and information will be addressed. However, this thesis is not in the field of the philosophy of science, mathematics or econometrics. In passing, we will discuss mutual influences among schools and the results of empirical tests of the presented theories. Such investigations are, however, subsidiary to the presentation of the evolution of argumentations.

1.3 Structure of the study

This overview presents ideas, concepts, and theories from several schools of economic thought. The various chapters are ordered as much as possible according to a specific style or school of economic thought. For the purpose of this study, the term style is to be preferred to the term school. A style may first and foremost be recognized by the dominant problem, the vision or the ideals which one wants to realize, and the techniques that are used (Zuidema 1986, 189). A style creates order in the minds of those involved. Moreover, a style creates order in the theoretical compositions, and it creates a tradition through the related scientific learning processes. A number of styles may co-exist. Because classifications are all somehow disputable, the most useful, i.e. suitable, classification may be introduced. It is no longer tempting to merely conduct a search for the largest common denominator, and run the risk of neglecting deviating opinions within a school. Furthermore, the homogeneity implied when discussing "schools" of economic thought artificially stresses the differences between different groups of scientists. For example, it will be stated in this thesis that fruitful mutual exchanges of thought take place between scientists committed to different sets of ideals. Finally, neither Schumpeter (1954) nor Blaug (1985) in fact portray schools as closed groups of authors which comprise a master and his students, which subscribe to a closed theoretical pattern with which they typify the world, and which tend to generate (over-) standardized solutions (Zuidema 1986, 184-5). Where the term school is used in this thesis it should not necessarily be taken to imply anything more than the term style of economic thought.

In this thesis we would like to concentrate on the following schools within economic thought: Mainstream economics, including New Classical Economics as its radical variant with regard to discussing uncertainty; Austrian economics; (Post-) Keynesian economics; and finally, Economic Game Theory. The prime reason for discussing a specific school of economic thought is to identify that school's characteristic way of paying attention to uncertainty, or not, as the case may be.

It has already been made clear that Knight considers the distinction between the simplified assumptions of economics and those of complex facts as crucial in understanding uncertainty and the unplanned profits/losses which may result (Knight 1921, 5, 30, 51). In chapter two, it is argued that the concept of uncertainty was finally fundamentally transformed in the interwar mainstream economic writings. By the close of this period, the concept of uncertainty had changed and acquired the meaning that one will learn more about the real distribution of the different outcomes as the future draws in. This position foreshadows discussions after the Second World War, and chapter three scrutinizes those developments. The relation between theory and facts was then discussed as trading upon probabilistically-ordered subjective opinions or beliefs about risk situations, as in Expected Utility Theory, or about possible future situations, as in Arrow-Debreu models. New Classical economics takes the implicit final step and bluntly presumes that people are aware of some "real" distribution of future outcomes. That economic uncertainty was effectively removed from mainstream economics is probably due to mathematical refinements, closed conceptions of the economic world and specific experimental designs.

In sharp contrast to these positions reflecting a reluctance to incorporate uncertainty in the analysis, economists within the Austrian School of economics take uncertainty as a positive indicator of entrepreneurial actions building the heterogeneous economy. The fact that the boundaries to the scientific understanding of how human endeavours are actually correlated, and the way in which they result in both expected and unexpected results, is regarded to be of prime importance. The self-contained person is considered to find the opportunities present in heterogeneous situations. Subjectivity of expectations induced by uncertainty finally requires the Austrians to qualify their uniquely positive attitude to uncertainty. This generally positive attitude towards uncertainty will be discussed in chapter four of the study. However, uncertainty may be thought of as opening perspectives for individuals in an evolving economy, as well as troublesome because groups may change their views on the possible ranges of future outcomes overnight. An external party may sometimes be necessary to help to stabilize opinions and correct undesirable results of local decision-making. The extensively discussed and diversely characterized factor of uncertainty carries a mixed connotation for Post-Keynesian economists, and will be discussed in chapter five. That chapter starts and ends with an assessment of the writings of Keynes and is intended to present the ensuing evolution in addressing uncertainty in Post-Keynesian thought. Here it is not so much the heterogeneity of situations but rather the uniqueness in time of decisions which is the subject of discussion. The different positions return in another guise in chapter six where economic game-theoretic writings are presented. There, in contrast to chapters two and three, the strategic aspect of interactions is brought to the fore. The closing chapter will include a taxonomy of the various positions adopted, vis-à-vis uncertainty.

Certain recent developments in economic theory, which have a bearing on the deployment of concepts of uncertainty, must remain outside the scope of this thesis. While we watch with interest developments in the theory of Fuzzy SubSets, Neo-Institutionalism and New-Institutionalism, and Evolutionary Game Theory, it is too early to fit them into the historical contest on which this thesis is constructed. Because this thesis traces the main developments in theorizing about uncertainty since Knight (1921) there is unfortunately not enough scope to do justice to these approaches.

Having presented the essential features of Knight's view on uncertainty we naturally proceed to trace the reception of his ideas during the interwar period. Knight (1921) played the role of a powerful catalyst. In order to find out whether the stimulus was productive we will now direct our attention to mainstream economic views in the interwar period.

2: Mainstream Economics and Uncertainty: The Interwar Period

'If we are to understand the workings of the economic
system we must examine the meaning and significance
of uncertainty.'

(Knight 1921, 199)

2.1 Introduction

Knight became known as the man who introduced the distinction between
uncertainty and risk, and used this innovation to break the deadlock on the
theory of profit. He achieved the status of a distinguished economist soon
after the publication of *Risk, Uncertainty and Profit*. However, one should not
therefore jump to the conclusion that, by the end of the interwar period
economics was coping effectively with both scarcity and uncertainty (Shackle
1967, 6-7). It will be shown in this chapter that one can describe the trend
in mainstream economics in the interwar decades as the submergence of
uncertainty! (Rowley and Hamouda 1987, 45) Within a few years of Knight's
publication, economists were distorting his distinction between risk and
uncertainty. Next, it was questioned whether the subject of uncertainty should
claim such a large part of the economist's attention; uncertainty thus became
a side issue. Finally, the Knightian concept of uncertainty was shunted into
a scientific railway siding. By the end of the interwar period, although
uncertainty itself was still alive in the minds of mainstream economists, in
that it carried negative connotations for them and they spoke of a "mere"
local influence of its consequences, its meaning had fundamentally changed.

2.2 Uncertainty before Knight

While Knight was the first economist to posit a distinction between risk and
uncertainty, several of the issues he explicitly brought to the fore had already
been taken up by some of his predecessors. The accents in this preparatory
work concur with the opinion prevailing by the end of the nineteenth century,
and probably facilitated the positive reception given to Knight's thesis. 'Risk
is universal', declares J. Haynes, in 1895, '...we abide in a perpetual state of
risk' (Haynes 1895, 410). By the end of that century many scientists were

rejecting strict determinism, but held onto the conviction that the laws of nature are probabilistic, thereby preserving the idea of individual freedom of conduct under a collectively determined flow of events (Hacking 1990, 116; Knight 1921, 221). As C.S. Pierce would have is: 'change itself pours in at every avenue of sense: it is of all things the most obtrusive' (Pierce quoted in Hacking 1990, 200).

In economic life, change and uncertainty are pre-eminent in entrepreneurial activities, the entrepreneurs being in pursuit of gain. Therefore, in search of a satisfactory explanation for profit and loss, writers on profit-theory laid bare some of the relations between change, risk, uncertainty. In order to add depth to the original perspective presented in Knight (1921), we will first outline a dynamic theory of profit, a risk theory of profit and a combination of the two. Although some steps are taken towards constructing the type of theory presented in Knight (1921), it will become apparent that the authors involved hardly discussed uncertainty as such; neglecting its origins, its theoretical representation, and its consequences. Knight himself evaluated a number of such theories but rejected them all. The grounds are further prepared by Schumpeter's publication on the theory of economic development, which is next to be introduced.

When discussing theories of profit, one is virtually obliged to consider J.B. Clark's dynamic theory of profit, with its stress on the importance of innovation-induced changes in the method of production. The introduction of new processes introduces dynamic change and results in a temporary profit for the entrepreneur, which is subsequently diffused among all members of society. The entrepreneurial incentive of the potential profit brings about such innovations. The entrepreneur He is the rightful first claimant of the result, because he coordinates the elements furnished by others (Clark 1893, 46). Knight, however, would deprecate this profit theory, because it seems to overlook the distinction between foreseeable changes and unforeseeable changes. In as far as there is '...general foreknowledge of progressive changes no losses and no chance to make profits will arise out of them.' (Knight 1921, 36). In the event, Clark's complete dynamic economics was never written (Hopkins 1933, 63).

In developing a theory of profit, one finds F.B. Hawley advancing a theory based on risk. What he calls the assumption of risk, better known as risk-taking, is supposed to be the distinguishing function of the entrepreneur (Hawley 1901, 75). His reward is profit, which is a residue, and its amount is supposed to be uncertain until a transaction has been completed. Hawley in fact treats uncertainty and risk as interchangeable concepts, as he does risk, profit and residue (Hawley 1901, 88-9). He fails to distinguish between the determinate risk and the indeterminate uncertainty (Knight 1921, 46).

J. Haynes elaborated upon a combination of the dynamic and the risk approach, when discussing the difference between "static risk" and "dynamic risk". If there is any doubt with regard to damage or loss, there is risk. While the distinguishing characteristic of risk is the fortuitous element, the boundary cases are said to be certainty of harm and certainty of security (Haynes 1895, 409). Static risks, e.g., storms, earthquakes, early deaths, bad debts, and fires, are present even in a stationary state of society. Dynamic risks are due to dynamic changes. The categories involved are changes in society's wants, and in the methods of production (Haynes, 1895, 412-3). The availability of statistics made it possible to support the position that what an insurance policy holder may regard as either an uncertainty or a risk, is virtual certainty to the insurer (Haynes, 1895, 442-3). However, probability linked to outcomes, incorporating the above-mentioned boundary cases, assumes a homogeneity of outcomes.

Parallels between the explicit and implicit ideas expressed in Schumpeter's *The Theory of Economic Development* (1911) and in Knight's *Risk, Uncertainty and Profit* (1921) are remarkable. For example, both relate uncertainty to the imperfections of theories based on marginalistic optimisation, and to profits. In our view, the similarity of atmosphere reflected in the themes found in these two books justifies extended treatment. This remains the case despite Knight making a number negative observations on Schumpeter's book.

The prime subject addressed by Schumpeter (1911) is the analysis of the process of economic change. Economic development is defined as '...such changes in economic life as are not forced upon it from without but arise by its own initiative from within' (Schumpeter 1911, 1934, 63). To put it somewhat crudely, we understand the object of such research not to be changes at the level of the weather or product specifications, but rather on the scale of the introduction of the railway, the car, and so on.

Schumpeter was clearly dissatisfied with the theoretical apparatus of circular flow analysis because it is fundamentally unable to explain the purely economic aspects of discontinuous changes (ibid., 61). The contrast between a-temporal equilibrium models and theories of economic development is considered to be fundamental because static models exclude from theory the possibility of change '...which so displaces its equilibrium point that the new one cannot be reached from the old one by infinitesimal steps. Add successively as many mail coaches as you please, you will never get a railway thereby' (ibid., 64n1). Circular flow analysis investigates '...given processes already in working order' (ibid., 36).

An innovative activity alters the data of the economic system, changes the traditional course of economic life itself, and starts an irregular movement of the economy towards a new, but yet unclear, stable position. Accurate calculations are, therefore, impossible: 'many things must remain uncertain, still others are only ascertainable within wide limits, some can perhaps only be *guessed*' (ibid., 85). Incalculable and irregular events, non-routine problems and speculation may occur at any moment.

More specifically, the concept of adapting to new combinations covers the following five cases: (1) the introduction of totally new products or of products of a new quality, (2) the introduction of a new, i.e. not yet experimentally-proven, method of production, (3) the opening up of a new market, (4) the securing of a new source of supply of raw materials or intermediate products, and (5) the restructuring of an industry (Schumpeter 1911 1934, 66).

The uncertainty about the future is caused by entrepreneurial activities. The entrepreneur is defined as the actor who introduces new combinations of inputs (ibid., 74-5, 83). An entrepreneur is, in principle, neither capitalist nor manager, but innovator. The often adduced qualities expressed by the words "initiative", "foresight", and "authority", incongruous as they are with circular flow models, would fit the entrepreneur as just defined (ibid., 75).

Schumpeter stresses the differences between entrepreneurial and routine-decisions. Consumers' decisions are the driving force behind circular flow. Consumers and managers, including the so-called established entrepreneurs, react to changes by incremental readjustments of their means. Knowledge of routine boundaries is transmitted by inheritance, teaching and environmental pressures. Because following accepted rules of conduct and traditions may help to save on the labour of cogitation, they are useful for planning already routinized behaviour.

The novel procedure is created by our imagination, but there '...will be much more conscious rationality in this than in customary action, which as such does not need to be reflected upon at all' (Schumpeter 1911 1934, 85). Entrepreneurial decisions result in the redirection of productive means.

In the absence of familiar data, the decision-maker must foresee and estimate further what familiar lines of conduct offer: 'Now he must really to some extent do what tradition does for him in everyday life, viz. consciously plan his conduct in every particular' (Schumpeter 1911 1934, 85).

As a consequence, reliable foresight supplying necessary arguments is absent at the moment of decision, e.g. deciding on the proper scale of business contractions or expansions. The entrepreneur's success is dependent upon a capacity to foresee the future, and to grasp its essential elements. However, Schumpeter does not elaborate on how rationality is involved in estimating the future value of the outcome of new combinations. No specific means of calculation for entrepreneurial decision-making is offered or even hinted at.

The assumption that conduct is prompt and rational is commonly considered to be fictitious but nevertheless useful. 'But this [assumption; EW] holds good only where precedents without number have formed conduct through decades and, in fundamentals, through hundreds and thousands of years, and have eliminated unadapted behaviour' (Schumpeter 1911 1934, 80). A new demand for goods is created "ad hoc" by supplying credit to the entrepreneur without a simultaneous creation of a new supply of goods. 'It temporarily substitutes, as it were, a fiction of this claim for the claim itself' (ibid., 106-7). This creation of demand *ex nihilo* is characteristic for the commencement of economic development emerging out of an equilibrium. The entrepreneur uses credit to outbid present producers and thereby acquires control over the factors of production, diverting them in a new direction (ibid., 106).

In order to delineate his dynamic theory of profit, Schumpeter divides risks into two categories, namely: foreseeable and unforeseeable risks. Economic plans will normally incorporate the former. The methods by which to spread foreseeable risks are: incurring costs to guard against risks, risk avoidance, and cost accounting, including risk premiums. In principle, these risks are not to be associated with profits or losses. 'Without development there is no profit, without profit no development' (ibid., 154).

Profits and losses result from risks which cannot be foreseen, or which remain unaccounted for, and are a surplus over costs. However, they are neither a return on capital, nor a rent as are the differential advantages in regular business. Profits are neither simple residues, nor the results of exploitation: '...the problem of profit lies precisely in the fact that the laws of cost and of marginal productivity seem to exclude it' (Schumpeter 1911

1934, 153).

Certain changes in data reveal changes in a situation and require adaptations. Discrepancies between costs and revenues are due to the time-consuming learning processes, the problems involved in decision-making, and the impossibility of perfect adaptation (ibid., 33). In time these discrepancies will be reduced and the temporary surplus eliminated, first, by the rise of exchange values of the means of production induced by the rise in value of the social product, and second, by the downward pressure on prices of new products due to emerging competition (ibid., 149-50).

The climate in which economic depressions occur is caused by uncertainties about data and values, and crises seem to be inevitable as complements to the continual emergence of new activities. The reason is that '...new combinations are not, as one would expect according to general principles of probability, evenly distributed through time -..- but appear, if at all, discontinuously in groups or swarms' (ibid., 223). The clustered appearance of new combinations is generated by the difficulties to be overcome by the pioneers, by the hasty imitation of an innovation by existing businesses within the same sector, and by the imitative behaviour of entrepreneurs active in other sectors of the economy (ibid., 228-30). Errors emerge as an accentuating circumstance at the start of a boom and during a depression (ibid., 85, 227). These uncertainties are only to be removed by way of learning from experience acquired under the new circumstances. The necessary adjustment process, which is in progress during the period of depression must, at least in theory, sooner or later arrive at a new equilibrium (ibid., 239).

If we restrict ourselves to what Schumpeter had to say about our subject, i.e. uncertainty, we must conclude that this 1991 publication is seriously flawed. In the first place, his theory of economic development neither properly defined uncertainty, nor convincingly distinguished it from situations of risk. He discusses uncertainties as denoting unforeseeable risks, but also as representing yet unknown but stable facts. Secondly, uncertainty itself was of minor importance in Schumpeter's book. Whereas he elaborates the problems of economic changes, he casually introduces uncertainty as if by accident when elucidating the circular flow of economic life and the fundamentals of economic development. Thirdly, he does not clarify how one may distinguish between (1) the dynamic implications of introducing new combinations (Schumpeter 1911 1934, 66), and (2) mere frictions in a situation of equilibrium (Schumpeter 1911 1934, 33, 36, 59-60n1, 61, 82).

Knight rarely refers to Schumpeter and when he does so, is dismissive (Knight 1921, 15n, 24, 33n), as when he attacks his dynamic theory of profit. Schumpeter is hardly explicit about the fact that profits and losses are conditional upon an absence of foreknowledge. As Knight would argue, there is no theoretical reason why profits or losses should be generated by changes if general foreknowledge of those changes is prevalent (Knight 1921, 31-6). Nevertheless, Schumpeter prepared the ground for Knight: first, by drawing attention to the importance of separating the analysis of development from the analysis of a situation, and second, by emphasizing the fundamentally different effect of changes as opposed to adjustments. Let us then turn to Knight (1921), the chosen benchmark of this thesis.

2.3 Risk, uncertainty and profit

Knight's *Risk, Uncertainty and Profit* can be read as '...tackling one of the most fundamental problems of epistemology and ethics' (Gordon 1974, 572), that is, uncertainty. Uncertainty is a neglected theme in economics, '...which we propose to put in its rightful place' (Knight 1921), 231). The confusion of ideas present in the notions of risk and uncertainty lies at the heart of the nature and methodology of economic science (ibid., 23). Uncertainty exemplifies the distinction between '...the perfect competition of theory and the remote approach which is made to it by the actual competition of, say, twentieth century United States.' (ibid., 19). Knight regards Marshall's emphasis on concreteness and his lack of interest in presenting and following his own theoretical structure as clearly as possible as symptomatic of the blurred contrast between theory and reality, between simplified assumptions and the complex facts of life (ibid., 15). As a consequence, Knight decides to define and elucidate the mechanisms of competition as if uncertainty were entirely absent, in part two of the book, before discussing the concepts of risk, uncertainty and profit, in part three. In search of a valid theory of profit, Knight places the problems which uncertainty and risk pose for competition at the centre of discussion. 'Uncertainty must be taken in a sense radically distinct from the familiar notion of Risk, from which it has never been properly separated' (ibid., 19).

Knight considers uncertainty as an aspect of the open future. While uncertainty may be an important characteristic of a decision-making situation, it cannot be regarded as a causal factor. Of course, he acknowledges that we may try to rein in the major economic consequences of uncertainty, which are sometimes apparent, but it is foolish to pretend to be able to predict the emergence of the underlying changes themselves.

As we have already stated in chapter one, Knight's definition of uncertainty states that in economic life, the fundamental uncertainties are the errors (1) in predicting the future, and (2) in making adjustments to future conditions (Knight 1921, 259). Such an understanding of uncertainty carries a negative connotation. Uncertainty is first and foremost all dependent upon change (ibid., 370).

Knight distinguishes the following three ideal-types of probability situations/cases and then discusses uncertainty in relation to the third:

1. *a priori* **probabilities** can be calculated from general principles. An example is the *a priori* or "real" probability of getting a 6 in throwing dice. This type of probability is virtually absent in economic behaviour (ibid., 215).
2. **Statistical probabilities** are derived from past experiences, and involve applying statistics to actual instances, to end up with empirically-determined classifications of instances. The example of the chance of a specific house burning down fits this category. Statistical probabilities are "extremely common" in business (ibid., 215).
3. **Estimates** or **guesses** are inevitable whenever a valid homogeneous basis for a classification of alternative outcomes is non-existent. Problems in selecting courses of action arise from the fact that we know so little about the future (ibid., 199). The uniqueness of the situation dealt with will, in general, imply the absence of a distribution of outcomes (ibid., 226, 233). For example, the profitability of an investment in producing a totally new product is uncertain, because we neither have general principles at our disposal, and neither has relevant experience yet been acquired (ibid., 209-32).

Both *a priori* and statistical probabilities enable us to know the distribution of outcomes in a certain group of instances. The first two of the three types of probability situations can be classified under the term "risk" (Knight 1921, 46, 216-25, 233; Orlean 1987, 10-1).

The forward-looking character of the economic process is at the bottom of the uncertainty problem (Knight 1921, 237-8) and consists of two kinds of expectations: first, in advance of any production one must estimate the resulting final quantities and qualities of output; second, the future demand which the producer is striving to satisfy with his products must also be estimated beforehand (ibid., 237-8).

With regard to reasoning about economic problems with a finite intelligence Knight holds the following two tenets; (1) the world is made up of "things" (ibid., 204) manifesting constant modes of behaviour; (2) there is a practically manageable number of distinguishable properties or modes of resemblance (ibid., 204-9). However, in reality these and additional logical requirements may not be met. For example, fundamental changes in the properties of things may frustrate the use of analogy or inference (ibid., 201-4, 209-12). Our powers of dealing with our total environment through knowledge are highly inadequate, making perfect knowledge of, and anticipation for, future developments impossible. Uncertainty relates to the troublesome matter of foreseeing the future. 'At present we are concerned only to emphasize the fact that knowledge is in a sense variable in degree and that the practical problem may relate to the degree of knowledge rather than to its presence or absence *in toto*' (ibid., 199).

Knight stresses the point that the relation between change and profit is indirect. Under perfect competition, demand and supply can be represented by the laws of diminishing utility and of diminishing returns respectively. A prerequisite if the scientist is to use the assumption of perfect competition is according to Knight, the absence of uncertainty. Consequently, profits and losses are conditional upon the presence of uncertainty. Profit is the effect of our imperfect knowledge of the future, itself '...a consequence of change' (Knight 1921, 198). Knight would come to summarize this position by stating that profits are the result of unmeasurable risks, changes and the ability of the entrepreneur (Knight 1934, 484). Lasting profits can result only from those changes for which (1) the law of change is not known, and (2) where there is no knowledge of what actual changes are about to occur, and (3) where there is no knowledge of the probability of any particular occurrence (ibid., chapters 2 & 7). Uncertainty forms the basis for a valid theory of profit and, outside monopoly considerations, appears to underlie the difference between '...the conditions which theory is compelled to assume and those which exist in fact' (ibid., 51).

An action under uncertainty hinges on two separate exercises of judgment: (1) the formation of an estimate of the probable outcome of any proposed course of action; (2) a subjective estimation of the amount of confidence to be placed in the conclusion reached (ibid., 226-7). For example, an entrepreneur will use the best estimate he can form of the outcomes of his actions, and here Knight disagrees with Irving Fisher, who stated that there is only the estimation of the subjective feeling of probability itself. Unfortunately for Fisher, a person is also liable to estimate the correctness of his estimates. 'The action which follows upon an opinion depends as much upon the amounts of confidence in that opinion as it does upon the favorableness of the opinion itself. The ultimate logic, or psychology, of these deliberations is obscure, .. We must simply fall back upon a *capacity* in the intelligent animal to form more or less correct judgments about things, an intuitive sense of values' (ibid., 227).

Nevertheless, Knight lists six economic means of reducing uncertainty (Knight 1921, 238-63, 347). In practice they are mixed, and mixed differently in different situations:

1. **Consolidation**. Uncertainties are often less prominent in group contexts. Statistical and *a priori* "uncertainties", i.e. measurable risks, tend to disappear with the increasing scale of coordinated situations. The institution of insurance serves as an example, converting determinate uncertainties of single situations into effective certainty (ibid., 46-7).

    According to Knight, even when we cannot find a valid basis for classification, that is, in the case of true uncertainty, we often observe some tendencies toward regularity. As an example he offers the institution of free enterprise itself.
2. **Specialization**. Due to different attitudes towards uncertainty, we are able to specialize the function of risk-bearing. This tactic intermingles with that of consolidation, because specialization involves concentration, which involves consolidation. Speculation and the division of parts of enterprises into a new enterprise are examples of this specialization.
3. **Control of the future**. The use of advisers and the promotion of better management make better control of the future possible.
4. **Increasing power of prediction**. Gathering, digesting and disseminating information enhances the quality of the resulting predictions. Better estimates of probable future changes and outcomes can be made by enlarging the quantity of relevant information.
5. The **diffusion of consequences** has, apart from its aspect of consolidation, an aspect of its own: the chance of losing a small fraction of total resources is less disconcerting than the chance of losing a larger part.

6. **Steering production towards less uncertain lines.** By concentrating on production which yields more certain results than other lines of production, one reduces uncertainty.

Consolidation, the first of the six economic means of reducing uncertainty, is the most important tactic. What individuals may regard as uncertain, but which actually involves known risks, can be reduced to any desired limit by developing organizations, such as insurance companies, in order to combine a number of cases (Knight 1921, 46-7). Increasing the quantity of related experiences will induce situations of uncertainty to be transformed into situations of risk. Under uncertainty, readjustments will be carried out by trial-and-error methods under the competitive motive to better oneself (ibid., 272). Thus, Knight states that in a stabilised economy, insurance and competition will perform effectively and cancel out losses and profits, although he does not discuss how the level of the minimal efficient scale of grouped activities might prove troublesome to the functioning of competition.

In real life situations, however, no objective line can be drawn between profits and other incomes, since economic life always involves economic changes and imperfections of competition. Under conditions of uncertainty, we find that the market brings labour and property services into a comparative value scale. All payments have some relation to uncertainty.

Decision-making under uncertainty would have been highly troublesome if suitable institutional arrangements had not evolved. In many economic situations, decision-making is frustrated by the large number of potentially influential factors and the need to assess their relative significance. A quantitative and exhaustive mathematical study is sufficient only in a small group of cases (Knight 1921, 210-1). 'The fundamental principle underlying organized activity is therefore the reduction of the uncertainty in individual judgments and decisions by grouping the decisions of a particular individual and estimating the proportion of successes versus failures, or the average quality of his judgments as a group' (Knight 1921, 293). Note the use of the term proportion of successes instead of a (probability) distribution of results. Effective institutions, under a "government of law", will spontaneously arise under the effective application of the principle of consolidation. Yet, the result cannot be calculated from general principles or past experience, but inevitably involves estimates or guesses.

The presence of uncertainty explains the existence of important characteristics of social organization, in particular production for a market, and the concentration of direction, responsibility and control of production (Knight 1921, 267-8). The existence of the enterprise as such is a direct result of uncertainty. In business contexts we find many unique problems regarding the future of the company, partly as a consequence of technological innovation. 'It is this *true uncertainty* which by preventing the theoretically perfect outworking of the tendencies of competition gives the characteristic form of *enterprise* to economic organization as a whole and accounts for the peculiar income of the entrepreneur' (Knight 1921, 232). However, Knight does not explain what historical differences explain why social organization in the capitalist era differed from the social organization for meeting uncertainty in the preceding period (Arrow 1951, 408-9). One may consider the disintegration or as Huizinga has it, the autumn of the relatively static and stable medieval society as a partial explanation for the large-scale emergence of enterprises.

The specialisation of what Knight calls the function of "responsible direction", combining the two elements of responsibility and control, is in his opinion the essence of enterprise. 'Any degree of effective exercise of judgment or making decisions, is in a free society coupled with a corresponding degree of uncertainty-bearing, of taking the responsibility for those decisions' (Knight 1921, 271). In principle, management is not different from routine work. A manager becomes an entrepreneur, however, when his judgments involve potential errors, and he is responsible for others subordinate to him.

The presence of uncertainty introduces specific problems in the field of hiring labour. 'With uncertainty present, doing things, the actual execution of activity, becomes in a real sense a secondary part of life; the primary problem or function is deciding what to do and how to do it' (Knight 1921, 268). As our attention moves up the hierarchy of a company we may observe that the job increasingly consists of judging, more by inference and intuition than by perception (ibid., 201-11), how subordinates err in their opinions about another person's knowledge. The crucial factor, or the essence of the uncertainty involved, becomes our estimation of another person's capacity to deal with a problem, not his knowledge of the problem itself (ibid., 270-1, 295-6, 309).

Uncertainty determines a fourfold inclination in the selection of personnel and the specialisation of functions. First, it involves personal adaptation to occupations on the basis of partial knowledge. Second, a similar evaluation occurs on the basis of degree of foresight. Third, there will be an hierarchical specialisation within groups. Finally, those with confidence in their own judgment will specialize in risk-taking (ibid., 270).

Hammond argues convincingly that one of the recurring points Knight is driving at in his methodological writings is that there is no literal and exact description in any science (Hammond 1991, 365). Knight considers it troublesome to link scientific concepts of, e.g. knowledge and competition, to the evolving real life situations, in which man is liable to error, and may adjust his opinions. As a result of uncertainty, an incongruity arises between the scientific concept of knowledge and 'the convictions and opinions upon which conduct is based outside of laboratory experiments.' (Knight 1921, 230). Differences in the derived conclusions are often to be observed. Knight repeatedly stresses that such unpleasant, but unavoidable, surprises are due to the existence of uncertainty (ibid., 19, 218, 224 226, 230, 232). Our world is full of contradiction and paradox (ibid., 217, 313, 348). 'In any case we *do* strive to reduce uncertainty, even though we should not want it eliminated from our lives' (ibid., 238).

It is acknowledged that some further foundation would be useful, but Knight explicitly stops short at intuitive judgment or "unconscious induction", and the mystery of life: 'We are so built that what seems to us reasonable is likely to be confirmed by experience, or we could not live in the world at all' (Knight 1921, 227). Again, when we return to the example of selecting human capacities for dealing with unforeseeable situations, Knight concludes with a paradox: such situations involve '...apparent theoretical impossibility of solution. But like a host of impossible things in life, it is constantly being done' (Knight 1921, 298).

This troublesome link between economic theory and economic practices hampered the "economist as philosopher" Frank Knight (Buchanan 1968, 425). It reflects Knight's approach present throughout his work. As Emmett states Knight (1921), on the one hand, wanted to defend the role of systematic analysis, while, on the other hand, it stressed the limitations of analysis (Emmett 1992). For example, he concedes that, in practice, all gradations except the extremes of perfectly homogeneous groups and absolutely unique situations exist. Hence, according to Knight, the element of uniqueness of any typical business decision applies to most decisions. In some cases uncertainty prevails more than in other cases. No experience is absolutely unique any more than any two things are absolutely alike. 'Yet it is true, and the fact can hardly be over-emphasized, that a judgment of probability is actually made in such cases' (Knight 1921, 226). In all sorts of situations, men form opinions as to their judgmental capacities. Moreover, one is perfectly well aware of the vagueness of the border separating statistical probabilities from estimates or guesses. One may then be forgiven for finding it odd to state that the theoretical distinction between situations of risk and uncertainty is of the greatest importance, and is clearly discernable in nearly any instance of the exercise of judgment (Knight 1921, 226-9). Since Knight could not solve this puzzle satisfactorily; he left himself open to criticism of his dubious concentration on a clear-cut distinction between theoretical extremes of an actually continuous sequence (as indeed he is criticized, e.g. by Little 1938, 39n2).

A key to some of the problems just mentioned may be found in the probability theory chosen. As we will clarify in next section, Knight uses various probability theories in his typification of probability situations, but is unable to link the ideal types to the complex practical cases.

2.4 Probability theory

From the emergence of the concept of probability in circa 1660 (Hacking 1975), it made slow progress, until in the 19th century it was propagated by A.-A. Cournot and J. Venn, among others, where it went hand-in-hand with a society-wide rise of interest in classification and enumeration (Hacking 1990, 2-3). The probabilistic laws were applied as physical properties, and by analogy to the laws of gravity, the concept of probability was thus drawn towards a deterministic perspective. The classical theory of probability which developed was considered inadequate by the turn of the century: doubts were even expressed about whether a satisfactory definition of probability could ever be arrived at (Mises 1928 1957, 67).

Classical theory defined probability as '...the ratio of the number of favourable cases to the total number of equally likely cases' (Mises 1928 1957, 67). This theory was used primarily for binomial distributions, also called simple alternatives, and since it depended upon *a priori* probabilities, it could only be applied to fairly simple cases. An imagined ideal coin, a dice or a tin can containing ball bearings are often used as explanatory means. An economic example, already referred to, might be the number of profitable transactions out a total number of equally likely transactions (Knight 1921, 293).

The classical theory fails on several grounds. First, the Poisson-distribution or the first law of large numbers using the classical definition of probability, does not lead to any statements about relative frequency and related probability. This theorem is no more than a statement about purely arithmetical regularities, not about empirical entities (Mises 1928 1957, 115, 116, 104-9). Second, undue emphasis has been placed on the importance of the *a priori* equality of the possibilities of different cases, also called the principle of indifference (Mises 1928 1957, 69-71, 78, 79). Closely related to this shortcoming is the criticism that the classical theory ignores important practical problems, e.g. life insurance problems. For the classical probability theory the complexity of such problems is too great to deal with. In short, the classical theory of probability cannot deal satisfactorily with distributions of outcomes and probabilities.

In the first decades of this century, the classical theory of probability was first questioned by the subjectivist theory of probability, and then by the soon prevalent frequentist theory of probability. The subjectivist theory was proposed and elaborated on by John Maynard Keynes in *A Treatise on Probability*, published in 1921. Richard von Mises provided a philosophical foundation for the frequency theory of probability, which is most clearly described in his *Probability, Statistics, and Truth*, first published in German in 1928 (Mises 1928 1957, 224). The explicit break with the classical probability theory, together with an unprecedented growth in the mathematics of probability, boosted advances in probability theory. During this period, probability acquired an air of freedom, and free will dominates within a collectively-determined flow of events (Knight 1921, 221; Hacking 1990, 116).

Mises defines probability not as an analytic but as a Kantian synthetic proposition. Probability is '...the limiting value of the relative frequency with which this attribute recurs in the indefinitely prolonged sequence of observations' (Mises 1928 1957, 221). It is important to note that the subject matter of frequency theory is the study of observable mass phenomena and repetitive events, not of individual phenomena and unique events (ibid., vii, 102).

Probability can acquire a precise meaning only within a neatly-restricted set (ibid., 18, 103, 221). A set appropriate to the application of the theory of probability must fulfil at least the following two conditions: (1) the relative frequencies must possess limiting values, and (2) the limiting values must be independent of place selection, i.e. conform to the principle of randomness (ibid., 24-5, 28-9). In cases in which the collective cannot be readily constructed, it is erroneous to employ the term probability (ibid., 20).

Although widely-acclaimed and commonly-used, the frequency theory of probability is not devoid of drawbacks either. First and foremost, the condition of randomness, the absence of place selection, can be neither proved in practice, nor in theory. The reason is that the notion of a countable infinite sequence of observations is in no way logically definable (ibid., 85). This notion is necessarily based on randomness itself, for we are unable to list and test all possible place selections (ibid., 91). We may quite possibly end up using a probability distribution of outcomes, in what is actually a case of a perfectly deterministic sequence of outcomes. Second, in a test situation we have to face the problem of the missing memory of the object. It is not illogical to throw an infinity of tails when playing heads and tails with a "perfect" coin. Mises, therefore, rightfully defines his law of large numbers as the "almost certain" inclination of the observed frequencies to tend to the unknown real values (ibid., 131). But what, other than intuition, can ultimately justify the presumption of neat distributions of outcomes around the real values and the x-percent reliability interval? In their search for constants or tendencies in economic activities, scientists inevitably employ the implicit assumption that the data are generated by a research object that has a memory of the data already produced.

A related criticism concerns the condition of possessing limiting values. This condition can only be applied satisfactorily in an ergodic world, under the actuality of the uniformity of nature. Most economists, including Knight (Knight 1921, 204, 230, 313; Knight 1935, 114) take it for granted, and hence neglect the following two consequences: (A) we are faced with the probability paradox; we have to meet the logical problem that with absolutely homogenous groups, that is, with ultimate uniformity of things, we have '...uniformity and not probability in the result' (Knight 1921, 218); (B) moreover, under the condition of possessing limiting values, scientists cannot deal with cases of non-ergodicity. Real changes must be considered impossible. By contrast, however, and especially in the social sciences, we are faced with results changing fundamentally over a longer or shorter period. It is the lack of relevant historical data that makes it necessary to estimate the result. It is here that Knight situates economic uncertainty, business problems, and the necessity to fall back on estimates. And it is precisely for such situations that Mises rejects the use of probability theory.

Let us return to Frank Knight and add perspective to his typification of probability cases. To summarize, on the one hand he discusses *a priori* probabilities which can be computed on general principles, and have the status of mathematical propositions (Knight 1921, 214, 224). On the other hand, the statistical probabilities are based on an empirical classification and the evaluation of resulting frequencies (Knight 1921, 214, 225). However, as Knight admits, neither *a priori* calculations nor empirical studies are of any use when discussing the cases of estimates. 'This form of probability is involved in the greatest logical difficulties of all, and no very satisfactory discussion of it can be given' (Knight 1921, 225). In his opinion, we are obliged to guess the ratio of favourable cases to the total number of cases, and supplement this with an estimate of how much confidence to put in such a ratio.

Knight's position may be characterized as having arrived at a transformation phase. First, he tried to link these different theoretical concepts to a heterogeneous mass of real life situations. The reader will recall that he essentially used three different probability concepts: the classical, the frequency, and the subjectivist. Next, he stated that in the economy we only have mixed cases of the three types of probability situations. But how should we deal with situations, whose basis for classification is equivocal? Knight (1921) seems to be in doubt about how to link the irreducible, ideal-typical probability concepts to the broad range of empirical situations, an example of the problem of how to relate theory to reality.

That Frank Knight's ideas had their roots in the classical theory of probability is indisputable. We find numerous characteristic passages in which he does not discuss a distribution of outcomes at all, but rather the confidence to be placed on one single outcome (Knight 1921, 212, 216-7, 220, 226-9, 231, 234-7, 293). For example, practically all decisions are supposed to rest upon opinions '...which on scrutiny easily resolve themselves into an opinion of *a* probability' (Knight 1921, 237; emphasis added). In other words, it is implicitly assumed that decisions are often not based upon evaluations of a probability distribution.

As well as drawing on the classical theory of probability, Knight also applies ideas derived from the frequency theory of probability and, in a point of fact, his six possible means to reduce uncertainty owe a great deal to that theory. For example, the discussion on consolidation and specialisation suggests the use of the distribution of the different outcomes from a group of instances. And yet, in Knight we do not find any statements about another axiom of frequency theories, namely the summing of probability to unity.

Knight's original, but in fact hybrid, taxonomic scheme of probability cases betrays the fact that his 1921 book was conceived in a transitional phase in the history of economic ideas. But would this mixed salad composed of elements from subjectivist, frequentist, and classical theories, be more appetizing if only one of these theories had been used? The answer to that question must necessarily be negative. For example, if we consider the frequentist and classical theories, uncertainty would first of all always have to be quantifiable. This is an unrealizable condition, for the seeds of non-reducible qualitative elements will germinate and sprout sooner or later. In addition, Knight's definition of uncertainty excludes the construction of the neutral collective and the application of the frequentist theory to changes. If uncertainty finds its origins in unpredictable changes, and is as prevalent as Knight presumes it to be, then we are unable to approximate the possible economic consequences of uncertainty by using the frequency theory of probability.

How have economists reacted to Knights 1921 publication? W.C. Mitchell was clearly impressed by it, and advised economists to disregard their "palate" to "taste the book". 'For the distinction between risk and uncertainty is not less valid to the realistic economist than to the pure theorist' (Mitchell 1922, 275). Did economists get excited by the flavour, or was it soon deemed to be too unappetizing? It is clear that we have now come to the point of discussing how Knight's ideas carried over into the writings of fellow economists.

In the period subsequent to the publication of Knight's book we may trace two main lines of thought in the discussion on economic uncertainty. First, as has already been mentioned, a change took place in the techniques chosen to "model" uncertainty and risk. The frequency theory would take the lead. Second, uncertainty, i.e., the necessity for acting upon opinion based on partial knowledge, as it was defined by Knight, would soon be shunted into a scientific railway siding. Moreover, the idea of drawing a distinction between uncertainty and risk provided fuel for discussion, but resulted in remarkably few critical or elaborative publications. A first indication of the existence of alternative ideas on uncertainty during the interwar period may be found in works of one of Marshall's supporters.

2.5 Uncertainty linked to risk

During the interwar period, a marked shift in economic theorizing took place, which was inspired by the spectre of Marshall. In his search for tendencies and realism, his bequest to economists was a heritage suited for exploration by those among them who were seeking determinate theoretical conclusions. Frederick Lavington (1881-1927) was the English orthodox economist who in the first few decades of this century elaborated on Marshall's writings, in particular on the businessman's problem of uncertainty, which was only implicit in Marshall's work (Shackle 1980, 19). Lavington aimed at no more than building on the work of his hero Marshall, as is reflected in one of his favourite dictums: 'It is all in Marshall, if you'll only take the trouble to dig it out' (Whithers 1927, 504). He published three relevant articles, which, taken together, may illustrate the development of economic thought on uncertainty.

In his 1912 article in the *Economic Journal*, later mentioned by Knight (Knight 1921, 199-200n1), Lavington did not relate economic uncertainty directly to profit, but rather to the rate of interest, whereby he stated that uncertainty is a form of ignorance as to the amount of gains or losses (Lavington 1912, 398). Where perfect foresight exists, the normal rate of return is equal to the net rate of interest and to the so-called "actuarial value". However, changes in the future environment can only be foreseen imperfectly, and in general the return on investment in an enterprise is uncertain. The greater the perceived uncertainty, the wider the spread of prospective rates of returns. Diversity among the perceived uncertainties is due to (1) the state of knowledge, (2) the rate of social change, and (3) the degree of immobility of resources (Lavington 1912, 398). As a consequence, readjustments are no more than a succession of approximations. The result is a preclusion of the optimal allotment of capital, or the proximate adaptation of investment-means to ends. A more proximate investment of capital presupposes a reduced degree of financial insecurity for the owners of resources, who accordingly, in general, require a lower compensatory increment in the rate of payment.

Lavington differentiates three categories within the social machinery for dealing with the important social consequences of what he calls the '...evil of Uncertainty' (Lavington 1912, 401, 409). First, we have the category of prevention. Examples may be the reduction of ignorance by investment in intelligence, and the institution of law and order which precludes certain kinds of changes. Second, those who suffer the results of uncertainty may transfer the effects, either by spreading the effects over a large number of capitalists, or, conversely, by directly compounding its effects or indirectly via insurance companies. The result of the latter method of transfer is not the reduction of uncertainty of any single event, but rather an apparent reduction in the amount of funds which must be kept in reserve to guard against eventualities (Lavington 1912, 401). The third, and conceivably the most important, category of means of dealing with uncertainty links up with the retention of reserve funds adequate to eliminate the residual effects of uncertainty.

The organisations engaged in the marketing of capital, such as the stock exchange and the banking system, reduce the cost of this third provision (Lavington 1912, 407). The banking system implicitly supplies capital on demand, an activity which corresponds to the explicit contracts in the insurance system, and which is based on the same principle. In fact, banks offer insurance against financial emergency, because their readiness to lend reduces the necessity for businessmen to hold emergency reserves. Furthermore, because they can substitute investments for parts of the emergency reserves, banks reduce the cost of cash reserves, i.e. the loss of interest (Lavington 1912, 404-9).

In this 1912 article, the consequences of the withdrawal of the assumption of completely mobile resources is highlighted; we may nowadays recognize it as the introduction of resource-specificity. The removal of the assumption of a stationary state, i.e. of the perfect calculability of the product of the resources, is emphasised in two articles published in 1925-1926 (Lavington 1926, 196-7). The importance of the lack of knowledge was thus introduced. That there is neither discussion of, nor reference to, Knight (1921), may be explained by Cambridge's insularity, although this is speculation. We can only verify that Knight's book was known in Britain at the latest by the end of that decade. The omission seems significant, however, because while the concept of uncertainty is prominent in the 1912 article, the concept of risk is dominant in the two publications of the 1920s.

In his two later publications, Lavington elaborates on a theory of business risks. The condition of incalculability of the results of the activities is due to the '...immense complexity of the processes by which the future grows out of the present' (Lavington 1925, 187). This complexity creates a tendency to error, at least in the short-run (Lavington 1926, 199), and impairs the close adaptation of means to ends. Due to the incalculability of the results certain real costs arise which are peculiar in two respects, of which the second is the more relevant for economic conduct. The first characteristic of these real costs is the fact that they are made up of two types: the real costs of risks and those of uncertainty (Lavington 1925, 198-9). The former category relates to the expectation of loss due to the misdirection or imperfect use of resources in the separate cases. The latter, that is the real costs of uncertainty, relates to the likely error in that selfsame expectation of loss. Such errors result in an incalculable irregularity in individual incomes, and necessitate the holding of reserves. The costs of uncertainty result from the less than complete satisfaction of one's economic wants, and from the personality of the individual, who is usually unwilling to countenance uncertainty (Lavington 1925, 192-3). From the pages of these publications, the judgment that the real costs related to risks are far heavier than the real costs of uncertainty leaps into view. The second and more important characteristic of incalculability is that the related costs arise from our imperfect understanding of economic conditions (Lavington 1926, 195). We may infer from these summary-statements that when it comes to analyzing economic developments, risk and our imperfect comprehension account for a large part of incalculability, with uncertainty relatively of only minor importance.

According to Lavington, businessmen charge prospective payments for accepting the aforementioned two real costs of incalculability. Theoretically speaking, three distinct charges are levied in view of: (1) the reduction in the efficiency of productive resources which is generated by their misdirection, the related charge being called the amortisation charge; (2) the possible future fluctuations in individual income, this being called the reduced efficiency of individual incomes (Lavington 1925, 192-4), which may result in a charge for uncertainty-bearing; and (3) the acceptance of risk, which results in a demand for organising faculties requisite to deal with perpetual readjustments and generates costs, the charges being the earnings accruing to management. The charge for uncertainty-bearing, due to the reduction in the income's efficiency, ordinarily becomes part of profits (Lavington, 1926, 194). The individual expectations of loss arising from the occurrence of these three real costs in total is defined as risk. The "risk charge" is the total of prospective payments just sufficient to induce a businessman to accept a certain risk, and it is a component of the price of the output (Lavington 1926, 194).

In the short-run, both the magnitude and the distribution of the realised losses resulting from taking some risks is random or arbitrary, since in that case there is no necessary relation between individual losses and the losses falling on society as a whole. However, experience is supposed to exert a corrective influence in the long-run. The tendency will be towards balancing the average realized loss against the average amortisation charge (Lavington 1926, 194-9).

Having read these two articles, one realizes that no vital distinction between risk and uncertainty is offered. The difference in importance of the two characteristics of incalculability is reaffirmed by the following corollary to Lavington's argument on the definition of the term risk: 'If its general drift were agreed to, it would seem possible to simplify the definition of Profits, in particular by avoiding the logical need for a separate factor of production – Uncertainty-bearing – and to bring the scope of the term more nearly into line with the meaning given it in America' (Lavington 1926, 194). This quotation illustrates a conflict between the primacy of the consistency of theory itself and the correspondence of theory with economic practices. Moreover, the direct link between uncertainty and profit, which was stressed by Knight, is downgraded to a link of mere logical importance. From Lavington's 1920s articles, we may conclude that the distinction between risk and uncertainty lost much of the clarity present in the 1912 article. On the other hand, this suggests that, by 1925-1926, the distinction presented by Knight was not prevalent. This position may, but need not, contrast with Hicks's opinion on the state-of-the-art, published in Britain only five years later.

2.6 Risk eclipsed uncertainty

Before we embark on an examination of *The Theory of Uncertainty and Profit* (1931) by J.R. Hicks (1904-1989), which is one of the few papers to comment directly on Knight's distinction between risk and uncertainty, we would like to allow ourselves a few remarks in passing. Hicks, who had been invited by Lionel Robbins to lecture on risk and uncertainty at the London School of Economics (LSE), proclaimed that Knight's *Risk, Uncertainty, and Profit* had broken the deadlock in the development of the theory of profit, and that with its publication, Frank Knight had finally got the skeleton out of the cupboard and given it a rattle. The theory of profit prevailing around 1930 resembles Knight's theory of profit. 'At the very least, that work has laid securely the first foundation on which any future theory of profits must rest – the dependence of profits on uncertainty' (Hicks 1931, 170).

With this remark, however, the praise ends, and the criticism begins. Hicks deplores the fact that Knight gave us a theory of profit based on metaphysics and psychology, while any such theory should be based on economics, supplemented with a handful of simple assumptions, e.g. about the application of probability to economics (Hicks 1931, 171). Disagreement between Knight and Hicks about the importance of uncertainty in economic activities, already existed, and according to the latter, Knight had not demonstrated why true uncertainties should claim such a large part of our attention (Hicks 1931, 171).

We venture the opinion that there is no testable final solution to this problem. It seems almost impossible to prove the extent of uncertainty, because it seems to be open for judgment only by analyzing its possible yet unforeseeable consequences. Moreover, how can we ever decide which profits/losses are the consequences of uncertainty and which result from the imperfect working of competition that is due to other factors?

Another aspect of the disagreement between Knight and Hicks seems to concern the different models of classification. Knight proposed three ideal types, and discussed them, starting with uncertainty and risk, and analyzing accordingly. Because of this typification, he is obliged to pay attention to uncertainty-type situations, and analyse economic cases using his ideal types. For Knight, uncertainty is an aspect of almost every practical situation.

In contrast to Knight, Hicks takes practical situations, and classifies and discusses them. He distinguishes between four groups of probability situations: (1) the cases in which a large number of identical operations are considered; (2) the cases in which identical partial operations can be identified; (3) all those cases in which we cannot talk about homogeneous operations, but where deviations are minor; (4) true uncertainties or "unmeasurable risks", as understood by Knight. He presents the principal characteristics of each of these four groups, but unlike Knight, he does not aim at tracing the essentials implied by this classification. Hicks believes that the problem of the heterogeneity of situations is of little practical importance for economic analysis, risk theory being a good enough method for dealing with it. Thus, part of the disagreement about the importance of uncertainty is defused by the adoption of dissimilar methods.

The congruence of the probability theories used is not without significance. After all, both Knight and Hicks rely on the classical theory of probability. This enables Hicks to elaborate on a point already hinted at by Knight (Knight 1921, 237) and Hicks duly comes up with the idea of an ordinal uncertainty-curve, relating the amounts of incurred uncertainty to the expected result. Uncertainty-curves for both supply and demand of resources can be drawn which are different for dissimilar terms and result in an ordinal equilibrium probability ratio or "chance" (Hicks 1931, 173-9). The shape of the individual uncertainty-curves is dependent upon, and will change with: the given technique, the scale of production, and the chosen means and ends of production. For example, one may use complementary methods of production in order to reduce instability in production, or use electricity instead of oil to diminish the risk of fire. This idea reflects an enhanced belief in the possibility of the containment of uncertainty.

Significantly, Hicks writes about the reduction, rather than the elimination, of risk. The extent to which risk changes, and the exact vector of such changes, may often be found only by empirical research (Hicks 1931, 174, 178). He thereby implicitly advocates the application of the theory of profit in most cases, as long as they are imperfectly homogeneous (Hicks 1931, 171, 175n).

Hicks was not in step with R. von Mises, who restricted himself, as we have stated in section 2.4, to discussing groups of operations. Indeed, the latter forbids the application of the frequency theory to single instances (Mises 1928 1957, 9, 11, 15). Hicks instead considers repetitive situations, using the law of large numbers, and derives conclusions for individual cases from the results (Hicks 1931, 173-4). According to Hicks, Knight does not so much examine frequently repeated situations as focus on those situations in which unpredictable changes take place (Hicks 1931, 175). However, still according to Hicks, scientists are able to discuss the chance of a particular result in a particular situation. Such a chance is '...the ratio of the number of cases in which that result occurs to the total' (Hicks 1931, 171). In fact, these are not cases of Knightian uncertainty, under which it is the absence of relevant data that causes the problems.

We conclude this section by stating that the absence of the term risk in the title of Hicks's paper, together with previous discussion, illustrates a gradual shift in the paradigmatic meaning of the term uncertainty. Knight conceived of uncertainty in dissimilar cases, in which grouping, by whatever means, may help to enhance the quality of projections. In Knight's view, one may divine specific results, but economics is of little use in such a process. The view taken by Hicks is the opposite: what may be derived from groups is, in his opinion, applicable to the individual cases which comprise them. Hicks's position reflects Robbins's methodological views on economics, which had then been published, and to which we will now turn.

2.7 Back to basics

In his acclaimed essay on the proper subject-matter of economics, Lionel Robbins (1898-1984) confronts economists with the mundane inconveniences which frustrate their efforts construct and apply relatively simple static models (Robbins 1932, 1935). He condemns the purported scientific status of the study of economic development, once so forcefully propagated by Schumpeter, to oblivion. Economists would do better to confine themselves to the study of equilibria and to, what were euphemistically called, equilibratory tendencies. We would argue that it is partially due to Robbins's argument that fundamental change and uncertainty became marginalized research subjects in mainstream economics. How could this have happened? Was not Robbins '...the main expositor of Knight's views at LSE' (Coase 1988, 20)? During the period 1933-1940, and thus under Robbins's auspices, the LSE reprinted Knight (1921) for the *Series of reprints of scarce tracts* in 1933, 1935, 1937, 1939, and 1940; five editions within the space of eight years.

We propose to discuss two arguments which may be found in Robbin's 1932 essay, each of which relegates uncertainty to the outskirts of economics. The first is that economists cannot treat uncertainty scientifically if they already lack stable economic elements. The economic system functions without predictable future production functions and without permanently stable elasticities of supply and demand. Robbins acknowledges that the economic system is "open", if only because some resources are devoted to marketing and research, transforming revealed preferences and technological know-how respectively (Robbins 1932 1935, 129). We may be able to explain changing relationships due to changes in individual values, but we cannot explain changes in the data itself (ibid., 127), because '...there are certain things which must be taken as ultimate data' (ibid., 135). In spite of the fact that everyone is free to speculate about legal and political changes, or venture guesses on changes in techniques and in the supply of demand, '...economic analysis can have little to do with it' (ibid., 133).

The theory of profit is an '...analysis of the effect of uncertainty, with regard to the future availability of scarce goods and scarce factors' (ibid., 77). This is the main postulate of the theory of dynamics. Robbins cooly restricts its domain to planning for the future (ibid., 79). It fits in with Knight's opinion on the development of economics during the 1920s, when dynamic economics had already become a term referring to the limitations of static analysis, '...a sort catch-all for stressing changes in given conditions.' (Knight 1935, 167). Robbins's devotion to lofty theory is consistent with his prime interest in part two of Knight (1921), i.e. the piece on perfect competition (Coase 1988, 20), which precedes the extensive discussion on risk and uncertainty.

Robbins's second argument is that the difficulties encountered in our search for the laws of equilibrium and equilibrating tendencies should already have forced economists to eat humble pie. An economist must necessarily start with the most convenient assumptions. Perfect foresight and perfect rationality are examples of such assumptions with an '...essentially arbitrary nature' (Robbins 1932 1935, 57), but convenient for economic research. The incorporation of uncertainty is clearly not as convenient in economics, for it would complicate research tremendously.

The popularity of the essay, with its preference for the choice of convenient concepts, and rigorous analytical research, illustrates and affirms the popularity of the mathematical approach and the antipathy felt towards "theoretical quibbling". It represents yet another effort in the endeavour to stave off the unpleasant surprises involved in discussing uncertainty.

Did Frank Knight change his opinion about the need to engage in a separate discussion about the forward-looking character of the economic process? Having examined the evidence, we would venture to answer in the negative. He re-established his point in the preface to the 1933 republication of Knight (1921): 'I still find a fundamental significance in the analysis of uncertainty in the essay, and am puzzled at the insistence of many writers on treating the uncertainty of result in choice as if it were a gamble on a known mathematical chance.' (Knight 1921, xiv).

Knight was to remain dissatisfied with the application of the marginalist analysis of the unforeseen meanderings of the economy. 'The case is somewhat like that of a river and its channel; for the time being, the channel locates the river, but in the long-run it is the other way' (Knight 1935, 142). In his 1935 article, Knight considers the question of whether the forces acting under given conditions tend to produce an equilibrium to be more important than the question about the equilibrium itself. Economics lacks such a study of the laws of motion, '...the kinetics of economic changes' (Knight 1935, 141). On the one hand, economics has no place for relations between force (i.e., motive), resistance (i.e., ignorance, prejudice, etc.), and movement (i.e., social processes). On the other hand, in mechanics '...mass and energy are *really* neither created nor destroyed' (Knight 1935, 167). In an elaboration upon the question posed, Knight distinguishes between four levels in the stability of data: (1) the price levels at a given moment in a speculative market; (2) the more or less stable production period, e.g. of crops; (3) longer periods of approximately a decade, with roughly constant populations, practices, total productive capacities and techniques. Disturbances and maladjustments are due primarily to uncertainty about, or ignorance of, the future; (4) the long term, given a reasonably stable set of cultural values. According to Knight, it is here that scientists must locate the problem of growth and change (Knight 1930 1935, 170-80; Knight 1935, 140-5). Accumulative processes, such as the growth of population, the growth of capital, the concentration of ownership and the expansion of wants, cannot be analysed properly with the notion of a tendency toward equilibrium (Knight 1930 1935, 177-84). 'Probably we must go further and reject entirely the use of the mechanical analogy, the categories of force, resistance, and movement, in discussing basic historical changes' (Knight 1930 1935, 185). Furthermore, although he would like to be positive, Knight is inclined to a negative conclusion when considering the usefulness of relativity theory in economics (Knight 1935, 162-67). Because he never rewrote his book on risk and uncertainty, we are unable to evaluate the wisdom of this position when related to uncertainty.

In the next two sections, writings which were published at the end of the interwar period are discussed. The publications set out various positions with respect to the introduction of uncertainty into mainstream economics. They should present further clues as to the impact of Knight's 1921 book on economics during the interwar period. We intend to direct our attention to a summary-publication which claims to describe the views on anticipations, uncertainty, and planning which were prevalent around 1940. First, we will introduce the Knight-Hutchison debate, which addresses, among other things, the relation between uncertainty and equilibrium theory.

2.8 Uncertainty versus Perfect Expectations

The book *The Significance and Basic Postulates of Economic Theory*, written by T.W. Hutchison (1912-..) and published in 1938, marks the start of the positivist epoch in economics (Caldwell 1984, 1), and the beginning of a brusque and fierce polemic with Knight (Knight 1940; Hutchison 1941; Knight 1941). Knight holds a subtle antipositivist view of science: Although the existence of bald facts cannot be denied, neither do observational data present themselves once and for all, nor do economists hold definitive test procedures (Hammond 1991, 370). Paradoxically however, the arguments which Hutchison presents in this debate are very much in line with Knight's *Risk, Uncertainty, and Profit*, and the role which uncertainty plays in his work (Coats 1983, 2) is evident in a number of Hutchison's early writings to which we will now turn our attention (e.g. Hutchison 1937a; Hutchison 1937b; Hutchison 1938).

Hutchison states that uncertainty is essentially the single factor that causes problems of conduct (Hutchison 1937b, 652). Furthermore, like Knight he considers the analytic distinction between absolute certainty and absolute uncertainty to be fundamental: 'where the consequences of all decisions can be perfectly foreseen, the maximum principle clearly works itself out in a very special way, which must be fundamentally distinguished from the only way in which it can work itself out when there is any uncertainty present, that is under conditions where people cannot conceivably *know* or *calculate* but can only more or less vaguely *guess*, which out of many possible lines of conduct will lead to the fulfilment of the principle' (Hutchison 1937b, 638; cf. Hutchison 1938, 87).

Empirically-speaking, this distinction presents us with a complicated question because the dissimilarity of "certain choices" and "uncertain choices" does not correspond to any clearcut distinction in choices among goods (Hutchison 1937a, 73). Most actual choices are mixtures of the two extremes. Nevertheless, a large number of choices, especially investment choices, must be located near the absolute uncertainty pole (Hutchison 1937a, 72). 'In a *dynamic* economic world many decisions cannot be simply *calculated* but must be based more or less on *intuition*' (Hutchison 1938, 182). Under conditions of uncertainty, the neoclassical assumption of rational conduct can no longer be the starting point for economic analysis. Economic agents are assumed to act according to their expectations, and the term "rational" is usually added to grace these expectations, or the process of arriving at those expectations. Men, however, do not act like automatons because risk, uncertainty, and more or less correct expectations about the future pervade and inform all action, economic or otherwise (Hutchison 1937b, 638, 640). Under absolute uncertainty all desirable alternatives are equally attractive and there remains little more than guesswork. Moreover, in such cases it is irrelevant how choices are actually made, and terms like "rational" and "irrational" lose their meaning (Hutchison 1937b, 638). Therefore, '...apart from the pure pleasure in gambling for its own sake– .. –*there is no advantage or significance at all in being free to make it* (a choice; EW) *oneself as against having it made for one*' (Hutchison 1937a, 72).

According to Knight, the postulate of perfect expectation is essential to equilibrium theory: 'the assumption of practical omniscience on the part of every member of the competitive system' (Knight 1921, 197). This omniscience about the future is what Hutchison means by the term perfect expectation (Hutchison 1937b, 645). Hutchison is in agreement with Knight's opinion, insofar as the latter rejects the postulate of perfect expectations, which are, according to Hutchison, only compatible with "optimal" markets under competitive conditions. The introduction of this postulate would often preclude the study of real world problems resulting from uncertainty (Hutchison 1937b, 644; Hutchison 1938, 162). The assumption of perfect expectations is incompatible with an interdependent economic system. Furthermore, Hutchison claims that profit maximization together with adjusting one's conduct under perfect expectations of another man's conduct is logically impossible; and by analogy, perfect knowledge of one another's expectations would mean that a game would not be played (Hutchison, 1937a, 73; Hutchison 1938, 97-100, 163).

However, having discarded perfect expectations, the assumption that people only "tend" to conduct the maximising analysis is not sufficient to realize equilibrium. Under such a weaker assumption, a person might not, for instance, even perceive the maximum position as such (Hutchison 1937b, 638). The derived conclusion must be that, under less than perfect competition, activities are dependent on necessarily imperfect expectations about the conduct of others. We note in passing that this argument speculates about interdependent decision-making, although lacking the necessary game-theoretical analytical instruments, which were awaiting maturation. We will return to that subject in chapter six of this research.

Hutchison disagrees with Knight insofar as theorizing on economic behaviour under uncertainty within an equilibrium theory is concerned. Knight holds that uncertainty cannot be linked to perfect expectations, and therefore not to equilibrium theory, either. In contrast to Knight, however, Hutchison asserts that uncertainty and equilibrium theory can be combined, because equilibrium theory can do without the perfect expectation postulate, which can be replaced by the postulate of correct expectations. Correct expectations are those expressing the correct relations between actions and results. With regard to the validity of equilibrium theory, it is not important how or why people should behave in a certain way. What is necessary is that people do behave in a definite way (Hutchison 1937b, 642). It is not the knowledge which inspired people to certain actions that is important, but rather the actions and conditions of an individual or community. Under correct expectations one may remain unaware of certain, possibly more profitable, opportunities. Economists should use the concept of correct, that is undisappointed, expectation, but shun the concept of perfect expectations (Hutchison 1938, 101).

According to Hutchison, uncertainty is influenced by (1) learning, (2) the period of production and (3) competition. Uncertainty increases with the lengthening of the processes of production. Likewise, the more "oligopolistic" markets are, the more important uncertainty is. Conversely, the reduction of uncertainty requires the enhancement of competition. As long as we do not have data on economic outcomes, the question of whether the countervailing power of learning ultimately results in more correct prognoses or not, remains an open and unimportant problem (Hutchison 1937b, 648). Errors have been made, are being made, and will also be made in the future. Consequently, equilibrium is better characterised by the "optimum maximum" condition '...whether or not the individual or community has been led to it (equilibrium; EW) by perfect expectations.' (Hutchison 1937b, 646).

Furthermore, in the presence of uncertainty economic theorizing requires an extra principle to flank rational conduct. This extra principle implies acting in a certain way, e.g. according to custom, without the necessity of recourse to "objective rationality" (Hutchison 1937b, 648). The formation of expectations must be incorporated in any model that claims to deal with uncertainty. The actions and conditions of an individual or community are important for identifying existing economic relations and outcomes, which inevitably fall short of the optimum maximum. There is no need to search for any psychological imperatives underlying such actions and conditions.

Hutchison thus nails his colours to the mast as a positivist. Economic principles do not have to be explained in psychological terms, since we can observe economic relations in reality. Testing is necessary in order to be able to divorce metaphysics, based on intuitions and convictions, from science, and therefore what is claimed to be described must at least be testable. Propositions should, in principle, be reducible to testable statements. Hutchison acknowledges that, contrary to the laws of physics, the conformity of actual behaviour to economic principles cannot be verified, and that economic magnitudes are at best estimates. 'The fact that human behavior is affected by error (..) necessarily means that there is a divergence between the formula or positive law which describes economic behavior and that which describes its purpose, motive or intent' (Knight 1941, 752). Hutchison nevertheless argues that if economists are to agree among themselves, the only way open is to adopt the methods of the more exact sciences, that is, by constant testing of their propositions (Hutchison 1941, 742-3). The only way to achieve this goal is '...to look and see' (Hutchison 1937b, 652). Hutchison considers statistics to be the problem-solving instrument in economics, and although cautious about the multitude of interrelated factors and the difficulty inherent in collecting accurate data, he persists in defending the view that more data results in better tests of economic postulates (Hutchison, 1941, 741). Hutchison would later acknowledge the rather naive optimism of his former view on this point.

The Knight-Hutchison debate illustrates the importance of the economist's (methodological) inclinations for his understanding of the evolving economy. Both Knight and Hutchison use modes with the prime intention of enhancing our understanding of reality. However, we may presume that by adopting his approach Knight, facilitated the avoidance of uncertainty in analyses. He is clearly a neo-classical theorist working with his hypothetic-deductive model. That is to say, for him, in principle, the primary function of economic principles is to understand reality by building and deducing from a "well-defined" model. In contrast, for Hutchison, testing propositions as quickly as possible is of fundamental importance. Such an approach would probably time and time again confront economists with the consequences, and with the non-quantifiable nature, of changes and uncertainties in economic life. Because of the prevalence of uncertainty about the future, deducing implications from some fundamental assumption within a static analysis would prove to be a waste of time. We would like to state that in view of the dominance of discussions concentrating on theoretical specifications and mathematical methods, while choosing concepts instrumentally, any discussion with regard to the intricate problem of uncertainty is bound to remain a marginal affair.

In 1916, Knight adequately stated that the taking of responsibility is a better term than risk-taking when discussing decisions involving uncertainty, because risk is used in connection with known changes and insurance (Knight 1916, 281). As he reaffirmed in Knight (1921), uncertainty has a meaning fundamentally different from risk. In sharp contrast, by 1938, mainstream economists hardly bother to define uncertainty: they seem to understand this term rather freely, consisting first of all cases of which Knight would relate to risk. Uncertainty-bearing and the elimination of uncertainty are used as generic terms relevant to '...a *wider* field than that of insurance' (Little 1938, 36; emphasis added, EW). We have no reason to question the merits of the Little article in presenting an adequate account of the dominant attitude towards uncertainty in the economy. It may very well present a common view among economists on what they understand as the correct uncertainty-concept.

By the end of the 1930s, it was also clear that Knight (1921) had the unexpected effect of boosting the method of grouping or the application of the law of large numbers to these economic questions: 'The distinction between insurable "risks" and uninsurable "uncertainties", which was first propounded by F.H. Knight, made conspicuous in economic literature this process of estimation through aggregation' (Little 1938, 38). Spatial and temporal grouping of many instances of one type of behaviour in order to yield a measurable anticipation of that behaviour, implies the ironing out of irregularities in a large number of instances. Little (1938) emphasizes the rise in importance of the '...habit of transforming observation of qualitative changes into quantitative estimates' (Little 1938, 45). But did economists concede that the entrepreneurial decisions about the future in general or speculators' guesses of forward prices in particular, fit the third category of Knight's classification of probability situations? An affirmative answer would impair the prevalent applicability of such concepts as off-setting risks and risks premiums, and curtail the scope and method of economics in general and the theory of risk in particular. However, a negative answer seems to be more generally subscribed to: the opinion seems to be prevalent that by and large even in such cases prices will be carried to the level where chances of gain and loss tend to cancel each other out. This opinion is expressed by several economists (Sweezy, 1938, 236-7; Eastham 1938, 106-10).

2.9 Is this uncertainty?

Hart's book *Anticipations, Uncertainty, and Dynamic Planning*, published in 1940, provides us with a good example of the prevailing approach to uncertainty among economists of this era. What became a bestseller '...was part of the rather substantial literature this approach produced between 1935 and 1940.' (Hart 1940, v). A.G. Hart (1909-..), who became professor of economics at Columbia University, had just finished his studies at Harvard and Chicago when he wrote this summarizing work. Providing us with a well-considered viewpoint, he explicitly tried to incorporate ideas gleaned from the writings, teaching, discussions and guidance of, among others, Knight, Hicks, and Boulding. This systematic and accurate monograph concentrates on the analysis of anticipations as the starting point for building a formal dynamic theory of the business firm. Thus, Hart obeys Robbins's admonishment to restrict the theory of dynamics to planning for the future (Robbins 1932 1935, 79). As we stated earlier, it would also imply that only the most convenient assumptions may be used.

While both Knight and Hart may be labelled 'literary pure theorists' (Knight 1921, 5-6n2), Hart is the more rigorous of the two in applying the hypothetical-deductive method of theorizing. The theoretical advantages of adopting this methodological strategy of augmenting details in an initially uncomplicated, ideal model are evident, and include standardised terminology, straightforward argumentation and convenient explanation. As a result, a major difference exists between Knight (1921) and Hart (1940) with regard to the logical rigour applied. Knight uses a discursive style of writing, combining theory and practice, while Hart is more of a stringent logician, discussing problems in a more "technical" economic language (Hart 1940, 4), and employing economic shorthand. Thus, in his 1921 work, Knight devotes three chapters, or 146 pages, to defining and analysing perfect competition, while summarizing economic theory, discussing premises, implications and arguments. By the end of the interwar period standardized phraseology and terminology was widely accepted and Hart is able to use abridged forms. To give an example; '...in the *timeless* enterprise theory of the textbooks the *data* with which the entrepreneur is confronted are market situations (under perfect competition, fixed buying-prices and selling-prices; under monopolistic competition, supply curves and demand curves) and technical input-output relations' (Hart 1940, 9). Likewise, the word "convenience" is used on numerous occasions for clarity of argument. The logical rigour applied, however, does not result in the kind of realism found in Knight.

We hope by now to have established that during the interwar period the understanding and treatment of uncertainty changed dramatically. Hart and Little invest uncertainty with a meaning which Knight would have labelled risk and Knight's distinction between risk and uncertainty had almost disappeared. Uncertainty had changed meaning: Hart would characterize it as '...the dispersion of anticipations around the expectation' (Hart 1940, 65). In Hart's idea of uncertainty, the elements (1) singularity of outcomes and (2) estimation of future events, stand out as crucial. The concept of risk enables the essential features of uncertainty to be clarified. 'Estimates about any future event which is not regarded as certain may involve either uncertainty or risk. The event viewed in isolation is always uncertain. But viewed as a member of a group of events so related that their joint outcome is more certain than the individual events in the group, it is a risk.' (Hart 1940, 51).

Hart refers to Knight (1921) for further discussion on the difference between risk and uncertainty, but his 1940 work nevertheless does not elaborate upon Knight's classification of probability cases. Moreover, risk and uncertainty are considered to refer to nothing more than different strata of a pyramid, distinguished by the level of aggregation. Uncertainty loses its characteristic of immeasurability. In short, for Hart risk and uncertainty differ only according to the dimension of the number of cases under scrutiny.

Risk situations exist in firms, that is, in organizations of productive resources for business purposes under a single actor's control (Hart 1940, 2), only when the firms carry on separate and comparable operations with independent outcomes. A reduction of the degree of uncertainty is defined as a decrease in the statistical dispersion of market anticipations (Hart 1940, 65). Insurance can virtually eliminate uncertainties which involve specific unfavourable contingencies.

This definition of uncertainty fits the Knightian types of probability situations gathered under the heading risk. It now has little in common with the estimates or guesses, which were formerly so relevant in cases of uncertainty. We may thus conclude that, by the 1940s, uncertainty has become encapsulated in risk theory, although the writing was already on the wall in 1931. The open future is relegated to denoting no more than the points in isolation on a probability distribution.

In the absence of uncertainty and risk, applying rationality to economic decisions amounts to what Hart calls '...operating on the marginal principle' (Hart 1940, 4). He makes light of the fundamental and practical problems involved in the acquisition of information, the formation of rational estimates and the establishment of rational plans, by simply assuming, that '...business plans are explicit and rational in the light of explicit estimates' (Hart 1940, 5). In his view the introduction of the dimension of time is not by itself sufficient to render the static extrapolation of optimising techniques obsolete. Given certainty about future developments, the introduction of a time-subscript does not remove economics from balancing "at the margin". It is still analogous to finding the optimum of the firm in static analysis: the quantities of various components must be varied in order to find the optimum plan in time (Hart 1940, 18).

Hart states that uncertainty introduces a distinction between less and more reliable data, at respectively lower and higher costs. Costs are involved in both the gathering of data, and in the processes of estimation and planning. The ability, *ex ante*, to accurately discover how profitable extra information is, '...involves an accurate forecast both of the final estimate and of the event — which obviously cannot be made on the basis of the preliminary inquiry.' (Hart 1940/1937..) In Hart's view information about future markets will always remain incomplete and unreliable. 'Unfortunately it must remain eternally a matter of guesswork just where the margin of profitable estimation and planning lies' (Hart 1940, 81). This guesswork is at the level of acquiring information about economic affairs, not at the level at which crucially relevant information is non-existent, e.g., in the case of innovations. Hart's model suggests that neat probability distributions will even be satisfactory means by which to conceptualize such guesswork situations.

According to Hart, the main reactions to a relatively high degree of uncertainty are (1) installing non-specialised equipment, (2) purchasing insurance, and (3) maintaining liquidity (Hart 1940, 72, 25). These reactions enhance the adaptive capacity of the firm enabling it to react in due time to new developments and to take advantage of yet unknown opportunities. The prime entrepreneurial means of meeting uncertainty is the postponement of decisions until more information is available, that is, '...the preservation of flexibility in his (the entrepreneur's; EW) business plan' (Hart 1937, 286).

Flexibility will have a minor role to play in planning under certainty, and when future losses are not feared, no insurance will be purchased.

Similarly, calculations of cash balances and inventories will render liquid reserve holdings redundant. However, flexibility in plant and organization may yield better results in the case of a prospective varying rate of output. Likewise, in the case of variable sales, the costs of production flexibility must be weighed against storage costs (Hart 1940, 25-7). Whenever it is expected that economic activities presenting more scattered outcomes will prove the more profitable, Hart recommends the more flexible system of production. Hart regards flexibility to be virtually essential in the face uncertainty and consequent capital-market imperfections (Hart 1940, 25). This introduction of flexibility as a response to uncertainty is in fact considered to be Hart's principal contribution to economics (Blaug 1986, 376).

With regard to the planning problem, Hart uses the frequency theory of probability, and favours the utilization of both the expected value and the distribution of outcomes. This may be contrasted with Knight's approach, since Knight used the classical theory of probability, and discussed the estimate of a specific outcome. Furthermore, Knight was well aware of the essential role played by intuitive opinions, alongside measurable information in economic behaviour.

Hart, however, explicitly uses cardinal probabilities, and sums them to unity. He asserts that the use of ordinal probabilities is to be considered insufficient for decision-making. Moreover, cardinality must enter somewhere into decision-making, e.g. in evaluating the equability of insurance premiums (Hart 1940, 53-4). The use of (1) the expected value of a probability distribution, together with (2) knowledge about the range of the distribution of outcomes, clearly makes the discussion of flexibility a brainchild of this theory-driven discussion on uncertainty. Hart criticises economists who only use the expected value, claiming that such an approach would result in unjustifiably static recommendations. The following two arguments may be found in favour of the expectation *cum* distribution view of expected outcomes. First, the entrepreneur may be non-neutral vis-à-vis risks. Hart considers both risk aversion and uncertainty to be of quantitative importance in economic behaviour (Hart 1940, 74). Second, planning at t_0 for all present and future activities of the firm is considered to be superfluous and foolish business policy. The combination of an open future and the costs of estimation and planning limit the "economic horizon" of the entrepreneur. Estimates of the near future may be more definite and detailed than estimates of the remote future, whereas more comprehensive information will become available with the passage of time. 'The very core of the uncertainty situation is the expectation of knowing more about the future as it draws in toward the present. In short, anticipations include the expectation that anticipations will change' (Hart 1940, 83-4).

In our view, this viewpoint carries with it the following crucial drawbacks: first, a necessary condition is the narrowing in time of the range of the distribution of estimates: 'The t_1 estimates must recognize no possibilities for later dates not contemplated at t_0. And some ... must have dropped out of consideration' (Hart 1940, 85). Thus, the unexpected appearance of once written-off or yet-uncontemplated possibilities is not allowed to take place. A surprise is impossible; there is always an encompassing basis for classifying all possible instances, and probabilities can be added to them. Consequently, Hart states that estimates and plans must be less detailed and concentrate more and more on decisions about durable equipment, the further they project from the present. The reason is that relevant developments become more indefinite in time. Anticipations are considered likely to change more often, or to a greater extent, as the element under scrutiny is located further into the future. However, at t_0 a once and for all decision takes place covering all contingencies, balancing all costs and all benefits and plans according to the optimal timing of specific decisions. A second problem we have with this approach is the exclusion of surprises. Flexibility, creativity of thought, and decentralisation of decision-making and responsibility may be promoted for the sake of facilitating some adequate action or reaction when something unforeseen and/or unexpected materializes.

Under what Hart calls conditions of uncertainty a zone of schedules, e.g. of probability linked possible receipts from sales in time will exist. This zone is wider for estimates further in future. As Hart puts it in 1937, '...estimates for the near future will normally display less diffusion than estimates for more remote dates.' (Hart 1937, 286). From these schedules one may derive the expectation schedule, weighing all estimated receipt schedules against the estimated probability of the contingency occurring, and summing the results for each date.

The model for discussing sales-"uncertainty" can be expanded to a discussion on the existence of several types of output, as well as on "uncertainty" of technology, of raw material prices, and of interest rates. Incorporation of each of these elements should result in plans that leave adequate leeway for changes (Hart 1940, 59-60). For Hart, the uncertainties on markets for inputs and on markets for products are almost symmetrical.

The latter makes it profitable to minimize stocks of durable inputs, to avoid long-term buying-contracts, to produce unspecialized, storable semi-manufactures, to opt for short production runs and to plan for rapid switching of production. Input-market uncertainty favours plans under which substitution of inputs is straightforward, input reserves are held as stocks and prompt production increases are possible (Hart 1940, 60-5).

According to Hart, the existence of a "stepped" capital-market is an important practical consequence of uncertainty, and capital-market institutions differ to a large extent because of that very uncertainty. 'The institutions of the capital-market are deeply affected by the investor's uncertainty' (Hart 1940, 40). Every entrepreneur is confronted with the following four sources of capital: (1) own capital; (2) outside equity participations, whereby limits are determined largely by investment banking practices; (3) borrowing via investment middlemen, such as bankers and insurance companies, whereby securities are commonly required as collateral; and (4) renting capital goods, a source which would make no difference to the entrepreneur in a free capital-market.

In fact, capital-rationing, i.e., where the limits set fall short of the volume of capital the firm would choose to carry on if free (Hart 1940, 34), is an effect of uncertainty. The causes are the possible dishonesty of the borrower, and the uncertainty for the entrepreneur and/or others, of business prospects (Hart 1940, 43). When a firm wants to borrow via investment middlemen, collateral is commonly required for two reasons: (1) to foster confidence among the ultimate investors, the savers; and (2) to eliminate the need for expensive investigations. Certain types of inventories or real estate, and certain balance-ratios, function as thresholds controlling entry to markets for capital. 'Hence investment specialists (..) have built up systems of more or less arbitrary rules, which are followed also by many private investors' (Hart 1940, 40-9). The entrepreneur obtains capital on this stepped market, whereby each step has its own interest rates, follows its own rules of thumb, and imposes fairly specific quantitative limits. Capital-market imperfections induce a modification of plans aimed at enhancing the respectability of the company. The hoarding of larger idle cash balances is induced by relatively more uncertain interest forecasts, more risk avoidance, and more uncertainty about the future availability of capital in capital markets (Hart 1940, 71). Cash balances and insurance-policy holdings may prove advantageous in increasing borrowing power or by reducing interest rates. This applies irrespective of whether or not the individual entrepreneur is affected by personal uncertainty (Hart 1940, 50).

We may draw the following conclusion with regard to the interwar development of economic thought on uncertainty: most pre-war mainstream-economists no longer see a relationship between the fundamental absence of knowledge and the necessity of acting upon an intuition-based range of possible outcomes. In spite of Hutchison, who adopts the opposite stance, Hart, who is probably representative for the majority of economists, regards the condition of lack of knowledge to be a relatively unimportant one (Hart 1940, 84-7). In other words, by 1940 the term uncertainty was no longer being used in the sense intended by Knight. One may argue that this extreme adulteration of the Knightian concept of uncertainty was caused by the dominance of the "technocratic" approach; when results appeared to be unclear, such information could always be dealt with by means of probability-distributions. Support for this explanation of the demise of Knightian uncertainty may be found in Hart's preface to his 1951 edition. The sequence analysis offered in the book is essentially concerned to present '...formally a *mechanical dynamics*, with an *expectational dynamics* between the lines' (Hart 1940, viii).

2.10 The submergence of Knightian uncertainty

The question posed in the introduction to this chapter may now be answered. In tracing trends in the treatment of uncertainty in neo-classical economics, following its introduction into economics by Knight, we have found two major trends. First, during the interwar period the Knightian concept of uncertainty was first of all restricted to the domain of profit theory; later, it became a side issue; and finally it was shunted into a scientific railway siding. Uncertainty, as Knight defined it, was submerged, and that it sank is due partly to the prevalence of theoretical exercises, and partly to the troublesome multi-faceted problem of arriving at a useful concept of uncertainty. During this period, the meaning attached to uncertainty changed, and its parameters changed from unmeasurable outcomes into unknown chances. Throughout this period, uncertainty retained its negative connotations, although they also changed albeit in a different respect: the dynamic approach offered by Schumpeter and Knight, who acknowledged the importance of changing patterns of economic behaviour, was eclipsed by the preference for one-shot optimisation.

The second trend, namely the gradual change in techniques, which itself was stimulated by a change in the probability theory used, facilitated the straightforward modelling of economic activities. It was supposed that uncertainty could be conveniently encapsulated in probability distributions. A terminological veil of so-called uncertainties has been draped around a Pandora's box labelled determinism and probabilism. Of Knight's ideas on uncertainty there remains little intact, save the idea of a unique event conforming to irreducible (Hacking 1990, 181-2) statistical laws which govern phenomena. The intricate problem of reconciling numerical data with possibly unmeasurable or unpredictable outcomes could thus be ignored. However, the resultant so-called stochastic determinism is unable to take account of major changes. We recall that Knight himself actually warned against what had evolved out of related discussions during the interwar period, pointing out that when scientists treat changes as following known laws, they explain uncertainty by explaining it away (Knight 1921, 313).

If we restrict ourselves to studying mainstream economics, we are inclined to conclude that by the end of the interwar period, economics was not so much coping with uncertainty as a range of outcomes deemed possible, but rather with sets of *ex ante* defined outcomes, each having a specific probability of occurrence. Neoclassical economics is unable to deal with situations which are unique to a high degree. The developments may best be summarized in the following quote: 'One characteristic of changes in economic theory during these two decades identifies the initial awareness of complexity, the gradual use of probability to represent complexity, and the ultimate summary of probability distributions by means and standard deviations so that analytical convenience is enhanced ... It seems appropriate to describe this development as the *avoidance of uncertainty*.' (Rowley & Hamouda 1987, 45). Furthermore, the development of ideas on uncertainty within mainstream economics is consistent with the spreading of the creed that the laws of nature are probabilistic, while sustaining the notion of individual freedom within the boundaries of a probability distribution. 'Probability is, then, "the" philosophical success story of the first half of the twentieth century' (Hacking 1990, 4). A hidden theme in this success is that the term uncertainty shed its meaning and became submerged in mainstream economics in the interwar period. We hope to show how neatly ideas about uncertainty in the mainstream economics of the postwar period, which is the central subject of the next chapter, dovetail with the ideas arrived at by the end of the interwar period.

3: THE NEGLECT OF KNIGHTIAN UNCERTAINTY IN MAINSTREAM POSTWAR ECONOMICS

'Today choice under uncertainty is a field in flux: the
standard theory is being challenged on several grounds
from both within and outside economics.'

(Machina 1987, 121)

3.1 Introduction

In chapter two of this study it was made clear that by the end of the interwar period, uncertainty had undergone a metamorphosis in its meaning; as a scientific term. The emphasis shifted from immeasurable outcomes, which Knight stressed, and came to lie with unknown chances, as Hart understood them. After the Second World War, a specific and promising domain of economic enquiry, the so-called economics of uncertainty, developed with its roots in the interwar evolution of economic thought. Soon after the war, neo-classical economists were commonly prepared to interpret uncertainty as denoting the negation of certainty. When studying economic behaviour under conditions of uncertainty, they are, in fact, assuming a world of risk. Probability is believed to be a property of knowledge or beliefs (Hey 1979). These postwar studies are similar in flavour to Hart's work on subjective probabilities which, he maintains, converge to the "real" or *a priori* probabilities as more information becomes available with which to amend or refine the original subjective probabilities (Hart 1940, 60).

Postwar research on individual choice and allocative market equilibrium under uncertainty, featuring the expected utility model and the Arrow-Debreu state-preference approach respectively, resulted in various elaborations, a number of insights, and advanced theoretical constructs. It proved to be a success story in economic analysis, and remained so until the end of 1970s (Hirshleifer and Riley 1979, 1375-6; Balch and Wu, 1974, 1; Hammond 1987, 280; Machina 1987, 121; Machina 1989a, 1622).

During the 1980s, however, the paradigmatic standard model of choice under uncertainty, i.e. the expected utility model of preferences over random prospects, was discredited by a large body of experimental evidence from the field of behavioural decision research. This evidence casts doubts upon both the descriptive and the normative validity of the standard choice model (Hey 1982, 130). Unfortunately, not one of the alternative theories put forward has proven itself to be compatible with all of the data to a satisfactory extent (Sudgen 1987, 22; Appelby and Starmer 1987, 42; Machina 1987, 121; Machina 1989a, 1622; Ford 1987). The Arrow-Debreu general equilibrium theory was also criticised; not so much for internal inconsistencies, but rather for its deficient representation of the economy. 'We have certainly arrived at an orderly destination, but it looks increasingly likely that we cannot rest there.' (Hahn 1985, 123). The evidence on missing and evolving markets, and the consequent importance of learning processes, particularly undermined the credibility of the Arrow-Debreu model (Hahn 1989a; Hahn 1989b). These events resulted in a redirection of research, and within the two dominant fields in the economics of uncertainty, the emphasis has shifted from the large-scale mathematics-oriented projects of the first hour toward problems of acquisition and dissemination of information, i.e. research which concentrates on how people learn to cope with uncertainty (Drèze, 1987, xxv).

The above-mentioned pair of dominant branches within the mainstream economics of uncertainty are the first topics to be discussed in this chapter. These branches concentrate on what is variously referred to as exogenous, technological or event uncertainty, while employing the traditional assumptions of costless exchange at market-clearing prices (Hirshleifer and Riley 1979, 1376-7). The (Subjective) Expected Utility theory will first be presented and criticised, after which we will turn to the state-preference approach.

In sharp contrast with the tendency away from giving priority to mathematically-oriented advances, voices were also heard to advocate its reversal. Proponents of this policy virtually ignore the growing amount of empirical research. and argue the virtues of prioritizing mathematical research. Adherents of this approach took a radical step away from discussing the acquisition of information with which to identify the objective probability distribution; since people are assumed to know that distribution from the start. Testing human abilities to deduce or discover probabilities is deemed to be of secondary importance. This group of economists regard it as their prime task to construct models of interactions in risky situations and deduce policy-oriented conclusions from them. The approach which this tendency represents is known as new classical economics and will be dealt with in the sections six to nine of this chapter.

3.2 The (S)EU -theory

The theory of preference formation under uncertain contingencies first appeared in Von Neumann and Morgenstern (1944),in whose pages it is formally proved that the maximization of expected utility is derivable from a handful of axioms (Schoemaker 1982, 531). Von Neumann and Morgenstern presented their Expected Utility Hypothesis, which is supposed to specify rational choice in the context of uncertainty. The Expected Utility Theory (EUT), a theory based upon the Expected Utility Hypothesis, relies on a number of outcomes, and, more importantly, on a distribution of probabilities. As we may recall from Knight (1921), under uncertainty there is no valid basis for classifying instances, and the EUT is thus better regarded as a model of decision-making under risk. However, economists working on these theories use the term uncertainty '...rather loosely as a blanket name meaning "the lack of certainty".' (Hey 1979, 41). Therefore, we need to bear in mind that we are discussing situations of risk masquerading as an economics of uncertainty.

The EUT provides us with a generalization of the expected value approach, itself proposed by Pascal and de Fermat in the 17th century. The expected value approach features prominently in chapter two of this study. Unfortunately, this approach could not explain the Saint Petersburg paradox, which asks: will Jean decide to play if he is challenged to toss a fair coin until it comes up heads, with a doubling of the payout for each extra toss? It turned out that there is hardly anyone who would take the bet, notwithstanding that the odds offer an infinite expected value. The paradox can be explained when one realises that Jean's risk attitude may be relevant to his decision to accept or decline the gamble. The expected value approach assumes that the attractiveness of a bet, with x_i as a, potentially multidimensional, outcome from a list of say n outcomes, and p_i as the associated probability, such that Σp_i over the n alternatives is 1, is given by the following monetary value:

$$\Sigma \; p_i x_i$$

Von Neumann and Morgenstern defined utility as that which represents preferences over the alternative outcomes x_i using a utility function $U(x)$ cardinally unique up to positive linear transformation. Accordingly there should be no influence of changes in the agent's wealth position. Structured by the axioms of EUT, utility became a technical term (Broome 1991), and while in EUT, the property of linearity in the payoffs is dropped, the linearity of the probabilities is retained (Machina 1987, 125). Instead of an expected value we now have an expected utility value:

$$\Sigma \ p_i u(x_i)$$

According to EUT, a risk-lover will always accept a fair bet. A risk-averse agent, however, will prefer any reward above the expected utility value of the gamble, i.e. the certainty equivalent, for playing the gamble, although this reward may be lower than the expected monetary value of the fair bet. The risk-premium denotes what one is willing to pay to replace the expected utility value by its expected monetary value. This formula for the risk-premium may be used to identify the agent's risk attitude. Furthermore, it may function as an index of risk-aversion, because a (more) positive risk-premium reflects a (stronger) risk-aversion (Hey 1984, 443-4). It may be orthodox to assume risk-aversion, but it is neither a rationality axiom nor a necessary component of economic analysis (Thaler 1987, 104). It may be depicted using a concave utility function: the marginal value of wealth falls with any increment of wealth, or to be more precise, the first derivative of the utility function is positive and the second derivative is negative. A convex (linear) utility curve, on the other hand, indicates a risk-loving (risk-neutral) agent, for example a compulsive gambler.

In economic situations, however, it may prove difficult, if not impossible, to identify and assign the real probabilities to the different alternatives. Because the price distribution of whole-meal sliced bread in town, or of airline returntickets Amsterdam-Chicago, is probably neither known nor listed somewhere, one has to find out by guessing, enquiring, or learning by doing.

According to certain EUT axioms, the decision-maker is assumed to assign probabilities subjectively to the utilities attached to the final consequences. Next, one may try to deal with the uncertainty, or more particularly with the ignorance of objective probabilities involved, by integrating acquired information. By taking such refinements on board, the more generalized Subjective Expected Utility theory (SEU-theory) increasingly replaced EUT proper (Hey 1984).

probability usually associated with Ramsey and Savage. Subjectivists assume that probabilities represent degrees of belief which are fundamentally internal to the individual. As a result, the subjective probability of an event, $f(p_i)$, may differ from the stated or objective probability of an event, p_i (Schoemaker 1982, 537). Subjective probability beliefs may be called prior probabilities, and express '...the observer's uncertainty about events of the outside world.' (Poirier 1988, 122). By the same token, the expected utility value is replaced by the subjective expected utility value:

$$\Sigma\ f(p_i)u(x_i)$$

Thus, SEU-theorists abandoned linearity in both the probabilities and in the payoffs. However, a non-linear probability distribution violates what is called first-order stochastic dominance preference, which relates to the summing of subjective probabilities to a value not equal to unity. This violation means that agents employing SEU are amenable to have a "Dutch-book" made against them. In the present context such a book states the following: when lotteries are adequately modelled it is possible for a risk neutral, or rational agent, to make money out of a risk-lover's preference for lotteries, and out of the risk-averse agent's preference for sure chances (Machina 1989a, 1634-5).

The introduction of communicated information in general will lead to a revision of the prior degrees of beliefs. The compromise or average of the prior and the observed likelihood function presents the posterior probability function. This revision of the probability beliefs is determined by Bayes's theorem. For each payoff i, the prior probability $f(p_i)$ is multiplied by the observed or conditional probabilities, $q(p_i)$. When the aggregate has been obtained, the denominator is then rescaled to bring the probability integral back to unity (Hirshleifer and Riley 1979, 1394). From Bayes-theorem it may be understood that greater, or as the case may be lower, confidence in an agent's prior beliefs that an outcome will be realized is reflected in a less or more dispersed probability distribution respectively, and agents consequently attach less or more value to additional evidence.

The main normative advantage of this method is the structured updating of beliefs by the use of feedback information. However, an immediate drawback of the internally logically-consistent Bayesian approach is that it inhibits creativity. Applying the straightjacket of Bayesian updating to their field of research would limit both the researcher's and the agent's to their field of research would limit both the researcher's and the agent's creative freedom in learning from data (Rust 1988, 149; Poirier 1988, 167). Furthermore, because the posteriors are averages of evidence and priors there always remains some influence of the choice of the distribution of subjective probabilities. Who decides on the priors in major household or enterprise decisions? Moreover, structural breaks in results may be observed but cannot readily be introduced by means of the Bayes's rule, reflecting adaptive learning. For example, how could Bayes's rule introduce the dangers of the rise of major environmental insurance claims?

Systematic errors are exposed in Tversky and Kahneman (1974), and explained with the aid of the "representativeness heuristic". Such a heuristic compares a specific case with the stereotype of the whole class. For example, when asked about a regular six-sided dice with four green (G) and two red (R) faces, a significant number of respondents would erroneously regard the sequence RGRRR as less probable than GRGRRR. Similary, in the case of a perfect coin, HTHTTH is thought to be more likely than HHHTTT. On the same lines, people prove to undervalue prior information compared to new information, thus violating Bayes's rule, since agents overestimate the representativeness of the present sample. In a dynamic world, overreaction seems to be the rule, as, for example, the excessive volatility of stock prices would seem to suggest (Tversky and Kahneman 1974, 20-6; Machina 1987, 147; Thaler 1987, 117-9; Schoemaker 1982, 551). An impressive number of such systematic deviations from SEU-rationality has been found (Frey and Eichenberger 1989).

A reasonable alternative to acquiring information by actively seeking it is to wait and see. In some cases information may automatically emerge as time goes by, for example in the form of national statistics. One may wait for such emergent information by adopting a flexible position (Hirshleifer and Riley 1979, 1398). Although Hirshleifer and Riley (1979) do not refer to Hart (1940), whose work is discussed in chapter two of this thesis, their arguments are essentially similar to his. One has to choose by trading-off the costs of waiting against the possible losses which might ensue from a mistaken early commitment (Hirshleifer and Riley 1979, 1398-9).

Empirical refutations obliged researchers to go beyond expected value and pass on via expected utility to subjective expected utility. However, over and above these empirical problems, which on each occasion were resolved by taking a further step towards generalising the theory, there remain fundamental refutations challenging the sets of assumption pertaining to preference orderings and to rational behaviour (Hey 1982, 131). A few of such empirically-based problems and proposed alternatives to them are next in line to be discussed. We intend to restrict that discussion because most of the alternatives which are in vogue very likely still take probability distributions for granted. That is to say that these generalizations of SEU-theory are, like SEU-theory itself, in fact merely studying deliberate decision-making under risk, although they likewise insist on calling their field of research choice under uncertainty. Such generalisations include SEU-theory as a special case, that is when objective probabilities are given (Hey 1982, 137).

3.3 Variations on a theme

An early and major falsification of expected utility theory is the Allais paradox, which was dismissed or neglected since it was presumed to '...belong to the family of "optical illusions".' (Drèze, 1974, 14). This paradox, also called certainty effect or common consequence effect, pertains to the assumption set on preference orderings. It relates to the varying valuations of the payoffs under given probabilities. The Allais-paradox may be operated by obtaining agent's preferred options from the following two pairs of gambling opportunities:

a_1:1.00 chance of $1,000,000
a_2:0.10 chance of $5,000,000 +0.89 chance of $1,000,000 +0.01 chance of $0
and
a_3:0.10 chance of $1,000,000 +0. 90 chance of $0
a_4:0.11 chance of $1,000,000 +0. 89 chance of $0

Except for the money levels of the results, the two plays actually correspond. To clarify this, we reshuffle the plays as follows:

a_1:0.89 chance of $1,000,000 +0.11 chance of $1,000,000
a_2:0.89 chance of $1,000,000 +0.10 chance of $5,000,000 +0.01 chance of $0
and
a_4:0.89 chance of $0   +0.11 chance of $1,000,000
a_3:0.89 chance of $0   +0.10 chance of $5,000,000 +0.01 chance of $0

Expected utility theory would predict that if gamble a_1 (a_2) is chosen in the first play, then gamble a_4 (a_3) would be chosen in the second play, because the risk attitude in the first play proves the agent to be risk-averse (risk-loving). However, extensive research yielded the following results. Agents often choose a_1 in the first play, indicating risk-averseness, while choosing gamble a_3 in the second play, indicating a risk-loving attitude. The pair (a_2, a_4) accounts for relatively less violations of expected utility theory. This shift in risk attitude is termed fanning out (fanning in) (Machina 1989, 284-6). Later tests showed that learning effects would not change the results as drastically (Machina 1987, 126-9). The agent seems to prefer a certain gain rather than a gamble with a higher expected value, but when the chances of winning are small one seems to prefer the gamble with the higher expected payoff. The certainty alternative is given too much weight by the agent.

Another well-known paradox is the Ellsberg-paradox. In this research, Ellsberg focused on the probability dimension. It was apparent from experiments that people may not formulate uncertain choice problems in a coherent manner regarding probabilities (Machina 1989, 294). Furthermore, if the prior probability distribution is actually given, subjects seem to evaluate on the basis of something more than the mere expected payoffs. Take a pair of urns, a_1 and a_2. The first urn contains 50 red balls and 50 black balls, and the second urn also contains 100 balls, some red and some black, but in an unknown ratio. Agents had to choose between betting on x_1, drawing a red ball from a_1; x_2, drawing a red ball from a_2; y_1, drawing a black ball from a_1; or, y_2, drawing a black ball from a_2. As there is no information on the probabilities for a_2 it is surprising to find strong preferences for x_1 over x_2 and for y_1 over y_2. It turned out that subjects somehow felt that the second urn offered riskier options (Thaler 1987, 103-4; Machina 1987, 147-8). These results cast doubts on the usefulness of probability distributions in general and on their application to situations of uncertainty in particular. Nevertheless, Ellsberg-type research is less often presented, stressed and elaborated upon in the literature than are Allais-type investigations focusing on the outcomes, that is the payoffs themselves.

Several models have been developed to incorporate these and other structural deviations from (S)UE-theory. A common element in most of these generalisations or variants of (S)EU-theory is their recent origin (see e.g. Machina 1987, 132; Machina 1989a, 1631). In fact, there is no best and simplest theory among them which is compatible with all of the evidence (Sudgen 1987, 22). Therefore, we feel unable to present and evaluate the different alternatives in this overview of research. We will only have the time to outline the best known amongst them, namely prospect theory.

Prospect theory is a descriptive model developed on the basis of experimental research (Kahneman and Tversky 1979). A framing phase and an evaluative phase are distinguished. Agents are assumed to value the payoffs and weigh the related probabilities before the overall values of the prospects are evaluated. Prospect theory is intended to accommodate certain observed anomalies, although it cannot resolve, for example, the Ellsberg paradox. It proved to make a difference whether agents are told to choose after first assuming a present wealth position of $300 or $500, even though the final expected asset positions are identical (Thaler 1987, 105). This confirms proposed evaluation of prospects in terms of gains or losses relative to some neutral reference point rather than in terms of absolute results. Hence a value function over edited prospects is taken for the utility function $u(x_i)$ itself; the function is assumed to be concave for gains and convex for losses, or S-shaped, i.e. there is loss-aversion (Tversky and Kahneman 1981, 125-6). Next to a revised valuation of the payoffs, prospect theory also presents an original treatment of probabilities: the decision weight $\sigma(p)$, which is to be multiplied by the respective prospects, is a monotonic function of p but is not itself a probability: although it is assumed that $\sigma(1) = 1$ and $\sigma(0) = 0$, the function is not well-behaved near the extremes; moderate and high probabilities are underevaluated to a degree which is more pronounced than the overevaluation of low probabilities. It turns out that, as the value function and the weighing-function are non-linear, different frameworks for establishing essentially similar probabilistic decision-problems may result in different choices (Tversky and Kahneman 1981, 126-8).

The second group of theories which we want to mention here focuses on the potentially negative feeling about consequences, after having played. It includes such theories as Loomes and Sudgen's regret theory (Loomes and Sudgen 1982), and Bell's disappointment theory. The models are consistent with placing relatively higher certainty equivalents on small-stake-large-prize plays than on large-stake-small-prize plays (Loomes 1988, 18). The notion of disappointment relates to the different possible outcomes available in the chosen play. The notion of regret, however, relates to the outcomes of forgone alternative actions (Sudgen 1987, 16). Regret theory is a theory of pairwise choice. The composite experience may involve regret or, its opposite, elation. The value function is essentially the intrinsic utility modified by regret or elation. Regret theory may allow for non-transitive preference-orderings and regards EU-theory as a special case (Machina 1987, 138-9), but is incompatible with, for example, the Allais paradox (Sudgen 1987, 21-2).

This brings us to a general conclusion about (S)EU-theory and its variants. In a largely critical article, Hey arrives at the following conclusion: 'Despite some rumblings of discontent, Subjective Expected Utility theory continues to reign supreme in the Economics of Uncertainty.' (Hey 1984, 454). However, unfortunately no SEU-theory nor any of its variants on decision-making under risk is compatible with all of the evidence gathered hitherto. 'Perhaps one [such model; EW] is waiting to be discovered by an Isaac Newton of economics; perhaps not.' (Sudgen 1987, 22). The trend seems to be towards formulating different models by relaxing various assumptions, including those on the probability side of the formula.

A pervasive problem in SEU-theory and most of its variants is that they all accept the fundamental assumption that the set of alternative choices is certain and known, that the list of possible states of the world, here the alternative elements in the plays, are certain and known, and that the list of final consequences is certain and known. Agents are presumed to use backward induction, that is evaluate all alternatives from the final consequences backward to the first decision to be made (Hey 1982, 137). One of the reasons for defending the presumption of backward induction is that otherwise agents are open to exploitation, for they would be open to '...making [a; EW] book against themselves.' (Machina 1989a, 1624). However, agents adhering to the, among economists widely-applied, SEU-theory are also open to exploitation: as is remarked above, such agents' risk attitude violates the attribute of separability across mutually-exclusive results. More importantly is the problem that applying backward induction in a dynamic or static context neglects to take account of non-separability of preferences in the dynamic case and the limited possibilities of projecting into the future in the static case (Machina 1989a, 1636-46). First, there may be complementarity of physical mixtures of commodity bundles. 'I may prefer the cake to the loaf while preferring half a loaf and half a pack of butter to half a cake and half a pack of butter.' (Sudgen 1987, 15). Second, the application of backward induction is troublesome, because the future is largely unknown. Third, the backward calculations from those final results which are known may be horrendously complicated (Hey 1982).

This criticism naturally leads us to a redirection of attention towards the non-probabilistic analysis of the descriptions of the world held to be true and the suggested means for dealing with this uncertainty about the future. Consequently, we may now turn to the other prominent theme within the economics of uncertainty, namely the macro-economic allocative market equilibria under uncertainty.

3.4 The Arrow-Debreu model

A large number of economists might concur with the following characterization of uncertainty, as they concentrate on the ultimate objects of economic choice: 'Uncertainty means that we do not have a complete description of the world we fully believe to be true.' (Arrow 1974, 33-4). Uncertainty consists in not knowing, from a set of mutually exclusive and exhaustive descriptions of the present and future world, which description of the world is the true one. A set of mutually exclusive and exhaustive states of the world or nature guarantees the existence of uncertainty. There is no need to define the set of descriptions as either very coarse or fine (Machina 1987, 148).

This understanding of uncertainty clearly excludes strategic uncertainty, because any agent is assumed to be unable to influence which state will actually occur. There is only external uncertainty. Thus an early advantage of the Arrow-Debreu model may be noted: in principle, the formal description of the model requires no concept of probabilities. They do materialise however in the contracts agreed upon on the basis of the agents' beliefs about the likely occurrence of a future state of the world (Hammond 1987, 282). Central in this theory is the contingent commodity, which adds to the definition of a good the element of possible future states of nature, which are comprehensive specifications of the environment: 'One is thus led to define a [state contingent; EW] commodity in this new context by its physical characteristics, its location, and its events.' (Debreu 1959, 99). The adjective contingent refers to the actual future availability of commodities, being conditional on the occurrence of a specific environmental event (Safra 1987, 22). The economic agents control decision variables and have information about the finite set of alternatives nature may choose from.

The related state-preference approach links foreseeable payoffs with the respective states of the world (Machina and Rothschild 1987, 227-8). It appears as if economic activities start only after the whole future is determined in a gigantic higgle-haggle: neatly ordered preferences combine with beliefs about an environment in present and future markets. The actions of consumers are fixed for the whole future with specifications for the preferred goods and services at each location, date and event, so as to maximize expected utility, subject to a budget constraint. The producers choose a production plan such that the present value of the shares of their corporations is maximized. Contracts involve agreements on quantity, quality, point of delivery and a time-and-place-specific event. Payments, in units of account, are made irrevocably and at present, although the actual delivery depends on the actual realisation of the event (Debreu 1959, 99-100). Thus, drawing upon theoretical elaborations, the result of which is known as the Arrow-Debreu theory of complete markets, it may be stated that uncertainty can be dealt with in principle by a system of competitive present and futures markets for contingent commodity claims.

Subsequent research essentially tried to take account of informational aspects and the incompleteness of markets (Radner 1987, 305). As long as agents possess different but fixed information sets on the environment there is no fundamental problem for the Arrow-Debreu-model, except that here the existence and optimality of the equilibrium is relative to these fixed information sets (Radner 1987, 309). The organizational costs involved in obtaining information, e.g. because a production plan requires more specific information at a certain date, and the increasing returns on information at low levels of information may create additional vital problems for finding an equilibrium in the Arrow-Debreu model.

Explanations for the missing-markets problem, that is why there are relatively-speaking so few (futures) markets, refer to the enormous accounting problem involved, the uncertainty about the agent's future tastes, transaction costs, adverse selection (Drèze 1985, 323), the refinements needed in the system of markets, and problems of moral hazards (Radner 1987, 309). 'Incomplete markets are the rule' (Drèze 1987, 323). As a result, one the one hand theory presents us with too many equilibrium outcomes, while on the other, once it is recognized that the market system is incomplete and actually consists of a sequence of markets, the latitude is created for discussing money and the stock market. As a consequence, the present situation, the information already acquired, and expectations about future market signals, are of influence on the agreements that will be made now for the present and future. History matters (Hahn 1989b). In fact there is no place for uncertainty but only for distributions of risks. This alternative approach of presenting the environment as being state-dependent, directs attention back to the uncertainty-reducing effect of purchasing insurance against deficiencies.

3.5 Some intermediate conclusions

We may already safely conclude that in mainstream Economics of Uncertainty, uncertainty as described in chapter one has in fact disappeared from the scene. With the exception of a mere handful of alternatives uncertainty is largely neglected. A remarkable finding in our research is that the use of probability distributions is almost universally regarded as being appropriate. Risk is considered to be an integral element of life, either as a probability distribution of utilities, or as distributed beliefs on each of the possible states of the world which can be traded in insurance markets. The problematic relation between theory and reality is solved at the cost of authenticity. Uncertainty is often neglected but it comes to knock on the door time and time again.

Largely due to the influence of research discussing the relation between theory and actual economic practices, the emphasis finally shifted from the large-scale mathematically-oriented research which was initially carried out in the aforementioned two dominant fields in the economics of uncertainty toward problems of reference points and the acquisition and dissemination of information. How do agents form expectations, make plans and use rules of thumb? These questions became urgent problems, since empirical research compromised essential concepts in the economics of uncertainty.

Even before the advance of such empirical research compelled a shift, an alternative parallel route became popular among a group of mathematically-oriented economists. In order to re-introduce expectations, while circumventing theoretical and empirical difficulties concerning the formation of (adaptive) expectations, rational expectations were simply postulated. To facilitate theoretical progress in their economics, the emphasis was placed on the abilities of market participants to arrive at correct inferences on the basis of received price data and non-price information. Since environmental events are exogenous and the conditional expected utility was well-defined in itself, one may in fact concentrate on learning from other participants' non-price information by arriving at inferences based on market prices. Economic agents have developed individual models of the economy and use observations and published data as feedback from the "true model" of the real economy to their own models. If these models are stochastically identical to the true model what is referred to as a rational expectations equilibrium may emerge (Radner 1987, 312-21). We will now proceed to concentrate on this approach which came to be known as New Classical Economics.

3.6 Uncertainty and New Classical Economics. A contradiction in terms?

New Classical Economics (NCE) has radically changed modern macroeconomics in the space of a few decades. With Muth as the charismatic leader (Perlman 1986, 23), and Lucas as the principal architect, constructor and advocate of this approach, adherents to NCE realized a re-appraisal of the assumptions of rationality and equilibrium. New Classical economists substituted dynamic and stochastic optimization for static and deterministic optimization, and were concerned not with disequilibrium analysis, but with dynamic rational expectations-equilibrium under incomplete information (Peeters 1987, 445). Furthermore, NCE explicitly endogenized expectations. Finally, the models were encompassing in the sense that more phenomena could be explained than previously, for example money illusion and business cycles. However, the NCE adepts's interpretation of the postulates (1) agents act in their own self-interest, and (2) markets clear continuously and instantaneously, raises doubts about the adduced weights in the balance between mathematical handiness and appropriate portrayal. In this context, we will attempt in this paragraph to discuss the position and status of uncertainty in NCE.

3.7 The rational expectations hypothesis

The New Classical interpretation of the postulate that agents pursue their self-interest is known as the Rational Expectations Hypothesis (REH). The postulate that markets clear at each point in time is used to support the well-known Phelps-Friedman Natural Rate of unemployment Hypothesis (NRH). The REH and the NRH are the basic building blocks of NCE (Buiter 1980, 34; Grossman 1980, 6, 9; Pesaran 1984 195).

The New Classical endogenization of expectations by means of general theoretical approach (Davidson 1983, 182; Grossman 1980, 9) draws on Muth's (1961) classic paper, which aims at explaining certain phenomena observed in statistics. Muth regards the only real test for his theory to be Friedman's instrumentalism (Muth 1961, 4, 18). 'It is sometimes argued that the assumption of rationality in economics leads to theories inconsistent with, or inadequate to explain, observed phenomena, especially changes over time ... Our hypothesis is based on exactly the opposite point of view: that dynamic economic models do not assume enough rationality.' (Muth 1961, 4). Continuing in this vein, he proposes the Rational Expectations Hypothesis. Although still nascent in the 1969 articles by Lucas and Rapping (1969a; 1969b), the REH has been characteristic of NCE, since its incorporation in Lucas's 1970 papers, which were published in 1972 (Zijp 1992, 150-6).

We may distinguish between four variants of rational expectations: (1) The first version may be called the "weak form of Rational Expectations": the agents are assumed to equalize benefits and costs of marginal, costly information when they form expectations. The specific equilibrium which results is dependent on the distribution of information because optimisation on costly information involves an infinite regress. This is in contrast to the three variants of the strong form of rational expectations, to which we will now direct our attention.

Two out of the three variants of the strong form of rational expectations are of the "as-if" form; The first of these two is (2Aα) Muth Rational Expectations (Stein 1982, 47): 'expectations of firms (or, more generally, the subjective probability distribution of outcomes) tend to be distributed, for the same information set, about the prediction of the theory (or the "objective" probability distribution of outcomes).' (Muth 1961, 5). In other words, '...expectations, since they are informed predictions of future events, are essentially the same as the predictions of the relevant economic theory.' (Muth 1961, 4-5). These two much-cited phrases do not imply that predictions and expectations of individuals, and the economic models used, are common to all and in accordance with economic theory (Snippe 1987, 5). This variant of the REH asserts that (1) the economic system does not waste information, and (2) the way expectations are formed depends specifically on the specification of the relevant model describing the economy (Muth 1961, 3-5). Thus, Muth (1961) presents a strong form of rational expectations, in particular the macro as-if variant (Snippe 1987, 5); The second is (**2Aß**) the micro as-if variant: 'The REH asserts that the unobservable subjective expectations of individuals are exactly the true mathematical conditional expectations implied by the model itself.' (Begg 1982, 30). It assumes that each individual economic agent acts "as if" he knew the facts and coefficients underlying income and price formation (Snippe 1987, 5); (**2B**) The third strong form-variant is the descriptive variant, and presents a more narrowly-formulated REH: private agents do gather and make use of relevant information on the specification of the economy itself and of information on past and current facts (Grossman 1980, 10). This variant, subscribed to by Lucas, is mostly implicitly used by proponents and opponents of normative conclusions derived from the REH in policy analysis. Agents are assumed to know, or have internalized, the basic elements of the "objective underlying model" of the economy (Hodgson 1988, 232). Thus, Lucas borrowed from Muth's macro as-if variant of the REH for a description of the formation of individual expectations. Moreover, Muth (1961) applies the REH to local markets using a partial-equilibrium framework, but, unlike Lucas (1972, 72-3), refrains from presupposing that agents know the structure of the economy as a whole. The introduction of the REH in a general equilibrium framework necessitates the assumption of other if not much larger information sets in the possession of the agents involved (Zijp 1992, 162).

The Natural Rate of unemployment Hypothesis (NRH) refers to the discussion about whether the actual rate of unemployment can structurally deviate from a natural or equilibrium rate of unemployment. According to Friedman, the actual rate can deviate from the natural rate only to the extent that price changes are unanticipated (Pesaran 1984, 196). What is known as the (Phelps-Friedman) NRH posits that the negatively-sloped Phillips curve merely reflects short-run expectational errors. Lucas derived an aggregate supply function of the following form, in support of this claim: the difference between the present real and the natural present rate of change in output deviates by no more than a disturbance term derived from a function of the difference between the present actual and the for next period expected rate of change in prices. The disturbance term is supposed to be serially independent with a zero mean and a constant variance (Pesaran 1984, 203), which implies the exclusion of short, medium and/or long term disequilibrium situations. The derivation of this aggregate supply curve assumes that each agent has knowledge of the, stochastic, processes that generate future prices and wages (Pesaran 1984, 198-9).

We may now deduce that agents acquire knowledge to create rational expectations (RE) endogenously about the true parameter values of the model. However, despite general agreement on the relevance of the learning process itself for the acquisition of knowledge, the learning process is never made explicit in NCE (Pesaran 1984, 204). Given '...the non-existence of a logic of induction, the assumption of rational behaviour is not sufficient to imply that economic agents should conceive of expectational errors as systematic and persistent.' (Snippe 1987, 10). If agents learn on the basis of possibly erroneously specified models or use the correct model but incorrect parameter values, the outcome of the learning process will not necessarily be the correct model and the Rational Expectations single-exit optimal solution (Buiter 1980, 38; Pesaran 1984, 202, 204). Moreover, when agents acknowledge the possibility of misperception, they may already have begun to behave in a manner inconsistent with what the Rational Expectations Hypothesis would suggest on the basis of their present information set. All the variants of the REH suffer from this argument, including Muth Rational Expectations and Lucas's REH (Snippe 1987, 12-5; Bausor 1983, 5-9). Furthermore, how does one discover structural changes? Because of the non-existence of a logic of induction, the mechanism behind the formation of expectations will only be revised if we assume, over and above RE itself, that agents somehow arrive at inductive inferences. All three of the strong variants of the REH are embarrassed by this conclusion. In fact, when one thinks of living creatures who are assumed to pursue their own self-interest, it seems at the least odd to suppose that they abstain from using relevant information not included in NCE-models, such as information on product quality and political tensions. Thus, economic rationality, being different from Rational Expectations, undermines '...the validity of models which are based on expectations functions which assume expectations to depend on only a limited set of variables and/or make use of expectations functions which are independent of these models.' (Snippe 1987, 9). Finally, the aforementioned variant (1) of the REH gets into trouble with the introduction of costly information, because individuals may then be trapped in a vicious circle of ignorance (Pesaran 1987, 271).

3.8 Business cycles

New classical macro-economists use Phelps's "island parable", which features the metaphor of separate "islands", and states that a number of perfectly competitive but isolated markets, will be served by messengers bringing information from other islands. Representative agents, i.e. every agent being representative of the homogeneous population on his own island, possess all current local information but may hold only incomplete global information, due to lacunae and time-lags. The resulting signal processing problem amounts to tracing the permanent and relative price movements, because these movements should induce the agent to respond. In other words, given a change in local prices, agents face the problem of deciding to what extent this change signals real, as opposed to monetary, disturbances. 'Yet, for the same reason that permanent and transitory relative price movements cannot be sorted out with certainty at the time, neither can relative and general movements be distinguished.' (Lucas 1977, 230). The presumed recurrent character of business cycles should allow representative agents to learn what is called the real probability distributions of monetary, or nominal, and physical, or real, disturbances (Lucas 1972, 78) As global information will be assimilated with a lag of x periods, expectational errors result only in transitory effects on the "real" variables. The conclusion must be that systematic monetary policy cannot be successful; only unanticipated monetary actions can, in the short-run, be successful. Thus, '... uncertainty arises not because of the problem of intertemporal choice but owing to the lack of *current* information.' (Pesaran 1984, 199).

Many tests have been conducted on New Classical Economics, especially by testing the REH and the NRH. However, there is little positive empirical evidence relating to these persuasive hypotheses and their derivations (Grossman 1980, 11, 15, 20; Kantor 1979, 1433-7; Peeters 1988, 466; Pesaran 1984, 213; Pesaran 1987, 242; Hodgson 1988, 96; Sargent 1973, 176-187).

3.9 Stochastic certainty

According to Lucas and Sargent, uncertainty associated with the state of nature may be called "exogenous uncertainty": the probability of occurrence of a given event is invariant vis-à-vis an individual's action. In order to prevent a model from "petering out" in future, the model's "nature" must be assumed to "innovate" change. This is modelled as taking independent drawings of lots from a fixed cumulative probability distribution function (Lucas & Sargent 1981, xi-xii; Snippe 1987, 11). Following this line of thought, we see that whereas the distributions themselves cannot be modified, it may be feasible to prepare for, counteract, or insure against the consequences of the stable probability distribution. The economy must be viewed as consisting of stochastic processes with probabilistically-determined events (Lucas 1987, 20). This approach has resulted in a stochastic form of perfect foresight (Arrow 1987a, 210).

The underlying model basically consists of structural behavioural equations. The representative agents have partial control over certain variables and they are faced with an exogenous nature, whose unanticipated "actions" agents learn of after a certain time-lag. In principle "nature" subsumes governmental policies. 'Insofar as business cycles can be viewed as repeated instances of essentially similar events, it will be reasonable to treat agents as reacting to cyclical changes as "risk" or to assume their expectations are rational.' (Lucas 1977, 224). According to Lucas, only in situations of certainty or risk is economic behaviour explainable in economic terms. 'In cases of uncertainty, economic reasoning will be of no value.' (Lucas 1977, 224). The reason for this statement seems to be that the REH is not applicable when one cannot find out which observable frequencies are relevant (Lucas 1977, 223). 'Under the disguise of a stable stochastic process, knowledge of the future masquerades as rationality.' (Bausor 1983, 8).

Such stochastic processes are also known as ergodic processes, assuming the existence of the "Law of Uniformity of Nature" (Pesaran 1987, 15, 270; Davidson 1983, 185; Snippe 1987, 12). Otherwise, changes in the, exogenous, environment would under Rational Expectations necessarily change the perception of the evolution of nature or change the projected distribution function of outcomes. Such modifications could reasonably be expected to alter the decision rule of the agent (Lucas & Sargent 1981, xii-xiii).

Thus, changes in the environment may indirectly change people's behaviour. Lucas and Sargent seem to dislike this result, because it implies that there may not be, stochastic, perfect knowledge of the actual future. However, the usual practice of excluding changes in the environment, in fact also excludes any amelioration of the economic structure, for example by means of infrastructural works undertaken by governments. In point of fact, Lucas views government as an impotent element in society (Lucas 1987, 9-10). Thus, the exogenous uncertainty allowed for is introduced in a very demanding form. We will return to such "games against nature" in chapter six of the thesis.

An alternative approach to this game against nature has been elaborated by Kydland and Prescott and is called the "Dominant Player game". In this Dominant Player game it is assumed that the government is the leader and private agents are the followers. The leader already incorporates the effects of his policies on decision rules of private agents. The following agents optimize by taking as given the governmental policy function for control variables (Lucas & Sargent 1981, xxxiv-xxxv). The leading preference most widely linked to governmental behaviour is minimizing the variance of a certain variable (Lucas & Sargent 1981, xxxviii). However, because of the REH, the agents find themselves in a game consisting of optimizing agents, anticipating each other's actions. We have a game between at least two rationally optimizing agents, the private sector and the public sector. 'Traditional optimal control techniques fail to take account of the impact of future policy measures on current events through the changes in current behaviour induced by anticipation of the future policy measures.' (Buiter 1980, 36). This may lead to '...time inconsistency of optimal plans' (Kydland & Prescott 1977, 619): changing the agent's mind at some future point(s) in time. For instance, the government can break promises given in the struggle for votes. It is only by introducing a constrained class of optimal policy rules over which the government can optimise, that we can calculate optimal plans (Buiter 1980, 37; Lucas 1987, 103-4).

If agents were faced with "endogenous", or "behavioural uncertainty" (Pesaran 1987, 12) human interference might alter or destroy existing probability distributions, that is situations of risk, directly. Individuals can, by the performance of choice itself (Davidson 1983, 192), and thus through their own actions, influence the Data Generating Process (Pesaran 1987, 15). In reality, all decentralized systems of economic decision-making are subject to behavioural uncertainty. 'In conditions where behavioural uncertainty is predominant, the best that can be hoped for is to detect past patterns of regularity, to attempt to understand such regularities and to watch for possible changes in society's institutions, customs and habits.' (Pesaran 1987, 16). Widespread adherence to institutional rules may reduce behavioural uncertainty to a certain extent (Pesaran 1987, 13), but entrepreneurial behaviour remains essential to an economy.

Entrepreneurs as traders discern discrepancies between different markets, because preferences and abilities differ, so they move commodities to places where they are needed, and thus try to make some money. Entrepreneurs as innovators and producers change the economic structure from the inside by redirecting resources, creating new activities, producing new goods or services, and selling wherever profitable. Such activity may start, bolster or merely enlarge one (sub-) sector of the economy, possibly to the detriment of others active in the economy. The entire interlocked economy surely and entirely changes, albeit slowly, as a result of such entrepreneurial activities. Who on Earth is already aware of the fitting education for a career including an as yet non-existent job, 20 years hence? 'In these circumstances it is doubtful wether the uncertainty surrounding economic decisions could be represented by stable stochastic processes, and Keynes's and Shackle's objections to the use of probability models as the basis for the formation of expectations is likely to be valid' (Pesaran 1987, 15).

NCE presents models with, at most, a number of communicating, but not trading, innovating or migrating, representative agents. Aggregation of the independent groups of homogeneous agents presents a national product based upon microeconomic qualities, but such aggregates tell us little about the operation of any macroeconomic system: the portrayed "islands" disappear, change, merge, and/or enlarge with new islands emerging out of the water. 'In aggregates it is significant that the parts are added; in a system it is significant that the parts are arranged' (Angyal 1981, quoted by Peeters 1987, 457). The system is an independent framework, which cannot be derived as an aggregate from the parts. There is no place for behavioural uncertainty in the stochastically deterministic new classical models. Mathematical developments, under the banners analytical simplicity and scientific usefulness, have priority. 'But technique is interesting for technicians (which is what we are, if we are to be of any use to anyone)' (Lucas 1987, 35). In fact, NCE largely consists of technical innovations (Peeters 1987, 461).

We must conclude that the Rational Expectations Hypothesis narrows economics down to at most risky events. Endogenous uncertainty is absent and what is called exogenous uncertainty is present only as independent drawings of lots from a fixed cumulative probability distribution function. The de facto exclusion of uncertainty enables far-reaching implications often derived from the new classical models. It opens up routes to discuss stochastically-optimal economic developments and knowledge of the long-run equilibrium. However living human beings face an ever-evolving economy, and there is no great latter-day Domesday book presenting the blueprints of time-to-come, let alone knowledge of the future in our heads. Nevertheless, we are all assumed to know stochastically what it says.

3.10 Conclusions

This chapter presents the evolution of thought among mainstream economists since the interwar discussion of uncertainty. By the end of the interwar period uncertainty had become a term referring to unknown chances. Knight's reference to unmeasurable outcomes was submerged. After the Second World War, this reformulation of the term uncertainty continued unabated. The discussion shifted to probability distributions held by the agents. Everybody is thought to have preferences about the distribution of possible outcomes. For example, the Subjective Expected Utility theorists concentrated on the form of the probability distribution, risk attitudes, and lotteries. The external uncertainty is now ignorance of the real probability distribution between, for example, red and blue balls in an urn. One is supposed to learn by updating subjective probabilities, until the real probability distribution is known. The macro-economic state-preference approach is not so much concerned with the actual existence, or not, of preferences about all those possible future situations, as it is with the elaboration of some justification for the theoretically predicted shortage of markets in the actual world. New Classical Economics even assumes that agents know some real distribution of outcomes, not merely the set of outcomes, but they may temporary be mistaken on, for example, whether a change in prices reflects local or global changes in prices. NC-Economists value such fixed cumulative probability distributions as useful means for understanding economic phenomena at large.

This chapter presented an understanding of uncertainty which carries a negative connotation. The link with innovative activities became weaker and weaker, until ultimately innovations, surprises, and changes were excluded from economic thought. The dynamic approach made way for a static approach. At the same time, non-optimal outcomes emerge as the result of a shortage of information, although in principle such information is present already.

We will now turn to examination of an approach which regards uncertainty with an outright positive connotation. Mainstream Economists, including NCE, share a belief in the agents' capacities to evaluate all alternatives rationally with adherents of this approach. However, in contrast to the former, supporters of this approach, which is to be discussed next, seriously search for theories linking uncertainty to dynamic developments and an open-ended future. This is the approach characteristic of the approach called the Austrian School of Economics.

4: AUSTRIAN ECONOMICS AND UNCERTAINTY: ON A NON-DETERMINISTIC BUT NON-HAPHAZARD FUTURE

'That man acts and that the future is uncertain are by no
means two independent matters. They are only two
different modes of establishing one thing.'

(Mises 1949, 105)

4.1 Introduction

In the chapters two and three we discussed uncertainty in mainstream
economics and in New Classical Economics. We noted the mathematical
drive to reduce the importance of uncertainty by fusing it with risk or
neglecting it altogether. But, the combination of testing the theories and
evaluating their requirements has resulted in a less optimistic mood about
how much economic theory can thus accomplish in more complex situations.
Uncertainty is usually referred to as a troublesome element for the
economists and the economy alike. We will now turn to an approach which
holds a more optimistic view on the dynamic developments of the economy
and the function of uncertainty therein, namely the Austrian school of
economics.

Uncertainty is taken seriously in the Austrian School of Economics.
In accordance with their statement that 'the pretence of the sciences' is often
unjustified, economists of the Austrian school of economics acknowledge the
prevalence of uncertainty in economic practices. With regard to future
conditions, uncertainty prevails in both long-term and short-term activities
(Mises 1962, 51). 'This uncertainty of the future is one of the main marks of
human condition. It taints all manifestations of life and action.' (Mises 1962,
65).

It will be argued in this chapter that the Austrians concentrated on
uncertainty in relation to the initiation of actions, the origination and
interpretation of information and the use of knowledge. Due to both the
dispersion of knowledge and to its volatile content, the coordination of
economic activities is not self-evident but should be the very subject of
scientific research. The emergence of an equilibrium may not be taken for
granted. In this context, Austrians emphasise that spontaneously-developed
institutions, in particular markets, will advance the emergence of valuable

outcomes of interactions. Substantial external interference may only hinder those who embark on potentially rewarding activities. More recently, adherents to this optimistic line of thought have stressed the need to distinguish between entrepreneurial and rule-governed behaviour.

As Knight (1921) is the starting point of this study, this chapter will also start at the beginning of the interwar period. Mises, sometimes called the intellectual father of the Neo-Austrian school, may be considered to be the first Austrian economist to stress the importance of uncertainty. Therefore, the discussion will start with his writings on the subject. The historical approach adopted in this study obliges us to concentrate more or less chronologically on the main authors in this area. Successively we will broadly introduce writings by Mises, Hayek, Kirzner, Lachmann, and O'Driscoll and Rizzo.

The focus of this chapter will be on answering questions about; (1) how uncertainty has been introduced into Austrian economics; and (2) what the consequent implications for the analysis of decision-making are. We intend to begin with a discussion of Austrian epistemology, since the relationship between uncertainty and economic theory was discussed at this fundamental level by Mises himself. His position, which was already stated in his interwar writings, was more clearly set out in several of his later publications, which will therefore also be used. The key problem resulting from this discussion will be the coordination of actions directed at an uncertain future. Hayek gained prominence precisely in this area by elaborating on the fact that information is scattered, and on the necessary means of facilitating the coordination of interdependent individual activities. We will see that the theoretical profundity of Austrian argumentation evolved and became refined during an interwar "capitalism-socialism debate", also called the "(socialist-) calculation debate" (Lachmann 1977, 192; Kirzner 1988). This debate may illustrate the confrontation of the rapidly maturing but strongly dissimilar Austrian and Neoclassical paradigms, of which the authors involved seemed to be unaware (Kirzner 1988, 2). Furthermore, it presents another illustration of how the dynamic conception of uncertainty came to be excluded from mainstream economics (Lavoie 1981a, 42).

Despite the originality and fruitfulness of the approach adopted by Hayek, he was unable to solve the problem of the open-ended context of the market process, leaving both the pioneering finding of new information, and the individual interpretation of market information hanging in the air. It was Kirzner who tried to solve the first of these two problems by arguing that it is the entrepreneur who creates the future by making decisions embedded in an alertness for potentially profitable opportunities. In turn, Lachmann confronted the second problem by investigating the formation of expectations. The two viewpoints have been integrated by O'Driscoll and Rizzo, who achieved this by distinguishing between the unique and the recurrent features of developments, which are related to entrepreneurial and rule-following behaviour, respectively.

4.2 Human action

Ludwig E. von Mises (1881-1973) linked uncertainty directly to his key epistemological concept, i.e. "human action". Fundamental to Mises's approach is his thesis that to act is to choose. Action is directed at improving the future state of affairs. 'The uncertainty of the future is already implied in the very notion of action. That man acts and that the future is uncertain are .. only two different modes of establishing one thing.' (Mises 1949, 105).

Human action is understood as being purposeful, as a teleological concept, and a concept which assumes that each individual uses means-ends frameworks. In other words, (1) action is caused by the desire to better one's situation; (2) it is directed at realising a subjectively imagined more satisfactory state of affairs; and (3) every individual must expect that purposeful behaviour can at least alleviate the uneasiness. For Mises, these are the general conditions for human action (Mises 1949, 13-4).

One must beware, however, of subsuming all human conduct under human action. In order for human behaviour to be regarded as human action, there must be scope for human interference. It is not possible to speak of human action when man cannot influence his situation. In other words, in the absence of the freedom to behave otherwise, human behaviour does not involve actions. A stimulus-response (S-R) approach towards human activities is out of question. By the same token, a conscious choice to do nothing in the presence of at least one alternative must be regarded as a human action.

Under these conditions, uncertainty is clearly a permanent attribute of all calculations and decisions. Where the category of action is deployed, the perceived future cannot at the same time be considered to be deterministic. Mises states, virtually echoing Frank Knight: 'If man knew the future, he would not have to choose and would not act. He would be like an automaton, reacting to stimuli without any will of his own.' (Mises 1949, 105). However, a man cannot predict all of the potentially relevant choices made by others. 'The future for which he plans will be codetermined by the actions of people who are planning and acting like himself.' (Mises 1962, 46). Thus, individual expectations about the future must necessarily remain uncertain and inherently involve guesswork.

As a consequence, uncertainty is regarded as an impediment with respect to the possibility of avoiding harm. As Mises stated, '...well-being ultimately depends on the operation of forces beyond man's wisdom, knowledge, prevision, and provision.' (Mises 1962, 66). Engineering merely marginally restricts the field of possible events, while natural sciences only supply us with information about the specific results of particular actions. Only in retrospect, *ex post*, do we know to what extent an action attained the desired end and whether it was the best possible choice.

4.3 Praxeology

Praxeology is '...the general theory of human action' (Mises 1949, 3). The fundamental axiom declaring the existence of human action sets praxeology apart from other methodological viewpoints. Furthermore, there are two fundamental postulates to be made: (1) a variety of resources exists; (2) leisure is a consumer good. The inclusion of the subsidiary postulates (3) that indirect exchanges are being made, and (4) that firms aim at maximising their money profits, permits the elaboration of the economics of the market (Rothbard 1957, 316-7). 'The science of human action that strives for universally valid knowledge is the theoretical system whose hitherto best elaborated branch is economics. ... It is, as it were, the logic of action and deed.' (Mises 1933, 12-3). That men purposively intend to bring about changes differentiates the subject matter of praxeology from its counterpart in the natural sciences (Mises 1949, 352).

Human thought and human action are generated by the same source, namely: the human mind. 'There is nothing in the structure of action that the human mind cannot fully explain. In this sense praxeology supplies certain knowledge.' (Mises 1962, 64). The categories of means and ends, causality, the law of diminishing marginal returns and the time-structure of production are immediate logical implications of the premise of the existence of human action (Mises 1949, 22, 64, 99; Rothbard 1957, 317).

According to Mises, the axiom of human action is a synthetic *a priori* proposition (Mises 1962, 8). He rejects the position adopted by logical positivists who claim that *a priori* knowledge is necessarily always analytical. Having rejected the logical positivistic approach, Mises argues that human action is a Kantian category, which supplies one with universally valid knowledge, and thus tells us something about reality as we may know it (Huussen 1989). *A priori*, to Mises, means independence of time and place, but it does not imply independence of potential experience. In this respect, Mises refers to universal inner experiences of introspection and self-examination; 'evidence is reflective rather than physical.' (Rothbard 1957, 318).

The following two implications may now be discussed: (1) praxeological predictions are totally unconditional and absolutely valid, but they do not tell us anything about individual future value judgments or about their influence on specific actions (Mises 1949, 65); and (2) praxeological theories are not amenable to empirical confirmation or refutation. To elaborate:

(1). Praxeological laws are regarded as being universally valid, referring as they do to the "form" of economic behaviour. Ultimately, all general knowledge is deductively derived from the *a priori* category of action. General knowledge refers to knowledge applicable to time-independent constellations (Mises 1949, 64). Nevertheless, praxeology presumes uncertainty with respect to means and ends. The latter are contained in the black box "producing" actions to better one's situation. The rationality involved is not rigidly deterministic, and is aimed at explaining and predicting individual behaviour. The rationality within praxeology deals with the logical patterns of purposeful behaviour. An example is the analysis of entrepreneurial activities in Mises's own business cycle theory.

(2). Concerning the second implication, it will be clear that Mises disagrees with Popper on the scientific status of praxeology. Praxeological laws do not relate to the ideal-typical economic concepts, which supply us with contingent laws. Praxeology provides us with necessary laws instead. Therefore, these laws do not lend themselves to empirical testing (Selgin 1988, 24). Moreover, if Popper's scientific demarcation-criterium is applied, all a prioristic theories, such as logic, mathematics, and praxeology, would be unscientific, for in principle they cannot be refuted by experience. The fallibility of our apprehension of sense data (Mises 1962, 71), and the problem of induction, oblige Mises to conclude against historicism and empiricism. 'There is no reason to ascribe to the operation the mind performs in the act of becoming aware of an external object a higher epistemological dignity than to the operation the mind performs in describing its own ways of procedure. In fact, nothing is more certain for the human mind than what the category of human action brings into relief.' (Mises 1962, 71).

Technology and the sciences may at best somewhat restrict the domain of pure chance. A more important enterprise is therefore finding out how the various economic activities performed by the individual agents are coordinated. The entrepreneur in particular must peer into the dark in order to appraise mutual effects actually brought about by an action, together with their respective degrees of intensity: he must deal with the relevance of each motive and each action. This is called "understanding".

4.4 Understanding

The uncertain future may be approached with the aid of (1) the faculty of understanding, and (2) the experience of past events. Experience of past events serves as no more than a starting point for a planning procedure. After trying to guess what is likely to change in the relevant future, man will adjust his actions as best he can to foreseeable future want satisfaction (Mises 1949, 210-4).

According to Mises, understanding, *verstehen*, is the only appropriate method for dealing with the uncertainty of future conditions. Understanding is the attempt to grasp what is going on in the minds of other men (Mises 1949, 118; Mises 1962, 50). It supplies one with expected future exchange ratios. It does not refer to the praxeological side of human action, but to the field of history: 'Understanding deals with judgments of value, with the choice of ends and of the means resorted to for the attainment of these ends, and with the valuation of the outcome of actions performed.' (Mises 1962, 48).

In principle, both scientists and ordinary mortals alike use the method of understanding. 'The methods of scientific inquiry are categorically not different from the procedures applied by everyone in his mundane comportment.' (Mises 1962, 48). Observed dissimilarities may be traced back to differences in refinement, as well as to the number of inconsistencies and contradictions.

Quantitative problems must be approached with understanding, based on incomplete knowledge. This knowledge will always be defective because we can never exclude the possibility that we have erred (Mises 1949, 112). Austrians seem unwilling to let quantities prevail over qualities. Valuations are neither necessarily constant nor continuous. In contrast, qualitative predictions may be based on praxeological knowledge. We must bear in mind that praxeological knowledge is deemed to be certain.

In parallel with Knight's distinction between risk and uncertainty as measurable and unmeasurable categories, Mises states that there are two different types of probability: (A) class probability; and (B) case probability. A statement is probable if our knowledge concerning its content is deficient: we do know something, but we do not know everything about the problem concerned.

(A) Class probability (or frequency probability) means: 'We know or assume to know, with regard to the problem concerned, everything about the behaviour of a whole class of events or phenomena; but about the actual singular events or phenomena we know nothing but that they are elements of this class.' (Mises 1949, 107). Insurance may be characterized by its practice of dealing with a whole class of events. It is based on pooling and distributing risks, in order to compensate for the losses which "regularly" occur. The word regularly denotes that: 'The amount of these losses is known as far as the whole class of the various items is concerned.' (Mises 1949, 109).

(B) Case probability means that '...we know, with regard to a particular event, some of the factors which determine its outcome; but there are other determining factors about which we know nothing' (Mises 1949, 110). Statements in this field deal with unique events which are not as such members of any class. Case probability is '...not open to any kind of numerical evaluation.' (Mises 1949, 113). The actual heterogeneity of situations seems to underpin this position (Lachmann 1956 1978, 26-7).

Mises is rather meticulous in distinguishing between the two types: the former is suitable for the field of the natural sciences, while the latter is a feature of the sciences dealing with human actions. Every human action, every experience, every event is unique, for each one of them changes our perspective. Unique events are no more than classes by themselves. This is called "methodological singularism" (Mises 1949, 45). Measurement and quantification in the sphere of human action are, consequently and inevitably, impossible. 'The fundamental deficiency implied in every quantitative approach to economic problems consists in the neglect of the fact that there are no constant relations between economic dimensions.' (Mises 1949, 118).

Mises's radical conclusion that the use of class probabilities in economics is to be rejected as being impossible originates in his adherence to subjectivism. In fact, it is often concluded that the most prominent feature of Austrian economics is radical subjectivism (Lachmann 1978, 1). We must, however, beware of equating this variant of subjectivism with the neoclassical one as used in relation to, e.g., subjective probabilities and marginal utility theory. In neoclassical theory subjectivism refers to numerical individual numerical comparisons and rankings. Radical subjectivism also differs from an alternative interpretation of subjectivism, which concentrates effectively on the isolation of the economic subject.

According to the subjectivist stance taken by Austrians, we know about the physical world from without only, but about the world of human action from within. The method of the social sciences is the method of understanding. However, no questions can be posed with regard to the veracity of chosen ends and means. The reason is that the facts of the social sciences consist of individual preferences and understood adequate means. 'Value judgments are necessarily always subjective' (Mises 1949, 395).

No ideal decision rule may be derived from praxeology, for what is the best course of action when dealing with truly unique events? It is the greater or lesser ability to understand the future which determines one's relative success or failure in this regard.

The future may be dealt with by gambling, engineering and speculating. With regard to the non-controllable influences, man is always the gambler, acting on incomplete relevant knowledge. When concentrating on engineering, economic man is trying to enlarge his knowledge and reduce uncertainty as much as possible. Technologically satisfactory solutions will, however, never eliminate the importance of the element of speculation altogether.

The prevalence of the negative connotation of speculation may be caused by the lack of noticing or acknowledging the existence of uncertainty. Every investment is really a form of speculation. This occurs because man tries to adjust his actions to the imperfectly known actions of others. 'Action is always speculation.. In any real and living economy every actor is always an entrepreneur and speculator' (Mises 1949, 253).

4.5 Economic calculation

In order to act in an economy with considered judgment one cannot dispense with economic calculation. For economists writing in the Austrian tradition, economic calculation implies the use of a common denominator: the only suitable one is money. Note that first and foremost Mises had investment and trading activities in mind, rather than the buying decisions of the consumer. Thus, monetary calculation is not based on individual subjective use-value, but on exchange-value, '...arising out of the interplay of the subjective valuations of all who take part in exchange' (Mises 1920, 97). Therefore, valuation is a social interaction and coordination problem, amd not an individual choice problem. The value of the money unit itself is subject to fluctuation, but money is still the best denominator for economic calculations, especially for practical purposes (Mises 1920, 97-9, 107-9).

'Economic calculation is either an estimate of the expected outcome of future action or the establishment of the outcome of past action.' (Mises 1949, 211). The purpose of the establishment of the outcome of past action is, according to Mises, merely to show the extent of the surplus free for consumption, and economic calculation does not offer certainty about the future. Moreover, economic calculation is, first of all, aimed at making plans for the future, but does not, by itself, supply any extra information about that future. Because economic realities are perpetually fluctuating, action will always remain speculative (Mises 1949, 215).

It will very probably improve our understanding of Mises's idea of economic calculation if we now look at the first stage in the socialism-capitalism debate. As early as 1920, Mises brought forward the problem of economic calculation to the fore in his fierce attack on socialist economic organization, which at the time he believed to be the nascent commonwealth (Mises 1920, 88; Mises 1922, 511-5). Moreover, in his opposition to his fight against socialism, Mises became more outspoken, lucid and consistent in his later works. As has been established already, in these later writings one finds most clearly the relationships between praxeology, economic calculation and uncertainty.

Mises's critique is generally interpreted as the denial of the "logical credentials" of socialism. Under socialism, it is expected that the community will determine the allotment of all means of production. However, even if the planners, who somehow represent the community, happen to know the actual needs of the population, it is still impossible for them to calculate the required production structure (Mises 1920, 107). The fundamental reason for this is the impossibility of finding a non-market alternative for homogenizing various degrees of capacity and dexterity of labour. The labour equalization process necessary in a socialist economy, '...is a result of market transactions and not its antecedent.' (Mises 1920, 115).

In addition, in the absence of private property rights, there is no motivation to search for the most efficient production methods and transactions. This inhibits the emergence of genuine relative scarcity prices for nationalised means of production. For example, it is impossible to find the cheapest way to produce under socialism, with regard to goods created in a combination of production processes, e.g. the building of a new railroad. 'But then we have the spectacle of a socialist economic order floundering in the ocean of possible and conceivable economic combinations without the compass of economic calculation.' (Mises 1920, 110). This rudderless vessel is bound to end up on the rocks.

It was soon shown that E. Barone had already solved the problems involved in proving the theoretical possibility of rational calculation under socialist economy by 1908. Drawing on work by Pareto, Barone demonstrated that a socialist economy could be modelled in a manner analogous to Walras's general equilibrium model of choice. His simultaneous equations model of a socialist economy includes such elements as a numeraire, a collective maximum and an equilibrium situation (Barone 1908, 245-90).

It was also claimed, e.g. much later in Schumpeter (1942), that a socialist economy may eliminate the internal uncertainties inherent in a market economy with its dispersed decision-making, the '...uncertainties about the reaction of one's actual and potential competitors and about how general business situations are going to shape.' (Schumpeter 1942, 186). The practical solution of economic problems would be more straightforward under socialism than under capitalism, since the economic efficiency of an economic system is reduced to productive efficiency, and the central planning board acts both as a clearing house for information, and as a coordinator of decisions (Schumpeter 1942, 186-9).

We may conclude that a general consensus evolved in support of the position that a calculation may in principle incorporate all the consequences from and for activities in other parts of the economy. Socialism was considered to be superior to capitalism in certain cases, for example, when an economy moves from one theoretically specified economic equilibrium position to another. What is more, in the case of reserve capacity: 'as a matter of blueprint logic it is undeniable that the socialist blueprint is drawn at a higher level of rationality.' (Schumpeter 1942, 196; cf. Schumpeter 1954, 989). Thus, the neoclassical general equilibrium approach provided most economists, including many socialists, with a satisfactory answer to the problem put forward by Mises.

However, according to adherents of a currently prominent, albeit radically different interpretation of the socialism-capitalism debate, there has been a critical misunderstanding of the point of Mises's argument. The misinterpretation may have been caused by implicit differences in the blurred conceptualization of the market (Kirzner 1988; Lavoie 1981; Lavoie 1981a; Keizer 1989). The Austrian version pointed toward the process view of the market. Economic problems by definition involve change. Therefore, the main task of economic calculation is '...not to deal with the problems of unchanging or only slightly changing market situations and prices' (Mises 1949, 213). On the contrary, the main task of economic calculation is to deal with changes. The misinterpretation of the concepts used by the Austrians was inevitable because their opponents subscribed another view of the market, namely one based on the Walrasian equilibrium approach: 'the static state can dispense with economic calculation.' (Mises 1920, 109). Economic calculation ceases to be a problem in the stationary and structurally unchanging economy. The neoclassically-oriented socialist model of the economy indeed holds such a static equilibrium view of markets.

However, even if one accepts the possibility of a static state, there is the additional argument that the transition towards a socialist state will itself change all economic data. In the actual economy, peopled with agents coping with an imperfectly known future, one cannot do away with economic calculation, if only because of the changing economic data.

According to the authors mentioned above, in the course of the debate Mises and his followers only gradually became aware of the fundamental differences between their view and the Neoclassical view: the controversy began with "dynamic" issues, and was diverted to statics by the market socialists. 'Where there is no uncertainty concerning the future, there is no need for any cash holding.. Money in itself is an element of change; its existence is incompatible with the idea of a regular flow of events' (Mises 1949, 414). Since Barone's work established the formal similarity between capitalism and socialism under static conditions, and nothing more than that, the Austrians considered it to be inapplicable.

Furthermore, it is claimed that no proper answer has yet been given by the socialists in regard to the necessity of using money prices for rational calculation. Other objective values such as labour hours offer no alternative for the price system. The price system inherent in markets is not only the best, but the only possible method of allocating resources.

Mises's later writings support this alternative interpretation. In them we find a Mises who is still highly dissatisfied with the way in which most economists deal with the fundamental problems involved in economic calculation. For Mises, the crucial problem is the disregard for the non-neutrality of the denominator; 'they do not comprehend that money prices are the only vehicle of economic calculation.' (Mises 1949, 202). The "money" he was referring to is money under an institutional system of dispersed private property and markets for means of production. His concentration on the role of prices in society and his neglect of any extensive discussion of the presupposed competition may be due to the diversity of the schools which he was simultaneously attacking.

Before we introduce and discuss Hayek's ideas, another element of Mises's thought needs first to be introduced: the element of coordination. The distinction between coordination and equilibrium is fundamental in Austrian economics.

4.6 Equilibrium versus coordination

From the *a priori* category of human action, Mises deduced that there is an equilibrium as soon as there is no longer any action, and thus no uncertainty. However, in the economy consisting of individuals coping with an uncertain future, it is almost always easy for them to imagine a more favourable situation. As a consequence, the relevant situations are those in which individuals interact while they are all striving for an individually preferred position. How then are these subjective calculations resulting in human actions integrated into one huge harmonious pattern which is congruent with the economic possibilities? Mises was unable to fit this coordination of entrepreneurial activities into his praxeological framework. This section will show that the introduction of coordination proved to be troublesome for praxeology. As a consequence the focus must shift to the role of knowledge and the function of learning in economic behaviour. In order to understand the difference between coordination and equilibration more completely, I propose to discuss Mises's views on economic equilibrium.

When one defines equilibrium as the absence of endogenous change, the informational structure becomes implicit; it is one of perfect information. Such an equilibrium is, for both Mises and Hayek, no more than a limiting case. According to Mises, discussing equilibria is redundant, since in such a situation there are no economic problems. In a praxeological sense, no one would "act" any more. Hayek, however, considers the study of equilibria as being useful to the study of some elements of economics.

In the absence of a feeling of dissatisfaction, there is no Misesian action, and thus a situation of equilibrium. Equilibrium is no more than an intermediate tool of thought, a heuristic, in analysing some logical aspects of how the economy works. It is not claimed that an equilibrium actually exists at a specific moment, because such a claim would be tantamount to stating that all economic problems have been solved. One may confidently state that Mises's conception of human action implies the existence of disequilibrium. In a situation of a disequilibrium there is a subjective feeling of not being in the most favourable situation possible. 'The statement that action is equilibrating merely refers to the logical proposition that action continuously accounts for changes in the imagined framework of means and ends, i.e. changes in the structure of imagined profit opportunities.' (Selgin 1988, 38).

As we have seen, Mises claims that the price system is necessary for establishing an equilibrating tendency. Market prices are necessary for enabling understanding, calculation, and subsequent human action. The price system, although imperfect, provides the framework for guiding competitors under disequilibrium conditions. Profits are the result of noticing and exploiting shortcomings in markets, and they direct the activities of entrepreneurs. Within the context of praxeology, profit opportunities only exist when agents understand them as such. Such an imagined opportunity will be eliminated by the logically subsequent action. In principle, the equilibrating tendency is devoid of a real world content, because understanding is a subjective element (Selgin 1988, 34). The profits involved are not necessarily equal to the profits in , e.g., fiscal accounting systems. For example, as a consequence it is perfectly possible to assert praxeologically the presence of an equilibrium, while simultaneously, and in reality, huge monetary profits and/or losses are being made. Understanding merely depends on subjective feelings of satisfaction.

The methodology of praxeology runs into fundamental problems when coordination is about to be introduced. The primary reason for this is that coordination, itself dependent on the reliability of expectations, is not a praxeological concept, and Mises did not discuss it. Moreover, coordination requires adequate foresight. The ambition to better one's situation does not, however, either by definition or by deduction, bring about perfect mutual, and thus social, coordination: 'While we cannot think of free action as non-equilibrating, we may conceive of actions that are non-coordinating.' (Selgin 1988, 43). It is the consequence of breaking up the relationship between the past and the future, and of introducing uncertainty with regard to the future. No mechanism for learning from past experiences was explicitly elaborated by Mises.

Without such a mechanism, praxeology, in principle, cannot refute the statement that the future is radically uncertain, or kaleidic. Kaleidics refers to the absence of stable linkages between different time periods. As in a kaleidoscope, a small change in the situation makes the prevalent conception of economic relations and how they interact entirely obsolete. The idea that the future is fully kaleidic, a position adopted for instance by Shackle and elaborated in next chapter, section 5.6, consigns human action to haphazardness (e.g. Shackle 1955). Admitting the presence of an imaginable but completely unknowable future would render praxeology merely tautological. As a consequence, the step from praxeology to man in his environment cannot be made without introducing historical aspects.

Mises wrote extensively on themes such as the economic process, and the role of the entrepreneur in society. However, praxeology appears to be mainly useful in studying understanding, calculation and action at the level of the individual. Ultimately, Mises must abandon his a prioristic viewpoint and introduce empirical hypotheses, in order to be equipped to link up his theoretical conclusions with market phenomena. Indeed, he has been criticized for this shortcoming, e.g. by Kirzner (Kirzner 1988, 7). Mises was unable to solve the problem of integrating subjective calculations into a coherent pattern. Other writers in the Austrian school of economics, concerned to question the empirical meaningfulness of the Misesean idea of praxeology, emphasize the necessity of introducing historical time-and-place elements into economic theorising. Their aim is to be able to make statements about the development of the economy, and about the possibility of coordination of actions under uncertainty. Friedrich A. von Hayek (1899-1992), Mises's pupil, directed the attention of economists to the empirical elements of locally scattered knowledge, and of human interactions. We may say that, in the period 1930-'35, his theories were the major alternative to the theories presented by Keynes (Hicks 1967, 202). But, for various reasons to be discussed in section 5.4, his ideas had fallen out of grace by the time they achieved a great lucidity (Wubben 1992; Wubben 1993).

4.7 Economics and knowledge

An important idea in Hayek's writings is the notion of the purposefulness of human action, i.e. that man is guided by expectations of an uncertain future (Hodgson 1989, 18). Hayek concentrated his investigations more on the consequences of starting with scattered bits and pieces of subjective knowledge, than on the consequences of uncertainty itself. He brought together problems of incomplete information, disequilibrium and expectations, which were already being energetically disputed during the interwar years (O'Driscoll 1977, 20). He proposed to emphasize the role of learning and thus elevate economics from being a science of human action to a study of human interaction, i.e. of coordination, as well.

Hayek's view of his relation with Knight is set out in his seminal article *Economics and Knowledge* (1937), delivered at the London Economic Club in 1936, and published a year later. It confirms a train of thought which first shone through in his 1933-Copenhagen lecture. The very article became the centrepiece of *Individualism and Economic Order* (1948), which together with his elaborations Hayek (1943) and Hayek (1945), and Hayek (1946), comprises his tetrad on economic coordination. Thanks to his publication on uncertainty, Knight is the solitary economist actually named in its core text. In a discussion on operationalizing the empirical element of economics, Hayek stresses the importance of the assumptions concerning foresight. 'The stimulus which was exercised in this connection by the work of Frank H. Knight may yet prove to have a profound influence far beyond its special field.' (Hayek 1937, 34).

Economics and Knowledge essentially discusses equilibrium concepts and problems relating to knowledge, but is also interesting for the epistemological stance adopted. We now propose first to discuss his epistemological stance because such an analysis will very probably enhance our understanding of his views on planning, coordination, and information.

With this article Hayek is thought to have broken with praxeology. Some supporting evidence for this version of events may be found in his famous series on economic coordination, written in the period 1936-1947, when he was deeply involved in the socialism-capitalism debate. For instance, these articles seem to suggest that Hayek accepts Popper's demarcation criterium (Hayek 1937, 33), which was anathema to Mises. T.W. Hutchison even speaks of Hayek's "U-turn" (Hutchison 1981, 215).

However, Hutchison's epithet is misplaced. How, for instance, can we link this interpretation to Hayek's opinion that the phenomena connected by means of a model can exclusively possess attributes derived from that model? 'Experience can never teach us that any particular kind of structure has properties which do not follow from the definition (or the way we construct it).' (Hayek 1943, 74). A theory, which is the mental construct for interpretation, cannot be verified or falsified by facts any more than mathematics or logic. It may '...only be tested for its consistency.' (Hayek 1943, 74).

Furthermore, Hayek states that knowledge of other minds is based on reasoning by analogy from one's own mind. One observes another agent's action and supplements the data by projecting our own classification of objects, but. '...we can understand less and less as we turn to beings more and more different from ourselves.' (Hayek 1943, 66). It is by means of the connotation of a concept that we form classes (Hayek 1943, 60-5). We may no longer understand the actions of others when we cannot apply analogies or patterns from our own way of thinking. Hayek's case for pattern predictions cannot be reconciled with Popper's philosophy because pattern predictions are immune to falsification (Paqué 1990, 282, 291). Pattern predictions are contingent projections into the future.

In view of this approach adopted by Hayek, it is not surprising to find that alternative interpretations have been put forward, which contradict Hutchison's. According to such points of view, Hayek did not abandon praxeology at all, but merely adjusted it, and support for this view may be found in several of his writings.

In the first place, Hayek receives his training in philosophy in the school of E. Mach and later at the feet of the logical positivists: 'Yet all this had the effect only of creating an awareness, which became more and more definite as time went by, that, certainly in economics, all the people who are universally regarded as talking sense are constantly infringing the accepted canons of scientific method evolved from the practice of the natural sciences.'

(Hayek 1943, 58; emphasis added). This statement was made six years after the publication of what promised to demonstrate the acceptance of Popper's demarcation criterium. He emphasized that natural scientists stepping into the social sciences either relinquished the methodology of the natural sciences, or came to a sorry end.

Secondly, when one wants to explain social processes, one has to introduce hypotheses on the actual acquisition of knowledge; in other words '...the question to what extent and how his [the agent's; EW] knowledge corresponds to the external facts.' (Hayek 1937, 47). It is essential to choose the most relevant or useful ideal types among the infinite variety of possible situations. Hayek, however, engages merely in conjectural history. He actually reduces the function of testing to finding out whether a theory fits actuality or not, a method of corroboration which does not, unfortunately, render the theory empirically true (Huussen 1990, 119).

Thirdly, the formal aspects of social processes are the elements from which to construct a theory for explaining social interaction (Huussen 1990, 125). They supply us with a causal explanation of social structures. According to Hayek, it is the task of psychology, not economics, to explain individual behaviour. Economics does not (need to) explain individual behaviour (Hayek 1943, 67).

Finally, what Hayek calls the pure logic of choice - and which Mises called praxeology - is acknowledged as covering all conceivable situations. It begins with facts common to all human thought that are universally applicable and therefore true in an *a priori* sense (Hayek 1937, 47-8).

Hayek's opinion of scientism is related to this epistemological stance (Hayek 1943, 58), and the struggle against it has always been one of his major themes. He believed that social scientific knowledge is fundamentally different from that found in the natural sciences. In *Economics and Knowledge*, Hayek introduced the distinction between scientific or objective knowledge, "knowledge that", and private or positional knowledge, "knowledge how". The implied conclusion is the impossibility of talking about subjective probabilities that tend to objective probabilities. The dimensions of "knowledge how" and "knowledge that" are not on the same footing but cover different "levels" of knowledge. 'To employ a useful metaphor: while at the world of nature we look from the outside, we look at the world of society from the inside; .. in the world of society at least some of the most familiar concepts are the stuff from which that world is made.. a common structure of thought .. is also the basis on which we all interpret such complicated social structures as those which we find in economic life or law, in language, and in customs.' (Hayek 1943, 76).

Hayek calls the result of this kind of theorizing the "compositive method", '...which *constitutes* the social *wholes* by constructing models from intelligible elements.' (ibid., 73). Theories are not about groups of facts, but merely serve to connect individual facts (ibid., 73). 'We cannot speak about the behaviour of wholes as wholes, because we never deal with the whole of reality but always with a selection made with the help of our models.' (ibid., 74). Theories constitute these wholes, but are not about the social wholes. The complex phenomena discussed in the social sciences '...are never found ready given as are the persistent structures in the organic (..) world.' (ibid., 72).

The following three objections to this compositive method may be raised:

1. The hierarchical order is broken once one acknowledges the existence of social and institutional influences on individual preferences and actions, even if social "wholes" are themselves explained in terms of individuals. This is even more relevant because of the process orientation Austrians adopt. The result would be an infinite regress leaving us with a chicken and egg problem.

   Writers in the Austrian tradition can present ideas of "observational individualism" and "ontological individualism" to support their position. First, an analysis of individual actions is considered to be the only means to cognition of social wholes, because we cannot observe social wholes as such (e.g. Mises 1949, 42-3). Against this we would argue that the explanatory power of formal mind constructs, such as companies, may be undervalued. It is often more appropriate to talk about social wholes, e.g. factory, corporate division, firm and government, than to talk about the individuals that people them, because laws, investments, etc., provide observed and relevant output for other collective wholes, and for the individuals involved. The second Austrian argument, i.e. that of ontological individualism, states that social wholes are no more than mind constructs, although potentially useful mind constructs. It is the individual who decides and acts, although he may act differently under different external conditions. However, we do not know how to discuss an individual outside a specific environment, since it is acknowledged that even his revealed preferences are situation-dependent.

2. The fallacy of composition, which hold that the whole is more than the sum of the parts, is a second point against the compositive method. The building blocks, the basic elements in the hierarchical structure, must inevitably be the human individuals. All activities in society must now be entirely explained by reference to basic elements and their interactions (Hodgson 1986, 220). We beg leave to disagree. The compositive method originating from Menger and elaborated by Hayek involves a Darwinian explanation. Social phenomena are explained in terms of their origin and their functioning, allowing for the unintended consequences of rational economic actions. Hayek uses a different method from the one discussed in combination with the fallacy of composition.

3. The parts do not function '...merely because of their inherent qualities, after taking in inputs (information, etc.) from outside' (Hodgson 1986, 221). There is an original and thus unpredictable element in choices. This may cause the supposed composition of social wholes out of smaller elements to lack a strong foundation in historical analysis.

As early as the 1930s, Hayek was distancing himself from the novel but soon to be common definition of the economic problem, as defined by Robbins, namely: economics as the problem of allocating scarce means to ends. More specifically, Hayek objected to the use of the standard assumption of complete knowledge on the part of all transactors, because it failed to do justice to the actual problem (Hayek 1937, 33; Hayek 1945, 89-91). For Hayek, the central question to be posed in the social sciences is the following: 'How can the combination of fragments of knowledge existing in different minds bring about results which, if they were to be brought about deliberately, would require knowledge on the part of the directing mind which no single person can possess?' (Hayek 1937, 54). Thus, the central research goal of economics as defined by Hayek is the problem of the usage of dispersed knowledge (Hayek 1937, 50-1). 'Throughout all his work he maintained his conception of the *economic problem* as a coordination problem, for the analysis of which the method of *logical implication* is the appropriate tool.' (O'Driscoll 1977, 28). Mises's pupil Kirzner was later to speak of "Hayek's knowledge problem" (Kirzner 1984, 407-8). Hayek's conceptions of the economic problem and the price mechanism continued to evolve until he completed his contribution to the calculation debate and especially the quartet of works on economic coordination.

In line with Hayek's non-conformist definition of the economic problem, is his plea for a reformulation of the concept of equilibrium. He objects to the '...excessive preoccupation with the problems of the pure theory of stationary equilibrium.' (Hayek 1940, 188). Equilibrium analysis is no more than a useful preliminary to the study of practical problems. It has no direct relevance (Hayek 1945, 91; Hayek 1946, 96). 'What is relevant is not whether a person as such is or is not in equilibrium but which of his actions stand in equilibrium relationships to each other.' (Hayek 1937, 36). An individual's actions remain in equilibrium with each other during the period in which his anticipations prove to be correct. Any change in the knowledge available to an agent which results in an alteration of his plan may be called a disruption of the equilibrium relation. Thus, subsequent actions are no longer mutually related (Hayek 1937, 36).

The main difference between an individual and a societal equilibrium may be traced back to a crucial difference in the nature of the data. Correctness of individual anticipation does not imply the usage of objective data, but rather the absence of a need to change relevant, subjective knowledge. Change is defined as '...any divergence of the actual from the expected development, irrespective of whether it means a *change* in the absolute sense.' (Hayek 1937, 40).

An equilibrium in a society at a given point of time means that various plans, framed by individuals for action in time, are mutually compatible. However, there is no need to restrict the discussion to a stationary state or to conditions of constant data (Hayek 1937, 41, 49). 'Hayek's view of the competitive process.. depends on progressive learning that must take place by virtue of the presumed stability of the market in question' (Boland 1986, 37). An equilibrating tendency implies that '...the knowledge and intentions of the different members of society are supposed to come more and more into agreement.' (Hayek 1937, 45). Men act on the basis of partial ignorance and engage in a learning process.

Hayek's view of the optimal social coordination of actions - the mutual compatibility of plans - is dependent on the presumed stability of the market system. A stable economic system is supposed to find, in one way or another, the best outcome by solving its own economic problems, such as deadlock situations.

As a consequence, correct foresight is not a mere precondition for arriving at an equilibrium. Moreover, correct foresight is the defining characteristic of the state of equilibrium. Such a static equilibrium will last as long as the external data corresponds to the common expectations of all the members of the society, '...as long as the anticipations prove correct.' (Hayek 1937, 42). When we want to discuss a process, foresight need only be correct insofar as it is relevant for the decisions of the individuals and Hayek here speaks of relevant foresight.

The institutional framework is of importance in the dissemination of knowledge. In contrast to models which assume perfect knowledge, Hayek's does not assume that decisions taken by various agents are optimal by definition. It raises the question of how we may create a situation in which the agents in possession of the knowledge suited to a particular task are empowered to perform that task (Hayek 1946, 95). No individual is able to grasp the totality of adaptive events. 'Nonetheless, the whole structure of activities tends to adapt, through these partial and fragmentary signals, to conditions foreseen by and known to no individual, even if this adaptation is never perfect.. There can be no deliberately planned substitutes for such a self-ordering process of adaptation to the unknown.' (Hayek 1988, 76).

Is it then, practically-speaking, impossible to plan an economy? That question is widely considered to be the principal point of discussion in the second phase of the calculation debate. The first round of the calculation debate, about the theoretical (im)possibility of a socialist economy, was considered to have been won by the socialists. The second round was to be concerned with the practical problems involved (e.g. Hayek 1935a; Hayek 1935b; Hayek 1940). The sheer scale of the collection of the necessary quantity of data from a myriad of heterogeneous situations, and the subsequent resolution of the large number of details necessary for a simultaneous equations model, would render a socialist economy impossible and, together with Robbins, Hayek was a prominent advocate of this viewpoint. According to the standard interpretation, this second round of the debate was effectively closed with Oscar Lange's publications in 1936.

Lange (1936) reflects the neoclassical viewpoint, offering the state as a substitute for the Walrasian auctioneer, and pointing to long-run average cost minimization as the leading principle for productive activities. He exposed the parallels '...in both the formal conditions for a determinate equilibrium and in the trial-and-error procedures for *finding* equilibrium, between the neoclassical perfect competition model and his market socialist scheme' (Lavoie 1985, 161). His market socialist approach has long been accepted as the definitive answer to the critics (Schumpeter 1942; Schumpeter 1954, 989n12).

Of course, the idea behind using the state as a substitute for the Walrasian auctioneer stands in sharp contrast with the Austrian view of the dynamic market. Dating the end of the debate at around 1937, while the development of argumentation on the Austrian side did not end until the 1940s, only serves to highlight the mutual misunderstanding. Other interpretations of the history of the discussion may be, and have been, given, and the interpretation below features prominently among them.

According to most writers in the Austrian tradition, the problem of central planning is the problem of using scattered information. 'Hayek's knowledge problem consists in the dispersed character of available information.' (Kirzner 1984, 410). It is acknowledged that a socialist scheme is logically compatible with a stationary economy (Mises 1949, 257). Such an "evenly revolving economy", as the Austrians termed it, is irrelevant to the calculation problem.

Hayek's knowledge problem is the collective analogue of the basic knowledge problem, functioning at the level of the individual. The basic knowledge problem consists in the inadequacies of an agent's knowledge of the relevant circumstances, and the central planner is subject to the same problems as the individual decision-maker. Moreover, he must also evaluate the adequacy of the available scattered bits of information, but lacks the instruments with which to do so. Furthermore, the knowledge problem confronting central planners cannot be solved by a mechanism like the market that resolves the basic knowledge problem of individual decision-makers (Kirzner 1984, 409-10, 414).

Mises, when contributing to the first round of the debate, and Hayek, in the second, are essentially discussing the same problem. Their arguments reflect the Austrian understanding of markets as involving a competitive discovery process. 'For Austrians, prices emerge in an open-ended context in which entrepreneurs must grapple with true Knightian uncertainty.' (Kirzner 1988, 14).

Hayek emphasises that prices perform two important functions; (1) they communicate information about the relative scarcity of resources; and (2) they improve the coordination of the transactor's plans under definite assumptions. These functions serve to guide the equilibrating and the coordination processes, respectively. He argues that the market system is the best possible method of allocating resources, because it is a relatively cheap communication network and functions as a system of signals (Hayek 1937, 45; Hayek 1945, 87). Without pretending to attain perfect adjustment, it is claimed that only by means of market prices may a multitude of individuals use dispersed, specific information. Viz., '...prices can act to coordinate the separate actions of different people in the same way as subjective values help the individual to coordinate the parts of his plan.' (Hayek 1945, 85). Knowledge with regard to valuation is scattered, but is reflected in the free communication system. 'The information created by means of the price system relates to changing market conditions' (Hayek 1945, 87). Although this mechanism is the result of human action, it not a product of human design.

Thus, while the market system is not perfect, it neither entails the economy-wide consequences of good, nor of bad, decisions which are inherent in a planned economy. Furthermore, the market system allows the individual the option of using unarticulated, non-price information. This individual economic freedom makes the market process flexible and adaptation to changes proceeds quicker than by any alternative decision-making procedure. However, the proof with regard to the best decision-making procedure is, according to Hayek, to be found in the eating of the pudding; that is, does a planned economy work?

In evaluating this position, one might say that Hayek discusses information at two levels. First at the level of the individual planner, and second at the level of the economic process itself. Economic agents are dealing with no more than distributions or series of prices, but Hayek neither explains how these agents recognize whether processes are either discoordinating or coordinating, nor how information about product characteristics and qualities is to be recognized individually. Given sets of prices alone, it is unclear how one induces relative scarcity, and takes those actions which enhance coordination. Hayek did not succeed in solving the problem of the open-ended context of the market process, namely the problem of coordination, which in turn may be considered to be his problem of uncertainty.

To conclude our discussion of the calculation-debate, we may at this juncture, state that we consider both the Misesian calculation critique of socialism, and the Hayekian relative inefficiency critique thereof, to be correct, within their own contexts, and review these criticisms as yet to be refuted. The Misesian calculation argument, which was under discussion among economists for the first time in the 1920s, is consistent with praxeological epistemology. The Hayekian knowledge argument refers to the inertia and ineffectiveness of a socialist economy in concentrating, calculating, and spreading local and partially-inarticulate information. Hayek discusses the influence of the structure of an economic system on its development. The panacea which he puts forward, the market system, is assumed to unfailingly mobilize the maximum of information. If the market cannot coordinate, neihter could any other economic system.

While Mises holds uncertainty to be concomitant with individual human action, Hayek stresses the result of uncertainty: the problem of coordination. Although, around 1950, Hayek was to leave London and economics in his wake to concentrate on law and politics, his unceasing interest in the problem of human interaction maintained his creativity in the choice of adequate concepts for understanding these actions. His later writings on cultural evolution, featuring group selection and social rules of conduct concur with this statement. There is a gradual and continual transformation in his opinions, but not a straightforward distinction between the Hayek extensively discussed here and the later Hayek.

However, Hayek in turn may be criticized for neglecting the economic problems relating to the perception of information, and the creation of information from scratch. Having decided to leave pure economics for what it was, he neither indicated how individuals obtain entirely new information, nor how they perceive existent information. Although economic coordination and the spreading of information are among the prominent themes of his main plot, Hayek assigned learning procedures and the generation of new data to unsatisfactory subplots.

As we have stated, Hayek disregards the influence of individual perceptions of the economic process. No explanation is offered to account for the discrepancy between data and knowledge. In fact, the two are not even distinguished. On the one hand, Hayek acknowledges his inability to answer the following question: 'What could lead the subjective knowledge of agents to come into conformance with objective reality?' (Caldwell 1988, 529-30). On the other hand, Hayek argues that it is the task of psychology to explain individual behaviour. This does not however seem convincing, since individual learning mechanisms and individual imagination fundamentally influence economic developments. For example, how and at what speed is one to learn whether a piece of information indicates some structural change or incidental error? Furthermore, learning in a state of disequilibrium is different from learning in a state of equilibrium: 'information, therefore, requires interpretation (the messages have to be *decoded*) in order to be transformed into knowledge, and all such knowledge is bound to be imperfect.' (Lachmann 1956 1978, 21-3). In this respect Hayek's ideas are in agreement with standard conventionalist choice theory, since both modes of reasoning take inductive learning for granted (Boland 1986, 37). We will discuss this problem and Lachmann's solution to it in paragraph ten of this chapter, but first we wish to concentrate on another problem which Hayek avoided.

Hayek may be criticised for evading the problem of the origin of (local) information. Is it by imagination or by observation that people come up with "new" information? It cannot be by purely subjective guesswork, imagination, that man comes to possess local information, because then we would have to wonder how, in such a situation, agreement between the guesses and reality can occur.

Israel M. Kirzner made an effort to provide an alternative analysis. Our understanding of economic processes can, according to him, be founded on the pure logic of choice, i.e. praxeology. Therefore, we do not have to wait for empirical results before we may discuss the economics of the market process. He devoted numerous articles and books to the discussion of subjects like uncertainty, discovery and economic understanding, and next, we intend to discuss his ideas on the problem of knowledge creation.

4.8 Uncertainty versus error

By the end of the interwar period, Lachmann and Hayek were the only remaining Hayekians at the London School of Economics. Austrian economists were to experience approximately three decades in the wilderness. Disillusioned, Hayek himself was to leave London and pure economics for Chicago and political philosophy. Lachmann continued to publish within economics after he took a chair at the University of Witwatersrand. But, '...the fortunes of Austrian economics were at low ebb.' (Lachmann 1956 1978, viii). However, at New York University, Kirzner succeeded Mises, his teacher, and created an important nucleus awaiting the revival of the fortunes of Austrian economics which indeed occurred in the 1970s.

Kirzner claims to step into Mises's shoes by refusing to explain action solely in terms of: (a) the Scylla of deliberately sought-out or learned knowledge, or (b) the Charybdis of pure coincidences, of luck (Kirzner 1979,

141-4; Kirzner 1981, 55-7; Kirzner 1989, ix). The first category is the subject of an extensive body of work known as "search literature". In this approach, a partial ignorance of knowledge is defended as potentially optimal, persisting until exogenous changes occur. Ignorance of information that is learned coincidentally, the second category mentioned, cannot be comprehended in terms of conscious individual decision-making. The reason is that ignorance of information itself signifies that we do not yet know what is already there, the '...sheer failure to notice what is there to be seen.' (Kirzner 1979, 145). A substantial part of knowledge, beliefs and expectations, results from such unplanned learning experiences (Kirzner 1979, 142). The knowledge acquired by economic agents, however, must mostly be located somewhere in-between. Although one does not exactly know what is to be learned, one is on the lookout for profitable information.

Uncertainty is defined as '...the essential freedom with which the envisaged future may diverge from the realized future.' (Kirzner 1982a, 151, 157; Kirzner 1985, 58, 66). Uncertainty reflects man's awareness that the correspondence between the envisaged and the realized future is far from adequate (Kirzner 1985, 55). Scope for the creative, unpredictable expressions of man's energy is to be found here.

Man must first of all select the relevant means-end framework because the actual economic calculation takes place within such a framework. However, one will never be sure of the adequacy of a chosen framework because the *ex ante* selection of one amongst a number of alternative frameworks takes place in an open-ended uncertain world. We all make errors of judgment when choosing a means-end framework (Kirzner 1979, 124; Kirzner 1982a, 147-8). Every agent is aware of the fact that he knows only some components of what will determine tomorrow. Different agents may, therefore, end up with different calculations from different frameworks. Deliberations about risks and probabilities are possible with reference to a specific, chosen, means-end framework only. As a consequence, it does not suffice to incorporate the acquisition of information into a framework. Purposeful limitation of the input of information, resulting in an optimum degree of ignorance, is beside the point. Experience may lead to a reappraisal of one's means-ends framework and subsequently of one's actions.

Kirzner argues that modern economic theory lacks a theory of error (Kirzner 1979, 121), despite the fact that '...economic analysis *depends* on this kind of error for its most elementary and far-reaching theorems.' (ibid., 131).

People do not intentionally fail to achieve the most preferred available outcome, but rather fail to notice relevant facts. Mises had admitted that man makes mistakes, but to him errors constitute irrationality, and cannot therefore be the subject of scientific research. Errors primarily exhibit a derived function, e.g. as the prime disturbing factor in the explanation of the business cycle, which is the result of erroneous impressions. Therefore, errors were of no particular interest to Mises (ibid., 121).

Error is defined by Kirzner as '...a decision being made in unwitting ignorance of pertinent information.' (ibid., 207). Contrary to Mises, however, Kirzner states that errors do not constitute irrationality. Although erring does imply ignorance, it does not necessarily imply uncertainty. In general, however, '...past error (..) may be attributed to the pervasive uncertainty that characterizes our world (and to the inevitably kaleidic changes responsible for that uncertainty).' (Kirzner 1982a, 147). Moreover, it is one thing to avoid ignorance, but dealing with uncertainty is another (Kirzner 1982a, 148). An equilibrium depends upon the absence of error, but any existent spread in prices is caused by sheer error (Kirzner 1979, 124-35).

Kirzner adopts a pragmatic attitude towards the resulting epistemological problem of the indeterminate future. On the one hand, he agrees with Lachmann on the troublesome predictability of human knowledge. We do not know how entrepreneurs attain a superior anticipation of unexploited opportunities (Kirzner 1979, 8; Kirzner 1984, 415). On the other hand, he states that the observed tendency towards opportunities being perceived and exploited results in a belief in a market process that is determinate (Kirzner 1979, 116-7): 'we do, in talking of human action, assume at least a tendency for man to notice those [facts; EW] that constitute possible opportunities for gainful action on his part.' (Kirzner 1979, 29).

The use of the perfect knowledge assumption or an information-gathering and information-distributing auctioneer makes the study of economic changes, price dispersions, information dissemination and dovetailing tendencies redundant (Kirzner 1979, 17-24). However, '...at any given time people will, on the one hand, be blissfully ignorant of opportunities staring them in the face; on the other hand, they will be delightedly proceeding to exploit newly noticed opportunities of which they had been unaware yesterday.' (Kirzner 1979, 33). Empirical research is useful only in revealing the details of the tendency to discover opportunities.

Metaphorically speaking, present uncertainty and past errors are merely two sides of the same coin, called entrepreneurship. The tension between present uncertainty and past error can be attenuated by the quality of alertness. The entrepreneurial faculty, '...of ensuring alertness to and awareness of the data' (Kirzner 1979, 116) is therefore called entrepreneurial alertness (Kirzner 1982a, 150-1).

4.9 Entrepreneurship

Entrepreneurial actors grapple with inescapable uncertainty by means of spontaneous, undeliberate discovery (Kirzner 1979, 137-53). While the failure to notice available information is a troublesome factor in decision-making, it is not inconsistent with purposefulness: 'there is nothing in purposeful action that by itself guarantees that every available opportunity must be instantaneously perceived.' (Kirzner 1979, 130).

Kirzner underscores the difference between discovering opportunities and learning facts (Kirzner 1979, 29). 'And it is the distinction between being alert and possessing knowledge that helps us understand how the entrepreneurial market process systematically detects and helps eliminate error.' (Kirzner 1979, 8). However, alertness is itself no guarantee for finding the truth - note our continuous erring. Dealing with uncertainty appears to be primarily motivated by the profit gained from avoiding possible adverse dicrepancies between the future reality and the individual vision of the future. Kirzner's entrepreneur is first and foremost alert (Loasby 1982, 119).

It is the concept of entrepreneurship, deduced from the concept of human action, that distinguishes a theory of market equilibria from a theory of the market process (Kirzner 1979, 7, 26-9). Entrepreneurship is absent in Robbinsian allocative activity, but present in Misesian human action (Kirzner 1982a, 146-7). 'Market entrepreneurship reveals to the market what the market did not realize was available, or, indeed needed at all.' (Kirzner 1979, 181). Thus, the analysis of the specific relationship between uncertainty and entrepreneurship, important for example to Knight and Schumpeter, has been furthered by Kirzner. Schumpeter considers development as disequilibrating, spontaneous, and prone to disjointed changes in which the entrepreneur generates disturbances in the circular flow situation. According to Kirzner, however, the entrepreneur ensures a tendency towards an equilibrium, responding to intertemporal profit possibilities, and grasping the yet unexplored available opportunities (Kirzner 1979, 117-9). The alternative affiliation of entrepreneurship is with the discovery of past error.

An explanation for the contrast between these viewpoints is to be found in the divergence of their respective understandings of the status quo. As Kirzner puts it: 'Instead of seeing how the entrepreneur has disturbed the placid status quo, we must see how the status quo is nothing but a seething mass of unexploited maladjustments crying out for correction.' (Kirzner 1979, 119). Or, '...at each moment, enormous scope exists for improvements that are in one way or another ready to hand and yet are simply not noticed.' (Kirzner 1979, 135).

Kirzner has been criticized by other Austrians for his interpretation of the relationship between uncertainty and entrepreneurship. The critique concentrates on the reduction of the entrepreneur, who is the bearer of uncertainty, to his quality of alertness. Mises defines the entrepreneur as follows: 'Acting man exclusively seen from the aspect of the uncertainty inherent in every action.' (Mises 1949, 254). Kirzner, in fact, agrees with this definition. The dispute about viewing the Misesian entrepreneur as the bearer of persisting uncertainty as opposed to the discoverer of mere errors, corresponds to the tension between present uncertainty and past error (Kirzner 1982a, 148). It must be acknowledged, however, that Kirzner often discusses the role of the entrepreneur coping with uncertainty in a static context, as if the entrepreneur is merely waiting for profitable opportunities to show up. This image is confirmed by his choice of metaphors, such as opportunities "lurking around the corner", or "staring them in the face", and entrepreneurs who "pierce the fog of uncertainty". Kirzner is aware of their mechanical flavour, but retorts: 'surely these metaphors are useful and instructive.' (Kirzner 1982a, 157). In fact, Kirzner is perfectly aware of the fact that in the multiperiod case, thereby multiplying the dimensions along which mutual ignorance may develop, an entrepreneur is more than a calculator. He needs '...qualities of boldness, determination and creativity.. to create the future in an uncertain world.' (Kirzner 1982a, 155). The entrepreneur plays an active role in giving shape to the evolving economy.

Further insight to Kirzner's understanding of the entrepreneur may be gleaned from his revised description of entrepreneurship. While it had earlier implied no more than alertness to opportunities, and subsequently implement, it later became the propensity, motivated by the lure of market profits, to formulate an accurate vision of the future, thereby enhancing consistency among different parts of the market (Kirzner 1982a, 152-3).

With regard to decision-making in the market economy two problems must be addressed. Firstly, we have the calculation problem of identifying the most profitable action. Secondly, there is the problem of ensuring that the best option is actually pursued. The former problem was treated extensively in economics, and is covered by the category of deliberate learning. The two problems are relevant to both the level of individual decisions and that of society. We need not express surprise at the fact that Kirzner concentrates on the latter problem: after all, it has to do with entrepreneurial alertness, which is no mere 'ingredient' in the decision-making process. On the contrary, entrepreneurial decision-making consists of making decisions structured by entrepreneurial alertness. At the individual level, the problem is how to ensure that one takes the necessary optimal action. At the social level, the problem is ensuring that existing opportunities will be found and exploited.

There are thus two levels on which entrepreneurship can be discussed. 'What the entrepreneurial element in individual decision-making is to the individual, the entrepreneurship is to the market economy.' (Kirzner 1979, 117). The correspondence between entrepreneurship at the level of individual action and in the context of the market is depicted in the following table (Kirzner 1982a, 148-53).

Table 1: Two levels of discussing entrepreneurship

Individual entrepreneurship	*Entrepreneurship in the market*
Endeavour:	
Consists of the endeavour to enhance correspondence between the individually envisaged future and the actual future.	Consists of the function of securing greater consistency in different parts of the market.
Scope:	
Scope determined by the individual uncertainty of the future.	Scope determined by imperfect knowledge resulting in price divergences.
Incentive:	
Avoidance of entrepreneurial error as not merely a matter of being more sagacious, but also profitable; the potential profit is the incentive.	The incentive seen as the pure gain to be won by market entrepreneurial activity.

There are some questions to be posed here. First of all, will widespread alertness preclude all the profit opportunities, and thus stop all human actions? (Loasby 1982, 117). The answer is, no, since entrepreneurship cannot be reduced to any kind of arbitrage – in general alertness does not remove all ignorance. The ubiquity of unnoticed profitable opportunities will leave the ideal of an equilibrium for what it is, i.e. no more than a limiting case in which '...each decision correctly anticipates all other decisions.' (Kirzner 1979, 110). An economy peopled exclusively by alert agents may ultimately result in a stable equilibrium.

Another question to be posed concerns what we would call the paradox of evident opportunities. In the presence of many alert individuals, all deciding on their own, it is unclear whether all, some, or none of them will take the opportunity to gain a profit. Kirzner's viewpoint with regard to entrepreneurship would require him to state that individually perceived opportunities should, in general, remain unnoticed for a while in order to make exploitation profitable (Loasby 1982, 117). Kirzner acknowledged this by stating that it is necessary that profit opportunities '...on the surface do not appear to exist.' (Kirzner 1979a, 149-50). Once they "become obvious" to many alert agents in the market the profit margin will be squeezed out. The presence of widespread ignorance is a sufficient and generally satisfied condition for making alertness profitable.

A third major problem related to Kirzner's entrepreneurial alertness argument is the possibility of economic losses. Of course, one may adopt the straightforward but simplistic argument that people look for and act only in the presence of profitable opportunities, and accordingly do not end up suffering losses. However, there is a difference between receiving and understanding information; the problem of interpretation. Mises dealt with losses by introducing the concept of understanding. He argued that profits and losses are corollaries, both being important in the functioning of the social order. Profits (losses) result from superior (inferior) foresight and judgment because opportunities are the only possible sources of income. Kirzner, in contrast, leaves us without an explanation for the possibility of the existence of errors and ensuing losses. The missing link is judgment, a factor which was eclipsed in Kirzner's approach to entrepreneurial alertness. Notice that alertness is not the same as, and cannot function well without, interpretation, i.e. judgment. Kirzner models his entrepreneur as if he is merely on the lookout for, and manages to discover, profitable opportunities (High 1982, 166-8).

Kirzner emphasizes, as did Mises and Hayek, that institutions matter. He is especially interested in the institutional arrangements offering opportunities to the agents who are most able to notice them; i.e. those agents who are most alert to them. Individuals differ to quite a considerable degree in their ability to notice what has so far been overlooked (Kirzner 1979, 148-9). Kirzner therefore reaches the following conclusion: 'Alertness thus appears to possess a primordial role in decision making' (Kirzner 1979, 131). As a consequence, entrepreneurship is a scarce resource of a special kind; costless; not a potential stock; and not something to be deployed in decision-making (Kirzner 1985, 20-9). Institutional circumstances must therefore be arranged so as to turn the discovery and exploitation of socially advantageous opportunities into personal advantages (Kirzner 1985, 19, 29). Kirzner sees the market process as being the most effective form of organization. The market process disseminates hitherto unknown knowledge, which must inevitably result in learning which was not sought after. If nothing else, we know that spontaneous learning will take place more rapidly when the opportunities seem advantageous to the agent involved (Kirzner 1979, 149-52). In a market economy, money '...represents a social arrangement with the ability to present existing overlooked opportunities in a form most easily recognized and noticed by spontaneous learners.' (Kirzner 1979, 150). The author wants us to recognize the '...extent to which both individual action and social coordination through the market can occur significantly despite the uncertainty of the future' (Kirzner 1982a, 156).

Profits are the result of noticing market shortcomings, and direct the activities of entrepreneurs. Entrepreneurs recognize the possibility of attaining a wealthier position. 'The Misesian theory of entrepreneurial profit may be described as an *arbitrage* theory of profit.' (Kirzner 1979, 94). The better an agent understands his environment the higher his profits, and the worse he understands it, the lower his profits or the greater his losses.

Let us take stock. We began this paper with a discussion of uncertainty in relation to individual human action, moved over to economy-wide dispersion of information, and finished with entrepreneurial alertness and individual spontaneous learning. Mises concentrated on the equivalence between uncertainty and human action. The actor tackles uncertainty with the help of experience and the faculty of understanding, to deal with the unique events of purposeful actions. Entrepreneurial activities take place only after monetary calculations have shown what outcome can be expected of an action. However, the problem of the coordination of entrepreneurial activities, a problem of dealing with mutually inconsistent expectations, was not solved by Mises. He was presumably unable to do so partially because the topic did not seem to fit in with praxeology, and partially because he concentrated on the decision-making individual, thereby underrating the importance of the acquisition of knowledge.

Hayek, on the other hand, focused on the assumption of dispersed information and the consequences for economics. Each one of us is guided by expectations of an uncertain future. Market prices are supposed to communicate scattered information, and improve the coordination of plans. An economic process evolves in a stable manner under relevant foresight only when the coordination is perfect, i.e. as long as the expectations are correct for the decisions at hand. One of the major fields of research neglected by Hayek concerns the creation or origin of information, and this has been taken up by Kirzner.

According to Kirzner, uncertainty reflects man's awareness of possible dicrepancies between the envisaged future and the realized future. Past error and present uncertainty are two sides of the same coin which is called entrepreneurship. The entrepreneur is alert for yet unnoticed profitable opportunities, i.e. existing maladjustments, but is unable to find them by deliberate search alone. The other major field of research neglected by Hayek is judgment, i.e. the linking of information to expectations, a field which has also been neglected by Kirzner. The question is how coordination may prevail when both errors and their concomitant uncertainties coexists? That question will now be turned to.

4.10 Expectations

Possibly as a consequence of the uncomfortable attempted resolution of the problem of dealing with mutually inconsistent expectations, that is of coordination of actions taking place under uncertainty, an increasing number of economists writing in the Austrian tradition came to concentrate on the problems related to the formation of expectations. Ludwig M. Lachmann (1906-1990) was the most prominent among them. From the 1930s onwards he wrote primarily about the problems of the subjectivity and diversity of expectations. His writings lend further force to the opinion that expectations and related problems have been taken seriously in economics since the 1930s.

Lachmann's ideas about economic activities were inspired by the views of Mises, Hayek, Weber, and Shackle. The latter writer will be discussed in the chapter on (Post-) Keynesian Economics. Shackle believed that economics may enhance our understanding of economic activity, but cannot provide us with useful predictions. The interpretation of economic activity as the result of human actions, implying changes and purposeful choices, must influence the perceived function of economics. Lachmann's position on the task of the social sciences, which he maintained for more than four-decades, is that social scientists ought to strive to enhance the intelligibility of human activities and not bother about their determinateness (Lachmann 1943, 14; Lachmann 1977, 71).

"Lachmann's Law", the name Boulding gave to Lachmann's view on prediction, asserts the following: 'The impossibility of prediction in economics follows from the facts that economic change is linked to change in knowledge, and future knowledge cannot be gained before its time.' (Lachmann 1977, 90). For Lachmann, to introduce time is to introduce a fundamental unknown into the analysis, for it introduces a categorical distinction between the present and the future (Garrison 1986, 91, 93). Although the future is not unimaginable, it remains unknowable (Lachmann 1976, 59); 'the present, in which we stand and judge, is but a thin veneer between an unknowable future and an irrevocable past, from which our knowledge is drawn.' (Lachmann 1956 1978, viii).

In an effort to synthesise Mises and Shackle, Lachmann stresses the negligence of Mises, Hayek, and Kirzner in failing to introduce expectations into their theories. In fact, Mises hardly ever mentioned expectations (Lachmann 1976, 58). In our evolving economy prices are assumed to transmit information about expressed expectations. Once transmitted, the information may be speculative or outdated. If only for this reason the decoding of price information is necessary (Lachmann 1956 1978, 20-2).

Expectations are '...acts of the entrepreneurial mind which constitute his (the entrepreneur's; EW) *world*, diagnose *the situation* in which action has to be taken, and logically precede the making of plans' (Lachmann 1956 1978, 15). Expectations are neither economic results, such as prices, nor data as consumers' tastes are. Furthermore, they may function differently in different markets. Expectations embody interpreted or "filtered" experiences.

The transformation process that takes place in the human mind, using experiences as inputs, results in indeterminate expectations. The "filter" is the subjective nature of our beliefs in the major forces causing and governing change in the economic process (Lachmann 1977, 66-73). Because of continuous and unpredictable change, expectations will differ among individuals. Divergent expectations are the individual images of new, but rather blurred, pieces of knowledge.

Lachmann's main proposition is that, because an undisputed single *ex ante* criterion of success does not exist, the market cannot generate and diffuse superior expectations. There is only a day-to-day balancing of "a-rational" expectations by anticipating man, *homo divinans* (Lachmann 1976, 58-61). A-rational expectations and behaviour are necessitated by the condition of genuine uncertainty. 'Market participants must make decisions without knowing what the relevant true probabilities are and even without knowing what the full range of possible outcomes are.' (Garrison 1986, 94).

One is able to comprehend all human action contingencies only by reducing them to a mental pattern of relative simplicity (Lachmann 1977, 71). What is commonly called the normal level, e.g. of prices and interest rates, is '...determined by what are believed to be permanently operative forces.' (Lachmann 1977, 78). In this respect, Lachmann was already discussing the phenomenon of price inflexibility in the 1940s. The analytical framework consists of a normal price range and an enveloping wider price range. Price movements are split between meaningless (functionless) and meaningful (significant) ones. One may also interpret this mental pattern as a distinction between minor or random forces and major or permanent market forces (Lachmann 1956 1978, 20-34).

Inelastic expectations will stabilize the price movements within the inner price range. As long as price movements remain within the "inner range", they will be disregarded and attributed to random influences. When prices stay within the "outer range", but are already outside the inner range, some market participants will take heed. When this situation continues for some time, expectations are bound to change sooner or later. The actual price will be interpreted as the resultant of a new constellation of permanent forces. If actual prices break through the outer range, a new diagnosis, and new expectations with regard to the various forces will be inevitable (Lachmann 1956 1978, 23-34; Lachmann 1977, 73-9).

The European Monetary System (EMS), as it functioned in the 1970s and 1980s, may serve as an illustration of an analogous construction. It featured a normal exchange level, as well as an upper and a lower exchange level limit, which implied accommodating actions by the central banks. In addition, there was an intermediate range, outside of which restructuring of the system would be necessary. Although the construction is analogous to his own, it is unlikely that Lachmann would have applauded this normative system. For him, it was only in the context of plans based on individual subjective judgments of information, and in the perspective of earlier expectations, that the establishment of normal price ranges was understood as useful.

Equilibrium will only be reached by chance. The equilibrating forces will be thwarted by unexpected changes. 'What emerges from our reflections is an image of the market as a particular kind of process, a continuous process, without beginning, or end, propelled by the interaction between the forces of equilibrium and the forces of changes.' (Lachmann 1976, 61).

Some convergence of expectations is ensured by the evolution of adequate market institutions. Interpersonal and time-dependent inconsistencies will be mitigated by the evolved institutions (Lachmann 1956 1978, 25). Expectations which are consistently disappointed will result in lower profits/higher losses, and will therefore be erased from the minds of agents in the market.

As we stated earlier, the importance of the adequate nature of institutions, as means of promoting the prevalence of expectations which accurately reflect the underlying economic reality, has also been stressed by other Austrians ever since the interwar socialist-calculation debate took place. For such Austrians, as for Lachmann, a market economy is the only useful mechanism, rewarding adequate expectations via the profits accruing from the ensuing actions.

4.11 Time and types

O'Driscoll and Rizzo brought together different lines of argument in regard to the relations between the future, the present, and the past, and especially those concerning the relations between explanation and prediction. In 1985, they published the book *Economics as a Coordination Problem* which is specifically concerned with the problem of economic coordination under uncertainty. They attempted to synthesize, and build upon, many of the writings and ideas which have been discussed so far in this chapter.

O'Driscoll and Rizzo use the term "genuine uncertainty" to refer to '...the recognition that all attempts to characterize the future involve both unique, and recurrent (typical) features.' (O'Driscoll and Rizzo 1985, 72). The main features of genuine uncertainty are (1) ignorance, or the inherent impossibility of listing all possible outcomes of a course of action, and (2) irreversible time, or the absolute endogeneity of uncertainty, (O'Driscoll and Rizzo 1985, 71; O'Driscoll and Rizzo 1986, 258-9). The neoclassical "counterparts" of these features are (subjective) probability distributions and the static concept of time. Genuine uncertainty not only stands in sharp contrast with the neoclassical conception of uncertainty and is incompatible with standard notions of equilibrium (O'Driscoll and Rizzo 1985, 4), but it is also inherently ineradicable (ibid., 66). We propose first to discuss the two features of genuine uncertainty, after which a discussion of the element of ideal types, which used to be part of O'Driscoll's en Rizzo's theory, will follow.

The first feature of uncertainty is ignorance. Individual decision-making is autonomous, although this does not imply that it is not dependent on what others choose to do. The Austrian interpretation of subjectivism makes this view explicit: 'A world in which there is autonomous or creative decision-making is one in which the future is not merely unknown, but *unknowable*' (ibid., 2). Action under uncertainty, i.e. what Mises called human action, and subjectivism are inseparable ideas. The economic future is unknowable, because the future is "underdetermined" by the present state of the economic world. The idea of ignorance cannot be grasped by reference to its counterpart, i.e. the presumption of perfect (stochastic) knowledge and foresight. Its fundamental aspect is the, albeit only perceived, impossibility of listing of all possible outcomes of a course of action. Since all outcomes are affected by other actors' activities, choices are never made with complete knowledge of their consequences. The possibility set itself is unbounded. Therefore, ignorance is not to be defined as merely incomplete knowledge (O'Driscoll and Rizzo 1985, 4).

Historical or "real" time is the second feature of genuine uncertainty. It may be contrasted with what O'Driscoll and Rizzo call Newtonian, or static, time. Both are special cases on a continuum. Uncertainty may be characterized by both time-independent and time-dependent features. Most economists rely on the Newtonian time concept, a perspective which is dominant when an economist speaks, for example, of a stable decision-making environment. Newtonian time may be characterized by at least three aspects: (1) time is homogeneous, and therefore it is a static category. Time may pass without anything happening; (2) time is mathematically continuous.

Each time instant is merely one bead in a string of beads and in principle independent of the others; (3) Newtonian time adds nothing to the world's content, and is therefore causally inert. The consequence of using the Newtonian time concept is the neglect of the problem of economic change, and of process (O'Driscoll and Rizzo 1985, 53-8).

Real, subjective, historical, dynamic or endogenous time is not perceived as some homogenous quantity, or as isolated points, but as a flow of events (O'Driscoll and Rizzo 1986, 255). It is the concept of time which Bergson called *la dureé*, i.e. duration (O'Driscoll and Rizzo 1985, 59). The continuous flow of novel experiences constitutes time. Memory and expectation are the structural components of historical time, connecting successive periods through their non-deterministic continuous influence on individual perceptions. Furthermore, as memory evolves one's present perspective changes. Finally, the perception of time is creative and causally potent rather than causally inert (ibid., 60-2). To sum up, O'Driscoll and Rizzo use the same metaphor as Lachmann: 'The growth of knowledge is the endogenous force that endlessly propels the system.' (ibid., 62). The effects of historical time are twofold. Historical time (1) is irreversible, and (2) produces unpredictable change. As a consequence "movements along curves" are no longer neutral in a given situation. Furthermore, there should be scope for surprise and for creative evolution (ibid., 56-62).

According to O'Driscoll and Rizzo, the critical underlying contrast in the uncertainty debate is between purely time-dependent, or endogenous, uncertainty and Newtonian, or time-independent, forms of uncertainty. Neither subjective versus objective probability, nor Knight's measurable versus unmeasurable uncertainty is the most fundamental contrast (ibid., 75).

Genuine uncertainty is ineradicable because actions aimed at reducing it can only transform it (ibid., 66). This will become evident when we refer to the gathering of information by, what Shackle called, "crucial" experiments. Such experiments affect the whole future course of relevant events but will not reduce uncertainty (Shackle 1955, 6, 63). Efforts to achieve a reduction of uncertainty may also be inhibited by certain characteristics of the markets, especially independent decision-making. Because of the eternal relevance of information on what others predict to one's own predictions, extra information will only result in an extra stratum of guesses and counterguesses (O'Driscoll and Rizzo 1985, 234, 72).

Different types of human activities occupy different parts of the time continuum. Maximizing behaviour is close to the Newtonian pole, while creative decision-making tends toward the real-time pole. The more explicit the solution to a problem, the greater the Newtonization of time, and the more narrow the mnemonic link. The leaping over logical steps, itself sometimes only clarified by means of reconstruction, is the creative element in a decision. 'Therefore, the actual content of the thought or decision-making process determines the appropriateness of the particular concept of time.' (O'Driscoll and Rizzo 1985, 67). An enlargement of the creative component goes hand in hand with a widening of the mnemonic link (ibid., 67).

Creativity, planning, and purposeful actions all create a paradox of uncertainty, because some degree of both indeterminateness and predictability is needed to enable creative activities (ibid., 11). The paradox of uncertainty may be stated more suitably as follows: 'While complete stability and predictability are incompatible with time, their absence is incompatible with action.' (ibid., 76). The fundamental problem inherent in any attempt to introduce a denial of regularity and uniformity is the necessity to refer to ideal-typical representations. Such representations already presuppose the existence of social causation and coordination (Selgin 1988, 46).

The solution to the paradox of uncertainty is to be found in the same critical contrast between endogenous and Newtonian forms of uncertainty. It is here that the writings of Alfred Schutz on the scientific interpretation of human actions come into play.

The philosopher and sociologist Alfred Schutz (1899-1959) applied Husserl's phenomenology to the structure of human action (Lachmann 1977, 96). Action, that is the execution of a projected act (Schutz 1932, 61), is based on a common sense scheme of reference consisting of unquestioned past experiences. This common sense knowledge is based on a basic fact of life, namely that '...we live in a world of more or less well circumscribed objects with more or less definite qualities.' (Schutz 1953, 307). This common sense knowledge is subjective, not necessarily coherent, and is altered by experiences.

Schutz emphasizes the distinction between the typical and the unique features of phenomena. In contrast to Weber, Schutz uses a narrow definition of ideal types, thereby signifying that all conceivable action conforms to these constructs. This definition makes his construction universally applicable and suitable as a foundation of praxeological theories.

Choices are made by way of a process of deliberation, that is a process by which combinations of selected knowledge components are created. The world is typically made up of a system consisting of more or less empty ideal types, to be filled by the unique features of the individual occurrence. It involves, what Husserl called, the idealisation of "I-can-do-it-again" (Schutz 1953, 319, 329).

According to Schutz, the basic uncertainty as to the outcome of rational action involving social interaction is reduced with further standardization of the prevailing patterns of action. The uncertainty is expressed in our hopes and fears. One orients one's actions in accordance with socially-approved standards of rules of conduct. These standards are embodied in norms, manners, and mores, and are supported by habits, traditions, organizational frameworks, rules, regulations, laws, etc. The overall framework of typical constructs is taken for granted by the in-group. The evaluation of projected interactions will always be informed by plausibility, by subjective likelihood, albeit not by mathematical probability. The reason for the latter omission is the undetermined future. The subjective chance that actions will be more efficacious is greater when the relevant behaviour pattern is relatively highly standardized (Schutz 1953, 325-33).

At this juncture, we need to consider a major problem which threatens to undermine this approach: since with regard to the question of choice, this approach denies a proper place for the novelty of circumstances, a factor of potentially crucial importance. It is not made clear how novel ideas and experiences change the ideal types which orientate the agents. In fact, Schutz more or less ignores an essential element of creativity, namely novelty.

Mises refers approvingly to the writings of Schutz (Mises 1933, 125-6n27), and promised to discuss his ideas in another paper. Indeed, he actually used the ideas of Schutz in another work: 'If an ideal type refers to people, it implies that in some respect these men are valuing and acting in a uniform or similar way. When it refers to institutions, it implies that these institutions are products of uniform or similar ways of valuing and acting or that they influence valuing and acting in a uniform or similar way. .. Ideal types are expedients to simplify the treatment of the puzzling multiplicity and variety of human affairs. In employing them one must always be aware of the deficiencies of any kind of simplification.' (Mises 1957, 316, 320). Although Mises's opinion on the integration òf these ideas in Austrian economics may have been interesting, he never published the promised discussion of Schutz's work and ideas.

Typification is the process of '...extracting what stability and regularity there is in the flow of reality. Stable features are called types.' (O'Driscoll and Rizzo 1985, 76). Events may be broken down into their (1) stable and typical, and (2) unique, aspects. This approach to theorizing in the face of genuine uncertainty enjoyed the support of, e.g., Langlois, Ebeling, and Selgin (Langlois 1986, 182; Ebeling 1986, 51-2; Selgin 1988, 46).

(1) Typical features are those elements of reality that we discover to be repeatable. Finding types or patterns is dependent on the stability of physical laws, and on mutual reinforcing and stabilizing effects of human interaction. The typical aspect may be anticipated with certainty or probability because it cannot be open-ended. The totality of possible alternatives is known. It enables pattern prediction.

(2) The unique aspect is the specific time-dependent element in a stable pattern. 'Unique features .. are the idiosyncratic, nonrepeatable aspects of reality, - that are tied to history and to particular concrete circumstances in which they occur.' (Langlois 1986, 182).

The unique aspect remains open-ended because the details are filled in as events occur. It constitutes, for instance, the endogenous market process. The typical features only change in the event of exogenous shocks, for example, a change in the institutional framework. Such shocks will produce a change in the class of results (O'Driscoll and Rizzo 1985, 85-7).

The interpretative-predictive schedule will inevitably change; (1) when the actual outcomes cause beliefs to change, (2) if a predicted typical event is falsified, and/or (3) when a unique event exerts major influence. O'Driscoll and Rizzo do not expect any rapid changes in these frameworks because types are, by definition, relatively stable elements (O'Driscoll and Rizzo 1985, 76-79), but they leave unanswered the lingering and urgent question about the empirical recognition of these three possible motors of change.

4.12 Entrepreneurship versus rule-bound behaviour

Both entrepreneurship and the adherence to rules reflect individual responses to uncertainty (O'Driscoll and Rizzo 1986, 253): accordingly, '...market economies do *not* rely solely on prices but depend on entrepreneurial activity, rules of thumb, contracts and other institutions to convey information and coordinate behavior.' (ibid., 256).

Rule-following behaviour is defined as a '...situation of the general type X, [in which; EW] a relatively specific action or a limited set of actions A is observed' (ibid., 258). These routines are the present representation of patterns of behaviour which have evolved gradually. A conscious explicit calculation with regard to individual costs and benefits will not be found in this case (ibid., 258).

Rules of thumb are adopted when the computational demand on maximization calculation is excessive, or when maximization is made impossible by the informational demands of time-dependent uncertainty. Such rules of thumb make behaviour more predictable by bounding individual behaviour and by providing regularities. They form a crucial factor in, for example, bargaining situations.

Continuous utility maximization, in the sense of ongoing, uninterrupted, recurring optimization at each moment, may yield in unpredictable results in a situation of uncertainty. An example would be Keynes's famous beauty contest, in which the appropriate expectation depends on guessing and counterguessing the expectations of the other participants; a process which, in principle, never ends. 'Rules may produce more satisfactory long-run results insofar as they reduce the errors attributable to fine tuning without sufficient knowledge, or insofar as they prevent destabilizing behaviour.' (O'Driscoll and Rizzo 1986, 258). Endogenous uncertainty is reduced by such rules in both situations, often resulting in relatively higher social returns (ibid., 259-63), and the authors therefore conclude that uncertainty, and not certainty, is the cradle of predictable or stable behaviour (ibid., 254).

The concept of entrepreneurship, as presented by O'Driscoll and Rizzo, is an amalgam of the Schumpeterian and the Kirznerian theories of the entrepreneur. Entrepreneurs may stabilize economic activities by "shouldering" uncertainty or by acquiring superior knowledge. 'The market function of entrepreneurial activity is to fill gaps in the knowledge of market participants. ..[It; EW] consists in "outguessing" market prices when the prices do not seem consistent.' (ibid., 257). O'Driscoll and Rizzo consider entrepreneurship to be, by and large, more of a stabilizing than a disruptive element in the economy.

The authors state that where information costs are other than zero, we will often experience sudden, if not catastrophic, changes (O'Driscoll and Rizzo 1985, 134-51). Quality-certificates, product information, etc., may be considered as supplying required information supplementary to that provided by prices (O'Driscoll and Rizzo 1985, 234). Deregulation, privatization, reorganization and other environmental changes render much previously accumulated knowledge obsolete. Such changes create great dangers to decision-makers because the need to adopt new behavioural rules necessitates a whole new learning process. This process, which is only partly manageable, involves the acquisition of new information and new learning functions. This learning process differs from the one referred to by Frank Knight, in whose opinion the process meant acquiring information on relevant prices and quantities.

Although they are at opposite ends of the behavioural continuum, entrepreneurship and rules of thumb are not incompatible. In contrast to what is commonly thought, they are mutually reinforcing. 'Entrepreneurial alertness, for example, may be the source of the perception of an opportunity, but rule following may be the only feasible way in an uncertain world.' (O'Driscoll and Rizzo 1986, 256).

A self-stabilizing circle may exist with regard to economic behaviour. In the face of genuine uncertainty one may find individual rule-following behaviour. Institutions are social crystallizations of these activities. The rules themselves bound individual behaviour, highlighting regularities while reflecting a high degree of uncertainty. Both the social institutions and the individual rule-following behaviour bound the economic system, thereby stabilizing economic activities. This may be a self-reinforcing circuit (O'Driscoll and Rizzo 1985, 6).

General equilibrium is no more than a conceptual tool in the mind of the economist. It does not exist in the real world (Rizzo 1979, 82). There is, in fact, a plethora of equilibria depending on the operative institutional processes (O'Driscoll and Rizzo 1985, 76-9). Because equilibrium concepts indicate directions for actions, via predictions, and are of use as a frame of reference, it is judged necessary to retain some sort of equilibrium concept as a tool of analysis. Introducing pattern-coordination may prove an enrichment of this conception whereby the Hayekian compatibility of plans and the distinction between unique and typical features could be deployed. 'Pattern coordination consists of coordination among the typical but not the unique aspects of individual behaviour.' (ibid., 114). There is a societal (stochastic) pattern coordination in cases in which agents have compatible plans insofar as the typical features of plans are (probabilistically) coordinated (ibid., 86).

The approach adopted by O'Driscoll and Rizzo may present a satisfactory solution to the problem of uncertainty, provided that we assume the stability of certain patterns of behaviour. However, this assumption has to be handled with the utmost caution, if overconfident conclusions are to be avoided.

4.13 Conclusions

We are now in a position to offer answers to the pair of questions posed in the introduction, the first being: how has uncertainty been introduced into Austrian economics?; and the second: what are the consequent implications for decision-making? We note that, in contrast to mainstream and New-Classical writers, writers in the Austrian school do not regard uncertainty as a negative factor. As Mises said, the same thing can be denoted both by stating that the future is uncertain and by asserting that man acts; uncertainty is a pervasive aspect of the economic process. If there was no uncertainty, an evolving economic process could not exist.

According to Mises, we handle uncertainty with the help of experience and the faculty of understanding. However, he could not solve the problem of dealing with mutually inconsistent expectations, partly because it did not seem to fit praxeology, and partly because he concentrated on the thoughtful individual, thereby underrating the importance of the distribution of knowledge via information. Therefore, we next concentrated our attention on problems related to the coordination of economic activities. It was Hayek who demonstrated the economic significance of the scattered-information assumption, and the necessity to analyse, within economics, the consequences of dispersed information. The actions of agents, in their unique circumstances, are guided by expectations of an uncertain future. Market prices are presumed to be means of communicating scattered information and improving the coordination of plans.

Hayek more or less ignored the origins of new market information. How do the agents who keep the economic process evolving, i.e. the entrepreneurs, come to find previously totally unknown opportunities? Kirzner tried to fill this gap. According to him, past error and present uncertainty are two sides of the same coin, and this coin is called entrepreneurship. Uncertainty reflects man's awareness of possible deviations in the envisaged future from the realized future. The entrepreneur is alert for yet unnoticed profitable opportunities and existing maladjustments, but is unable to find them solely by deliberate learning.

One wonders, however, how coordination might prevail when errors, and their concomitant uncertainty, are coexistent. It is in this respect that one must discuss economic judgment, i.e. the decoding or transformation of (price) information into individual expectations. This is the second major element neglected by Hayek. According to Lachmann, filtered experiences result in indeterminate expectations. The market cannot generate and diffuse superior expectations because there is no *ex ante* criterium of success. Events may be broken down into stable aspects and unique aspects. As a consequence, within price movements individuals can distinguish minor or random forces from major or permanent market forces.

An important contribution made by the Austrian school of economic thought is that individual decision-making about an uncertain future is related to economic development in a systematic way. Economies must be modelled so as to furnish the agent who is best suited to perform a particular task with an adequate information-finding mechanism. The importance of the adequate nature of institutions, that is to say, a market economy with profits and losses so as to promote the prevalence of expectations which are in agreement with the underlying economic reality, has been stressed by the Austrians ever since the calculation-debate.

More recently, there has been a strong inclination to stress the necessity of analysing both entrepreneurial activities and the adherence to rules as individual responses to uncertainty. These analyses are directed at synthesizing ideas put forward by Kirzner with ideas developed by Lachmann. Rules make behaviour more predictable, by bounding individual behaviour, and by providing apparent regularities. The function of entrepreneurial activity is to fill in gaps in the knowledge of market participants. Rule-following behaviour and entrepreneurial activities together propel the economy into the uncertain future, by enlarging our knowledge and, at the same time, transforming situations.

To conclude, Austrian economics may be regarded as representing a middle-ground position on the point of uncertainty, knowledge, decision-making, and predictability. This middle-ground lies between the extreme viewpoints of a deterministic universe and a haphazard or kaleidic future. The Austrians adopt a more radical position, however, on the capacities of the individual in evaluating what is the best action for him, on the likelihood of the market coping with external and interdependency effects, and on the rapidity with which new activities may be undertaken in a market economy. Because of the extremity of this position, it is attractive to turn to the alternative viewpoint which, on the one hand, stresses rule-following behaviour, while, on the other hand, disputing the trust on markets and individual capacities. This position has been elaborated in Post-Keynesian Economics, to which our attention will now be directed. Uncertainty is an important element in for example Keynes's en Shackle's worldview in particular because uncertainty fundamentally influences decision-making. Adherents to this approach stress the importance of opinions and conventional behaviour in the making of the economy. In next chapter, it will also be shown that although crucial contrasts remain pertinent, Austrian and Post-Keynesian opinions tend to converge on a number of important issues within economics.

5: Uncertainty and (Post-)Keynesian Economics: Imagination, Expectation and Decision-making

> 'Uncertainty, as opposed to mathematical risk, is a pervasive fact of life.'
>
> (Lawson 1985, 909)

> 'The future is not there to be discovered, but must be created.'
>
> (Shackle 1961, 16)

5.1 Introduction

The positions adopted by Mainstream, New Classical, and Austrian economists in discussing uncertainty differ in many respects. In particular, the preference of advancing a probability concept, and the negative connotation of uncertainty among the proponents of the Mainstream and New Classical approach are aspects which are entirely foreign to writers in the Austrian tradition. Furthermore, in contrast to the former groups the latter group of economists understand the economy as involving processes of ongoing transformations. Nevertheless, the different schools seem to concur that uncertainty is influential albeit more at the local level. There is no need to redesign the whole model or the conception of an economy when, for example, a price signal results in a rise of uncertainty about market conditions. Uncertainty is thus not regarded as a potentially destructive force. A large number of those who did appreciate this macro-economic aspect of uncertainty are called (Post-) Keynesian Economists.

At the time when Hayek evolved to a position stressing the spontaneous coordination of economic actions, John Maynard Keynes (1883-1946) moved to his soon famous position stressing the interdependency of people's opinions. This interdependency may sometimes become problematic and create a need for governmental interference, because the future is not there to be discovered but is rather created in an unsteady flow of expectations-driven human activities. Whenever economists refer to the writings of Keynes, there is usually a reference to his famous albeit "untidy" book (Blaug 1985, 670), entitled: *The General Theory of Employment, Interest and Money*, in which Keynes elaborates upon this position. The proper understanding and relative importance of uncertainty in Keynes's theories has been one of the main bones of contention in ensuing disputes ever since.

Three currents in Keynesianism sprang from the same source, but cascaded down the mountain in different directions (Shackle 1983, 242). Supporters of a first interpretation, including such eminent economists as Hicks, Samuelson, Modigliani, and Tobin, take as their point of departure the Hicks-Hansen Investment Saving/Liquidity Money (IS/LM) apparatus. It facilitated their goal of making Keynes's work amenable to comparison with alternative theories. This interpretation, which has been disseminated since the Second World War as Keynesian Economics, may be characterized by the label "Hydraulic Keynesianism" (Coddington 1983, 102). Advocates of a second interpretation, notably Clower and Leijonhufvud, stress the originality of Keynes's *General Theory*. Their "Reconstituted Reductionism" boils down to the opinion that economists should no longer concentrate on the concept of equilibrium itself, but rather address the problem of actually attaining a state of equilibrium (ibid., 105-11).

The third current to be distinguished is called fundamentalist Keynesianism, featuring Shackle, Townshend, S. Weintraub, J. Robinson, and P. Davidson (ibid., 91-100). A more suitable label may be "Post-Keynesian Economics", since Keynes's words as such are not enshrined and a diversity of approaches is involved (Dow 1985, 76). A characteristic frequently found in Post-Keynesian writings is the account taken of the role of time, i.e. of the difference between the uncertain future and the fossilized past (Robinson 1978, 12). In this chapter we will concentrate on the first and the third currents, since the ideas presented by adherents of reconstituted reductionism, the second current, had little or no impact on the debates on uncertainty.

This chapter concentrates on the main ideas concerning the meaning and content of uncertainty as they evolved out of the aforementioned book. Thus, the question posed in this chapter is the following: How has uncertainty been introduced into (Post-) Keynesianism? In order to arrive at an answer to the question we first attempt to lay bare the body of the *General Theory*. Next, contemporary views are discussed, illuminating the direct and profound differences among the various interpretations. Subsequently, the relation between the two dominant interpretations of Keynes's writings, that of Hicks and that of Shackle, and their respective "breeding-places", will be identified. The discussion about the first current ends with an illustration of the disappearance of uncertainty in the mathematics of hydraulic Keynesianism. Thereupon, the emphasis will shift to the Post-Keynesian current: in particular, Shackle's theory of uncertainty will be elaborated. Next, the downstream assimilation of existing ideas and theories will be examined. The chapter will be concluded with a discussion of Keynes's writings as they surface in the (dis-) continuity debate.

5.2 Keynes's *General Theory* on uncertainty

As stated in the introduction, in this section an attempt will be made to pinpoint uncertainty in Keynes (1936). Its theoretical framework will therefore first be presented, before proceeding to locate uncertainty within that framework.

The *General Theory* is primarily a study of the forces which determine changes in the scale of output and employment in a monetary economy. The addition of the element money is of importance, because money links the present and the future (Keynes 1936, 293). We may thus leave the theory of stationary equilibrium behind and construct a theory of shifting equilibrium, '...meaning by the latter the theory of a system in which changing views about the future are capable of influencing the present situation.' (Keynes 1936, 293).

Keynes distinguished between the following three basic, independent variables: (1) the wage-unit as determined by wage bargaining, (2) the quantity of money, and (3) the following three psychological factors: 'the psychological propensity to consume, the psychological attitude to liquidity and the psychological expectation of future yield from capital-assets.' (Keynes 1936, 247). The quantity of money is assumed to be constant. These variables, together with certain exogenous factors, determine the national income and the quantity of jobs.

The portmanteau function "propensity to consume" (ibid., 96) is '...the functional relationship X between Y_w, a given level of income in terms of "wage-units", and C_w the expenditure on consumption out of that level of income.' (ibid., 90). As a rule X is a stable function with the marginal propensity to consume out of Y_w somewhat smaller than 1.0 (ibid., 113-5). The exception to the rule is presumed to entail abnormal circumstances in which there is extreme uncertainty concerning the future (ibid., 94).

Saving is defined as '...the excess of income over consumption.' (ibid., 62). By defining saving as an excess, Keynes wants his readers to appreciate the optical illusion involved in the notion that people will always spend their money, in one way or another (ibid., 20). 'They are fallaciously supposing that there is a nexus which unites decisions to abstain from present consumption with decisions to provide for future consumption; whereas the motives which determine the latter are not linked in any simple way with the motives which determine the former.' (ibid., 21).

After having decided how much of his income to withhold from consumption, each individual will await a second decision (ibid., 65). This is the decision on the form of saving. The quantity of wealth a person prefers to hold in cash, his "liquidity preference", on the one hand earns no interest, but on the other enables an immediate command over goods and services in general.

The liquidity preference together with the independent "quantity of money" variable determine the actual or money rate of interest. The money rate of interest is defined as the percentage excess of a sum of money contracted for forward delivery over the spot price of the contracted sum (Keynes 1936, 222). This reward for sacrificing the convenience of liquidity for a specified period (ibid., 167-8), is a measure of the unwillingness to defer immediate command over money. It discloses the psychological "attitude to liquidity", the propensity to hoard beyond what is needed as a precaution and for transactions (ibid., 170, 194-209). 'A rise in the rate of interest is a means *alternative* to an increase of hoards for satisfying an increased liquidity preference.' (Keynes 1937, 111). Thus, the rate of interest is not a return for saving or abstention from consumption as such, but 'the "price" which equilibrates the desire to hold wealth in the form of cash with the available quantity of cash.' (Keynes 1936, 167).

The necessary condition for the existence of a liquidity preference is '...the existence of uncertainty as to the future of the rate of interest, i.e. as to the complex of rates of interest for varying maturities which will rule at future dates.' (Keynes 1936, 168). When nobody feels any uncertainty about the future rates of interest, the propensity to hoard will be zero (ibid., 208-9).

Monetary authorities may endeavour to establish the desired rates of interest via the quantity of money available in the economy. A monetary policy, for example to reduce the long-term rate of interest, will succeed in a case in which it is considered '...as being reasonable and practicable' (Keynes 1936, 203), and is promoted by an authority expressing representative opinion. However, if public opinion expects monetary policy to be liable to change or to be unsafe all extra money supply without theoretical limit will be hoarded in response to a small reduction of the interest rate, and a future rise awaited. Nevertheless, in general '...the rate of interest is a highly conventional, rather than a highly psychological, phenomenon.' (Keynes 1936, 203). Because of this conventionalist basis, the long-term rate of interest may be a fairly stable one.

Uncertainty comes into play primarily in the domain of investments. Current investment is defined as '...the current addition to the value of the capital equipment which has resulted from the productive activity of the period', which includes increments in capital goods and in entrepreneurs' stocks of finished consumption-goods (Keynes 1936, 62, 52; cf. Keynes 1979, 238-9). The individual propensity to invest depends partly on the rate of interest, and partly on the schedule of the Marginal Efficiency of Capital (MEC) (Keynes 1936, 136-7). The MEC is '...that rate of discount which would make the present value of the series of annuities given by the returns expected from the capital-asset during its life just equal to its supply price.' (ibid., 135). On the one hand, the current supply price of the capital-asset is given. On the other hand, the psychological "expectations of future yields" from capital-assets are based upon both (1) the facts known more of less for certain, e.g. the existing stock of types of capital-assets, and (2) '...future events which can only be forecasted with more or less confidence' (ibid., 147), e.g. future changes in taste among the consumers. Keynes listed the following factors which he considered relevant, at any rate in the nineteenth century: (1) The growth of population; (2) The proliferation of inventions; (3) development of virgin land; (4) The frequency of war; and (5) the level of confidence (ibid., 307). In so far as past expectations are so embodied and taken in conjunction with today's expectations they determine today's employment (ibid., 50).

Keynes is explicit on the necessity of distinguishing long and short-term expectations. The latter relate to decisions about daily output given the existing stock of capital equipment, itself the result of investment decisions, based on past states of expectations (Keynes 1936, 47, 50, 148). The process of revision of short-term expectations is generally a gradual and adaptive one. Although actually realized results in the production and sale of output are in principle irrelevant in the light of current expectations (ibid., 47), it is often practically sensible to base '...expectations on the assumption that the most recently realised results will continue, except in so far as there are definite reasons for expecting a change.' (ibid., 51). In the case of durable goods, the short-term expectations are determined by the current long-term expectations of the investor (ibid., 51).

Uncertainty features prominently in relation to the state of long-term expectations. This depends on the best forecast we can make and on the "confidence" with which we make our forecast, i.e. '...on how highly we rate the likelihood of our best forecast turning out quite wrong.' (ibid., 148). For example, our confidence in a forecast is low when we are very uncertain as to the exact form expected changes will take. It is in this context that Keynes stated; 'by "very uncertain" I do not mean the same as "very improbable".' (ibid., 148n1). Thus, the schedule of the MEC is based on the best forecasts we can make, and on the related state of confidence. There is not much to be said about this prevalent state of confidence *a priori* (ibid., 149).

The investor is interested in future developments, and must therefore try to guess what the prospects are, and act accordingly. However, there is no sound basis of knowledge on which to base our long-term estimates of prospective yield. 'Our knowledge of the factors which will govern the yield of an investment some years hence is usually very slight and often negligible. If we speak frankly, we have to admit that our basis of knowledge for estimating the yield ten years hence of a railway, a copper mine, a textile factory, the goodwill of a patent medicine, an Atlantic liner, a building in the City of London amounts to little and sometimes to nothing; or even five years hence.' (Keynes 1936, 149-50). Consequently, long-term expectations are liable to sudden revision, for 'they cannot be checked at short intervals in the light of realised results.' (Keynes 1936, 51).

In his renowned chapter 12 of the *General Theory* Keynes concentrates on decision-making in financial markets, although he extends the conclusions to the broader fields of political and economic decisions. He distinguishes between speculation and enterprise. Speculation is '...the activity of forecasting the psychology of the market' (Keynes 1936, 158), i.e. outguessing to higher degrees the average opinion of the market (Keynes 1936, 156). He appropriates the term enterprise for the '...activity of forecasting the prospective yield of assets over their whole life.' (ibid., 158). The relative importance may differ from market to market. Enterprise is a combination of reasonable calculation supplemented by "animal spirits", i.e. our innate urge to action rather than inaction (ibid., 161). We may calculate where possible, but, whim, sentiment, or chance, to a large extent determine our decisions and ensuing activities, and thus the future yields on investments. 'We are merely reminding ourselves that human decisions affecting the future, whether personal or political or economic, cannot depend on strict mathematical expectation, since the basis for making such calculations does not exist.' (ibid., 162-3). Our ignorance of the future may be somewhat mitigated by entering into long-term contracts, monopoly privileges, and public investments (ibid., 163).

As a consequence we often fall back on conventions, more or less rooted in secure knowledge (ibid., 152-3). Although logically-speaking incorrect, we seem to assume that the market valuation '...is uniquely correct in relation to our existing knowledge of the facts which will influence the yield of the investment, and that it will only change in proportion to changes in this knowledge.' (ibid., 152). The precariousness of a convention, however, is accentuated by the fact that the mass psychology underlying a conventional valuation is liable to sudden fluctuation of opinion due to almost irrelevant factors, and that there is a short-run advantage in outguessing "the market" (ibid., 149, 152-8). Stability and continuity will last '...so long as we can rely on the maintenance of the convention.' (ibid., 152)

Keynes arrives at the following four conditions of stability, supported by actual experience and arguments of plausibility (Keynes 1936, 250-4): (1) There may be a, probably narrow, range within which instability with regard to the consumption multiplier of real income does in fact prevail; (2) Furthermore, the change in the rate of investment, following changes in the prospective yield of capital-assets, is bounded by uneven costs of production and quantities of surplus resources, although establishing upper rather than lower limits; (3) The money-wage changes proportionately follow changes in employment; (4) Only in due time can the stock of capital-assets be fully adjusted to changes in the MEC, because the '...capital-assets are of various ages, wear out in time and are not all very long-lived.' (Keynes 1936, 253). But these four conditions of stability '...are a fact of observation concerning the world as it is or has been, and not a necessary principle which cannot be changed.' (Keynes 1936, 254)

The fluctuations in employment must be explained by means of the psychology of investment markets. Such fluctuations are due first of all to the wide fluctuations in the psychological expectations of future yields insufficiently offset in the short-term by fluctuations in the rate of interest. The '...association of a conventional and fairly stable long-term rate of interest with a fickle and highly unstable marginal efficiency of capital' (Keynes 1936, 204), frustrates the free market maintenance of full employment. During a boom the estimation of borrower's risk as to actually earning the prospective yield and lender's risk are possibly underestimated (ibid., 144-5). Increasing doubts, a lowering of confidence, as to the reliability of the prospective yields of capital-goods may suddenly arise and spread rapidly, and may end the economic boom (ibid., 317). A constant or declining population is, in itself, likely to depress the spirits of entrepreneurs. 'Moreover, the dismay and uncertainty as to the future which accompanies a collapse in the marginal efficiency of capital naturally precipitates a sharp increase in liquidity-preference - and hence a rise in the rate of interest.' (ibid., 316). Subsequently a collapse in investments will take place. The rise in the rate of interest will take place only after the fall in the MEC has already started the crisis (ibid., 315-6). A decline in the rate of interest together with a recovery of the MEC would finally, even without any interference, but only after a certain period, end the slump (ibid., 317-20).

Keynes is unhappy with this danger of wide fluctuations in employment under conditions of "laissez-faire": 'I conclude that the duty of ordering the current volume of investment cannot safely be left in private hands.' (Keynes 1936, 320). Otherwise, prices may become highly unstable, workers and machines simply lie idle, and business calculations may prove futile. Keynes concludes that with regard to maintaining full employment and given actual practices, '...the money-wage level as a whole should be maintained as stable as possible, at any rate in the short period.' (Keynes 1936, 270).

The essence of the viewpoint just presented was already present in his deliberations since approximately 1933. For example, in a radio talk on poverty, subtitled *Is the Economic System Self-Adjusting?*, Keynes ranges himself with the heretics '...who reject the idea that the existing system is, in any significant sense, self-adjusting.' (Keynes 1934, quoted in Eatwell 1982, 43). Keynes (1936) provides their argument against the citadel of orthodox theory with some intellectual weight.

5.3 The reception of the *General Theory*

Although the long-awaited book was immediately widely read and debated, Keynes (1936) proved to be a troublesome book when it came to comparison with the writings of his contemporaries. This was due to no small extent to Keynes's use of several models, and unclear distinctions and connections. For example, Kregel distinguishes three models on the basis of their differing assumptions about expectations (Kregel 1976, 214-6).

The disparity between the two interpretations of the *General Theory* which are presented in the following section reflects these difficulties. Hicks and Townshend stress different parts of the book, each one of them signalling a starting point of a current in Keynesianism. The non-academic Townshend may aptly be regarded as a trailblazer for the interpretation provided and propagated by Shackle.

5.3.1 In time or out of time? That's the question

In an early book review, Hicks identifies the innovations introduced by Keynes (1936) as being (1) the explicit incorporation of people's expectations of the future, and (2) reduction in the complexity of the factors determining output, '...by grouping complex factors together into bundles.' (Hicks 1936, 240). Changes in expectations, both in degree and kind, determine changes in demand and supply. They are, therefore, relevant in economic analysis. 'But this generally means that there is a psychological unknown. We must not expect the most elaborate economic analysis to enable us to see very far ahead.' (Hicks 1936, 241)

In order to discover what the fuss was all about, Hicks wrote his classic article, which he presented at a meeting of the Econometric Society in September 1936 (Hicks 1937). Partly due to the convenient simplifications made, Hicks distilled an analytical core of the *General Theory* which has primarily become known as a didactic instrument under the name IS/LM. What became of uncertainty once this model was widely introduced into the economic discourse? We will see that the emphasis shifted from the investment-uncertain expectations relation stressed by Keynes to the investment-interest rate relation stressed by Hicks (Weintraub 1975, 530). To be able to understand the change in emphasis we must first examine the framework. What is the framework of this model and how does it work?

The basis of the framework consists of two curves, denoting equilibria in the commodity market and the money market respectively. On an interest rate-national income graph, the IS-curve displays the downward sloping relation between income and the corresponding investment rate of interest. Any change in the propensity to consume or in the inducement to invest will result in a shift of the curve. The LM-curve, which Hicks called the LL-curve, drawn on the same interest-income graph, depicts the upward sloping relation between income and the money rate of income. The LM-curve will shift when a change in monetary policy or in liquidity preference occurs. Income and interest are determined at the intersection of the curves, where the investment rate of interest equals the money rate of income (Hicks 1937, 113).

The crucial difference between Keynes and the neoclassical writers, according to Hicks, concerns the slope of the LM-curve. The Keynesian variant has a horizontal part, reflecting interest inelasticity of money at some minimum rate of interest, and a vertical part, indicating an asymptote in nominal income which can possibly be financed out of a given quantity of money. If the intersection of the IS curve with the LM-curve is in the vertical part of the latter curve, an increase in the quantity of money would lower the interest rate and raise income and employment (Hicks 1937, 110-1). Keynes does not concern himself with this case, but rather with a second case, in which an intersection of the IS-curve with the horizontal part of the curve may, on the one hand, leave room for a rise in the subjective schedules of the MEC, and thus in income and employment, while leaving the rate of interest constant. On the other hand, in such a case any monetary policy to stimulate investment via the interest rate channel is frustrated: we are faced with a "liquidity-trap". This contradicts the classical theory, which has it that a rise in the MEC would not only raise income and employment, but also increase the rate of interest (Hicks 1937, 109-10). A rise in money supply would lower the rate of interest, and thus stimulate investment.

In response to Hicks, Keynes appeared to have '...next to nothing to say by way of criticism.' (Keynes 1973, 79). However, two elements of disagreement surfaced in related correspondence: (1) Interest has to do with the supply of and demand for money, that is with liquidity-preference, but not with loans. (2) Hicks overemphasized the influence of current income on the inducement to invest. It seems that Keynes increasingly came to appreciate the discrepancy between the underpinning mechanisms as the correspondence on the subject proceeded and time went by.

With regard to the first element, i.e. the one on the rate of interest, Hicks reiterated his view on several occasions: interest is determined by savings and investments, i.e. by means of a theory of loans (Hicks 1936, 245-7; Hicks 2 September 1936, 1973, 73; Hicks 9 April 1936, 1973, 82-3). At first, Keynes could not grasp what Hicks meant by liquidity preference (Keynes 31 August 1936, 1973, 72; Keynes 8 September 1936, 1973, 75). At a later stage, Keynes was clearly dissatisfied with Hicks's orthodox ideas: 'They regard the rate of interest as a non-monetary phenomenon.' (Keynes 31 March 1937, 1973, 80). Accordingly, Keynes disagreed with the credit-based determination of the interest rate as proposed, for example, by Hicks and Ohlin. Keynes declared his intention to publish a damning critique against Hicks and some other economists (Keynes 11 April 1937, 1973, 83): In the *Economic Journal*, Hicks, Ohlin and Robertson are accused of lending their allegiance to a superficially similar, but in fact radically different theory, '...altogether remote from my contention that the rate of interest .. equalizes the advantages of holding actual cash and a deferred claim on cash.' (Keynes June 1937, 1973, 206).

With regard to the introduction of current income into the MEC-equation, Hicks acknowledges the mathematical convenience which it provided. However, he also claims the following: 'I remain impenitent about including income in the marginal efficiency of capital equation' (Hicks 9 April 1937, 1973, 82). Keynes holds that present income does not exert such a causal and significant influence over the inducement to invest. 'Whilst it may be true that entrepreneurs are over-influenced by present income, far too much stress is laid on this psychological influence.' (Keynes 31 March 1937, 1973, 80-1; cf. Keynes 1937, 118-9).

It was only since the 1950s that Hicks became aware of, and acknowledged, the shortcomings involved, whereupon he withdrew part of his support for his IS/LM-model (Hicks 1979, 990-1): 'That diagram is now much less popular with me than I think it still is with many other people.' (Hicks 1976, 289-90). For example, it is true that income was introduced primarily as a parameter in the MEC schedule because of the mathematical expediency, '...but the temptation would have been better avoided.' (Hicks 1982, 101). An important, and possibly the most important, reason for Hicks's dissatisfaction with the IS/LM model has to do with the stock-flow method of analysis involved. In bookkeeping terms, the model elucidates a flow relation, expressed in the IS curve, together with a balance-sheet relation, expressed in the LM curve (Hicks 1980, 150-1; Hicks 1982b, 328-9). In an equilibrium of flows, all expectations must be fulfilled, which leaves no room for uncertainty. In the light of this stable IS-curve, however, there is no reasonable justification for speaking of liquidity preference, and thus for the inclusion of the LM-curve: 'For there is no sense in liquidity, unless expectations are uncertain.' (Hicks 1982b, 330).

The problems seem to be incipient in the *General Theory*, for '...uncertainty *as to the future outcomes* is all over the book, but so is stability.' (Hicks 1982, 259). However, for Keynes, uncertainty is a kettle of fish entirely different from instability. He does not consider instability as an important real factor in actual economic affairs, and he is equivocal about the prevalence of uncertainty about the future: 'In particular, it is an outstanding characteristic of the economic system in which we live that, whilst it is subject to severe fluctuations in respect of output and employment, it is not violently unstable.' (Keynes 1936, 249). In a letter to J. Robinson, Keynes again stresses the necessity not to confuse instability with uncertainty (Keynes 1973, 137).

In his later writings, Hicks agrees with this position. He had moved from the partial "IS/LM Keynesianism" to a Keynesianism in a much wider sense (Hicks 1979, 990-2). Hicks was to come to write about expectations using the idea of ranges of equi-probable expected outcomes, and refers to Shackle as working along this line of thought (Hicks 1980, 153; Hicks 1982b, 330).

We may conclude with Hicks, that Keynes's theory itself is a hybrid, for it only has one foot placed "in" time. The equilibrists therefore swallowed it whole, without knowing that they were being challenged: 'The "Keynesian revolution" went off at half-cock.' (Hicks 1976, 289).

5.3.2 Expectations and conventions

An alternative interpretation of the *General Theory* appeared as early as 1936, the year of its publication. It offers us an interpretation which concentrates on the dynamic part of Keynes's theory. The first economist to pursue this alternative line of thought was Hugh Townshend (1890-1974). As a mathematician, Townshend had been one of Keynes's pupils before he joined the Post Office. In several letters, Keynes explicitly agrees with Townshend, who is said to expound excellently on Keynes's own point with respect to the relation between investment and saving (Keynes 1973, 16; Keynes 1979, 238-9).

The crucial point Townshend makes, as early as in 1936, is that activities and income react only in the period immediately following a savings-consumption shift, *ceteris paribus* (Townshend 1936). When, for some subjective reason, savings rise (fall) relative to consumption, investment will react with corresponding increases (decreases) in investments in entrepreneurs' stocks of finished consumption-goods. Entrepreneurs who at the end of the period become aware of this unintended change in investments will adjust their estimations and their expectations of the MEC, subsequently restricting (expanding) production. This results in falling (rising) employment and incomes, until the previous consumption-savings ratio is arrived at. National income and employment stabilize at lower (higher) levels than before the savings-consumption shift. Meanwhile, the propensity to consume and the rate of interest are considered to remain constant. We may conclude from this argument, that the economic system is not inherently stable, that is, it does not automatically re-establish full employment (Townshend 1936, 647).

In 1937, Townshend published two short articles in the *Economic Journal* in which he presented his view of Keynes's ideas (Townshend 1937a; Townshend 1937b). For him, the central idea of Keynes (1936) is '...the *direct* causal influence of expectations on *all* prices.' (Townshend 1937b, 324). Prices may fluctuate independently of physical conditions of production, and of movements in money-balances. The contrast with the marginal theory of value becomes most clearly apparent when the rate of interest, i.e. the price of monetary assets, is under discussion. The interest rate is the liquidity-premium for forgoing liquidity. It is not causally determined at the margin by supply and demand for new loans (Townshend 1937a, 157). Not only so-called old loans, but also other durable assets such as houses and cars, carry a liquidity-premium; a category which refers to the value in future exchange. The liquidity-premium is a strictly relative concept. What varies is the subjective net balance in the individual minds about retaining and relinquishing liquidity.

In principle, all goods carry a liquidity-premium. For services and perishable or readily and cheaply produced goods the liquidity-premium is virtually zero. The liquidity-premium value of goods for which there are few substitutes and long lead times, in formal terms exhibiting low elasticity of substitution and of supply, will be significant and change with expectations about future developments (Townshend 1937a, 159-60). The ratio of new loans and new goods to existing stocks is low. The influence on prices of such "secondhand" durable assets (bonds, shares or capital goods) is attributed to '...quasi-unanimous changes in expectations.' (Townshend 1937b, 323). Even rapid physical production of new capital can never take place fast enough to be in step with the vagaries of purely subjective revaluations of existing assets, because those revaluations do not carry any time lag at all (Townshend 1937a, 164). Thus, changes in expectations do not simply influence demand and supply schedules for new assets. On the contrary, the supply and demand schedules for new assets will change until prices of old and new goods and loans are equalized (ibid., 159-60). 'The influence of expectations about the value of existing loans is usually the preponderant causal factor in determining the common price.' (ibid., 158)

In the long-run, money-prices vary unpredictably. First of all, competitive forces influence and/or distort shifting price levels. Secondly, the accountant's notion of maintaining the money value of assets intact is a chimera, as this value fluctuates at random (ibid., 169). Even in the short-run, the actual price of a house is still not precisely determined: unknown changes in liquidity-preferences may influence prices, even in the shortest period (ibid., 164).

A convention of stability is, however, necessary for any denominator to be useful. In the short-run, expectations are stabilized, for money values do not fluctuate wildly. There are two main reasons for this: (1) There may be a conventionality of outlook, causing stability of expectations as to developments in the money value of durable assets of certain kinds. (2) Some sort of conventionally stable wage-unit is actually maintained (Townshend 1937a, 161-2). A conventional outlook or money-price stability helps to stabilize the inherently unstable economy.

All economists who adopt a dynamic approach must assume a convention of price stability, or index-numbers (Townshend 1937a, 163). Other prices are then determined by the adjustment of supply and demand in new production on the one hand, and by the revaluations of existing assets on the other (Townshend 1937a, 162).

The first analytical instrument to be ruled out is the mathematical expectation of outcomes. 'The prospect of future returns (..) is not expressible as a *mathematical* expectation.' (Townshend 1937b, 325). The reason underlying this is the undetermined future. In other words, an economic expectation is not uniquely correlated with a single statistic (Townshend 1938, 523), for agents would be foolish to abstract from what the future has in store for us with confidence. The very existence of liquidity originates from doubts as to what may happen. To assume that nothing unforeseen is to be expected, i.e the notion of an indefinitely short interval, is to throw the essential feature of (non-) liquidity in expectational economic analysis overboard. To assume that intervals are finite is to acknowledge that we must use a series of numerical possible courses of events during the interval, each carrying a probability. These series are usually reduced to certainty equivalents. However, such reduction either neglects the weight of the evidence, or introduces evidence as a probability of a probability. According to Townshend, no method has been found for mathematically assessing a determinate course of maximum profitability. 'The elimination of the probabilities depends on the elimination of all instants of future time but one instant.' (Townshend 1979, 291). Thus, we end up in exposing fallacies, without a hope for the better (ibid., 293).

The second category which this way of reasoning causes to fall by the wayside is "classical theory". Strictly-speaking, the postulate adopted by classical theory on the constancy of a category cannot be stated at all, because its constancy does not exist (ibid., 257). All these forms of dynamic classical theory '...describe a world in which *risk exists without uncertainty.* The economic man is supposed both (a) to know the future and (b) not to know it, at the same time.' (ibid., 257-8). As a result, one is presumed on the one hand not to keep inactive balances, while on the other one earns profit merely by risk-taking (ibid., 258). Keynes agrees with Townshend on this point. The Achilles heel of classical theory which invalidates it is the fact that it obfuscates the problem of distinguishing between risk and uncertainty (Keynes 1979, 258).

Keynes elaborates on this point by discussing the probability-weight distinction. Economic theories introduce numerical estimates in principles of human conduct. Ordinary daily life, however, confronts us with the predominantly non-numerical nature of probabilities, if any, in mundane existence. 'When all is said and done there is an arbitrary element in the situation.' (Keynes 1979, 289). In order to avoid the predicament of Buridan's ass, which could not decide which pile of hay was preferable and perished, we fall back on motivations such as habit, instinct, will, etc. Keynes wants to distinguish between a risk-premium associated with probability and expected to be rewarded, and a liquidity-premium associated with weight. A liquidity-premium is not a reward, but a payment for increased confidence during a period (Keynes 1979, 293-4). The distinction affects every choice. We can only try, as far as possible, to evaluate the consequences of activities rationally. The last letter reprinted in Keynes's Collected Writings had been sent to Townshend, and in it Keynes draws the following conclusion: 'Generally speaking, in making a decision we have before us a large number of alternatives, none of which is demonstrably more "rational" than the others, in the sense that we can arrange in order of merit the sum aggregate of the benefits obtainable from the complete consequences of each.' (Keynes 1979, 294).

5.3.3 Keynes's supplement

In order to pursue our subject we will now centre on Keynes's reaction to his critics in '...an important supplement to the *General Theory*.' (Blaug 1985, 692). In this summary restatement of Keynes (1936), published in the *Quarterly Journal of Economics* in 1937, Keynes acknowledges that he is more attached to the fundamental ideas which underlie his theory than to the particular forms in which the ideas are embodied. Therefore, and in reaction to some critics, he took the opportunity of '...trying to reexpress some of these ideas.' (Keynes 1937, 209-10). In the light of these facts, the large proportion of the "supplement" devoted to discussing the consequences of uncertainty must be regarded as significant.

It is in this paper that Keynes finally and explicitly defines uncertainty. It is a state of the absence of a '...scientific basis on which to form any calculable probability whatever.' (Keynes 1937, 114). The game of roulette is not subject to uncertainty, while both the weather and life expectation are only slightly uncertain. Truly uncertain are, for instance, the prospects of a war, the price of copper in 20 years time, the obsolescence of a new invention and the position of house owners 30 years hence. In many cases, we cannot actually arrive at a scientific comparison. In the case of uncertain knowledge one cannot find any calculable probability, although this is unjustifiably abstracted by classical theory, since it underestimates the role of sentiments resulting in fluctuations in economic activities (Keynes 1937, 113-4, 122). In his Galton lecture, in which he stresses the problematic of the growth of population, an important determinant of the Marginal Efficiency of Capital, Keynes reaffirms this position: 'The future never resembles the past- as we well know. But, generally speaking, our imagination and our knowledge are too weak to tell us what particular changes to expect. We do not know what the future holds.' (Keynes 1973, 124). It is clear that Keynes, whether he was aware of it or not, was fully in step with Knight as regards characterizing uncertainty to a situation of numerically immeasurable probability (Lawson 1985, 48).

For Keynes, non-economic and economic man alike decide and act under uncertainty, by force of habit, instinct, will, etc. Since we are unable to make a "rational" evaluation of consequences, we need motives of another kind in our formation of expectations (Keynes 1979, 294; Keynes 1937, 114). 'We tend, therefore, to substitute for the knowledge which is unattainable certain conventions.' (Keynes 1973, 124). Convention acts as a surrogate for reason in the absence of adequate data.

Three important techniques are summed up (Keynes 1937, 114), which had been discussed somewhat differently in the *General Theory* and other writings (Keynes 1936, 148-58; Keynes 1973, 125):

(1) Keynes puts forward the opinion that it is reasonable to be guided, to a considerable degree, by facts about which we feel more confident, even though they might be less decisively relevant. In practice, we therefore take the existing situation and project it into the future, corrected for known and more or less definite changes. We have more or less confidence in the resulting expectations according to how far we expect that our best forecast will turn out to be wrong. We largely ignore the prospect of future changes about which we know nothing in terms of their actual character.

(2) We assume that the present state of opinion with regard to future prospects is summed up and expressed correctly in prices and production.

(3) We might try to fall back on the judgment of the rest of the world which might be better informed. This leads to conventional judgment and behaviour, informed by the behaviour of the majority or the average actor. This is evidently an inherently unstable strategy.

We construct practical theories about the future based on these three principles. A marked characteristic of these theories, due to their weak foundation, is their proneness to sudden and radical revision (Keynes 1937, 114-5).

The relation between conventions and economic behaviour runs via money, with changing liquidity preference and liquidity-premium, that is the interest rate, reflecting the weakening of conventions (ibid., 115-7). Given the propensity to hoard, it is the amount of investment which is the factor '...most prone to sudden and wide fluctuations.' (ibid., 121). We know little about the factors determining the opinions concerning future yield. Moreover, there is no reason to suppose that there are any offsetting tendencies in fluctuations in the propensity to hoard and opinions of the future yield. The result may be shifts in levels of employment and output (ibid., 121).

5.4 The London School of Economics

It is remarkable to find that two of the dominant interpretations of Keynes's writings originated in London rather than in Cambridge, namely those interpretations written by J.R. Hicks and G.L.S. Shackle. It is also remarkable to notice that both draw on Keynes and the Swedes, especially on Myrdal and Lindahl, who themselves followed Wicksell. Therefore, this paragraph will concentrate on the London School of Economics (LSE), which is a constituent part of the University of London, and its influence on the original responses to Keynes.

Directed from October 1929 onwards by Lionel Robbins, the LSE brought together, at the outset of the thirties, a group of teachers and researchers. The Robbins circle consisted of economists such as F.A. Hayek (since 1931), J.R. Hicks (period 1926-1935), A.P. Lerner, U. Webb, Rosenstein-Rodan, Edelberg, R. Allen, V. Smith, M. Bowley, R. Sayers, and N. Kaldor, L.M. Lachmann, and G.L.S. Shackle (1935-1937) (Shackle 1966, 53; Hicks 1979b, 356; Masera 1990, 292). While such people were working at the LSE, Lindahl, and a large number of other foreign economists, paid several visits to London (Hicks 1982a, 10).

Robbins invited Hicks to give lectures on uncertainty and risk, '...starting of course from Knight.' (Hicks 1982a, 5). Robbins had succeeded A.A. Young, Knight's doctoral-thesis supervisor at Cornell University, which would result in Knight (1921), being highly appraised by Robbins. Even as late as the 1970s, Robbins is still praising the '...profound discussion of the nature and effects of uncertainty in Frank Knight's brilliant *Risk, Uncertainty and Profit*' (Robbins 1979, 998). This early classic fostered Hicks's interest in the relation of money to uncertainty. 'Hayek was making us think of the productive process as a process in time, inputs coming before outputs.' However, his account of intertemporal relations was confined to a model relying on perfect foresight, in his 1928 article, or merely on monetary disturbances, in his 1932-book (Hicks 1979b, 359). With perfect foresight and the correct expectations, the economy would be in equilibrium and there would be no place for money. 'One must introduce uncertainty, before one can introduce money.' (Hicks 1982a, 7).

An article written by Hicks on the relation between uncertainty and profit was rejected for the *Economic Journal* by Keynes himself. Later Hicks came to acknowledge its rather crude view of numerical probability as a useful instrument of analysis, and was to alter his opinion in a direction indicated by Keynes (Hicks 1931, 11; Hicks 1983a, 375; Hicks 1979c). In fact, at least during the first half of the 1930s, there was not much dialogue with Cambridge on these matters (Hicks 1982a, 8).

Hicks was deeply influenced by Swedish economics, by Keynes and by Hayek (Hicks 1982a, 10; Hicks 1979b, 358-9). Nevertheless, he abandoned his research on the relation between money and uncertainty, and allowed himself to be sidetracked from it for nearly thirty years (Hicks 1982a, 7-9), until he returned to this topic in his '...Post-Keynesian, or (as it has turned out) neo-Wicksellian phase.' (Hicks 1982, xiii). With the advantage of hindsight, he would later state that it would have been better to have stuck to his subject. On an invitation from Pigou, Hicks took a job in Cambridge in September 1935. Unfortunately, he found himself in the "anti-Keynes" camp (Hicks 1979b, 359-60).

Shackle, who had obtained an external degree at the University of London, went to the LSE to write his PhD-thesis. He arrived by the first of January 1935, i.e. '...at the height of its splendour' (Shackle 1990a, 193). By a stroke of luck, he was just in time to attend the lectures on the Stockholm School delivered by Brinley Thomas, the latter having just returned from Sweden, where he had sat at the feet of Lindahl, Ohlin and Myrdal. The 31-year-old Shackle was well-equipped with knowledge of the debates going on in economics, and possessed the ability to assess the information brought over by Thomas on its merits. Shackle also attended Hicks's lectures, on what was to become the dynamics section of *Value and Capital*, and participated in Robbins's Monday seminar and Hayek's Thursday seminar (Harcourt 1990, xix). Hayek was changing his views on how to understand the coordination of human actions in favour of the position presented at length for the first time in *Economics and Knowledge* (Hayek 1937), which we discussed in the preceding chapter.

In October 1935, at an ad hoc seminar in King's College, Cambridge, Shackle attended a lecture delivered by Joan Robinson, who laid bare the *General Theory*, and another by Richard Kahn, on the paradoxes in the orthodox theory. Hayek, Shackle's supervisor, released him to work on Keynes's themes, in particular on recasting several of Keynes's arguments in Myrdal's terminology (Shackle 1990a, 194). So irony of ironies, this Keynesian started his career with a dissertation on Keynes supervised and examined by Hayek, Keynes's most profound opponent.

Shackle and Hicks share the same opinion on a conservative shift made by Keynes in this period. Hicks asserted that '...the technique of this work (the General Theory: EW) is on the whole conservative: more conservative than in the Treatise.' (Hicks 1936, 253). Shackle states that it may be the temptation to fight the enemy with his own weapons that made him discard valuable parts of the *Treatise* (Shackle 1974, 80-1), but remarks that 'Keynes made it entirely plain in the Quarterly Journal of Economics. He rode the race to a finish.' (Shackle 1983, 251). Here Keynes is more lucid on the essentials of his *General Theory* (Shackle 1988, 78); and 'declares unequivocally that expectations do not rest on anything solid, determinable, demonstrable. "We simply do not know."' (Shackle 1973a, 2).

Both Hicks and Shackle link Keynes (1936) to the work of Swedish economics. In his review of the *General Theory*, we already find Hicks alluding to a congruence between some of the ideas expounded in it and those found in Swedish economics: 'And an even closer analogy to Mr. Keynes's work is to be found in the methods which have been common in Swedish economics for several years.' (Hicks 1936, 240). As Shackle has it, '...the *General Theory* was anticipated by Myrdal's book in its scheme of thought and largely in its conclusions and this by a sound instead of an illusory method of reasoning.' (Shackle 1938, xv-xvi).

Shackle's first book, dealing with business cycle theory, '...was an attempt to graft the Swedish *ex ante/ex post* framework onto a Keynesian comparative statics model.' (Weintraub 1975, 165; cf. Shackle 1938, xviii). Shackle was to declare it a strange paradox that Myrdal's "binocular" method was ignored by Keynes (Shackle 1958, 75). Keynes would only acknowledge that an investment decision may be called an investment *ex ante* (Keynes 1937, 207). With the advantage of hindsight, Shackle was to state that Myrdal had anticipated Keynes in the scheme of thought, although they had pursued distinct paths (Shackle 1938, xv-xvi, xxxvi; Shackle 1988, 157-8, 222-3). While errors in foresight played a central part in Lindahl and Myrdal's construction, uncertainty itself was '...not given that basic and essential importance which it found in Keynes's ultimate expression of his ideas.' (Shackle 1961, ix).

It is here that the Hicks and Shackle embark on different routes. Hicks holds that '...we have to change, not so much our methods of analysis, as some important elements in the outlook which we have inherited from the classics.' (Hicks 1936, 253). Shackle adopts an alternative viewpoint in the form of sequence analysis. Sequence analysis is essentially the analysis of the thoughts prevailing in different minds at some single moment about interacting courses of conduct (Shackle 1938, xiv).

How could it happen that at the LSE, "the hotbed of socialists" (Hicks 1979b, 357-8), such a group of market adepts could take over? Moreover, how did two important interpreters of Keynes emerge from this group? Firstly, the ethos at the LSE has traditionally been relatively tolerant (Hicks 1979b, 358). Secondly, the Keynesian impact on some of the research students of the LSE in the late thirties did not "convert" them from "Hayekism", '...for Keynes was discussing deflation and Hayek was describing inflation.' (Shackle 1966, 55). The latter position was an odd one to adopt at that time; the idea of over-ambitious capital investments due to easy credit had no real-world equivalent in this period (Hicks 1967, 210-215). Thirdly, Hicks switched his focus of interest from the long-term problems, on which Hayek was concentrating, to short-run problems, which were Keynes's focus of attention (Hicks 1982a, 10). However, at the beginning of the thirties they all shared a common faith; a belief in the free market (Hicks 1982a, 3), from which both Shackle and Hicks were to depart. Thus, in that respect they changed their viewpoint (Hicks 1979b, 359).

5.4.1 Monday's weekly markets

Hicks's *Value and Capital* had little to do with his activities at Cambridge, where he took up a position in the autumn of 1935; 'it is a systematization of the work I had done at LSE.' (Hicks 1979b, 360). It links up with the writings on the IS/LM-diagram, because both are a product of his "Walrasianism" (Hicks 1979, 990). *Value and Capital* contained a flexprice theory in the Swedish tradition, i.e. one distinguishing flow accounts as estimates and realizations (Hicks 1979, 991), and in the book Hicks distinguishes between economic statics and economic dynamics. The former includes those parts of economic theory to which dating is irrelevant. The latter includes '...those parts where every quantity must be dated.' (Hicks 1939, 115).

The foundation of dynamic economics consists of (1) the "Hicksian Week", (2) individual plans, and (3) expectations. The "Week", a concept related to Marshall's "Day", is defined as '...that period of time during which variations in prices can be neglected.' (ibid,. 122). Price changes take place at regular intervals, that is on each successive Monday, when the markets are open for business. Assuming that there is perfect knowledge about relevant current prices, Monday's prices will reflect a position of temporary equilibrium and govern the disposition of inputs during this week (ibid., 121-3). The week is the planning interval, and the Mondays are the planning or decision dates, upon which new information is introduced. By Monday evening, each person has arrived at a mix of purchases and sales which he subjectively perceives as being most advantageous. Minor alterations may be introduced during that week, but they are negligible (ibid., 123-4). Plans depend upon current prices and upon anticipated future prices. 'Generally, then, it is uncertainty of the future, and the desire to keep one's hands free to meet that uncertainty, which limit the extent of forward trading under capitalism. .. in any type of society uncertainty is likely to produce "planlessness."' (ibid., 139). Hicks assumes that every individual has definite expectations of any price in any future week. Although people may sometimes entertain both their probable values and the related variations, Hicks supposes them to have extremely precise price-expectations, as they should already incorporate risk allowances. 'Now the farther ahead the future output is, the larger this risk-allowance is likely to become, just because the uncertainty of the future price increases' (ibid., 225). Hicks is aware of the necessity of constructing an economics of risk which goes beyond what is worked out in his own book (ibid., 124-6).

The process of change is treated as consisting of series of "temporary equilibria". On Mondays, plans are reconciled on the markets, while during the week plans will become effective themselves via production plans. When discussing terms *ex ante*, i.e. those terms relevant for conduct and decision-making, nothing is said about the actual realization of an expectation. *Ex post* calculations cannot be performed until the end of a week. The latter cannot be relevant to decisions taken in the present week, although they do influence decisions pertaining to the subsequent Monday's planning. The *ex ante* income concept excludes windfall gains, which, in contrast, are incorporated in the *ex post* income definitions (Hicks 1939, 181-4). Consequently, the situation at the beginning of a new week is inevitably different from that pertaining one week earlier. Thus, the essentials of static analysis, including such concepts as market equilibrium, are transferable to the dynamic field (ibid., 127).

If we redirect our attention to "equilibrium over time", it is the divergence between expected and realized prices, which is important. In contrast to Keynes, Hicks assumes that if short-term prices are fairly steady '...the system is likely to be quite adequately in equilibrium' (ibid., 133). He lists the following four potential causes of disequilibrium: (1) different individual person's price-expectations are inconsistent; (2) plans may be mutually inconsistent; (3) people may foresee their wants incorrectly, or make erroneous output estimates; and, (4) one's foresight may not inspire confidence (ibid., 134). Those causes may thus result in production plans which differ from those which would be framed if full confidence in one's anticipations. The last two causes of disequilibrium must inevitably be present in any economic system, since such systems cannot escape the uncertainty inherent in the vagaries of harvesting conditions, technological innovations and political upheavals.

We have both a temporary equilibrium within any week and equilibrium over time when prices are constant over time (ibid., 132). However, it is precisely this fluctuation in prices and the problems involved in arriving at equilibria which interested Keynes. For Keynes, the short-term was therefore probably something like a year, a time-period condensed by Hicks into his Week. The idea of building a model for these very short-run equilibria had originated in Sweden (Hicks 1982a, 10).

Hicks assumes the interchangeability of money and securities to be fundamental to dynamic economics. This mechanism is reflected in the working of the system of interest rates (Hicks 1939, 170), and Hicks disagrees with Keynes on whether the rate of interest is based on conventions. Interest is partly to be attributed to default risk, and partly, but not entirely, to uncertainty vis-à-vis the future course of interest rates (Hicks 1939, 163-4). Savings, e.i. planned demand for securities including money, and investments will be equal for the community as a whole during the week. Over any longer period this is not necessarily the case. 'Equality between savings *ex ante* and investment *ex ante* is then one of the conditions of equilibrium over time.' (Hicks 1939, 133-5, 183-4).

Hicks's investigations proceeded in the direction which Keynes had indicated, i.e. in the direction of changing expectations. Due to changes in expectations, both in degree and kind, following important changes in, or the creation of new, data, we have to face the relevance of this distorting factor in economic analysis. For example, the upward revision of price-expectations during a boom would result in a fall in unemployment (Hicks 1939, 296).

Hicks distinguished three types of influence on price-expectations: (1) Non-economic influences, such as political developments, the weather, and individual's psychological states; (2) economic influences ranging from market superstitions to indications of likely future movements of supply and demand; and (3) actual economic experiences. The first two are treated as autonomous factors (Hicks 1939, 204).

Hicks offers a measure of the influence of current prices on expectations: the "elasticity of expectations", which is defined as '...the ratio of the proportional rise in expected future prices of [a commodity; EW] X to the proportional rise in its current price.' (Hicks 1939, 205). Inelastic expectations occur in the case of fixed expectations. An elasticity of unity occur when people exactly adjust the level of expected future prices to the new level. When people recognize a trend (or a peak), elasticity will be greater than unity (negative) (Hicks 1939, 205). High elasticity is destabilising factor, but an elasticity close to zero is stabilising.

If the elasticity of expectations is taken into account, the stability of the system is perceived as being in jeopardy. Possible stabilising factors are the rate of interest and price rigidities, e.g. wages (Hicks 1939, 258-66). Interest rates may rise to offset a general rise in prices, and in the case of a high interest rate the opposite may occur when prices are falling. However, although interest rates may rise without causing any problems, they cannot fall without doing so. If the interest rate is considered to be low, interest rate control may no longer be effective. The same goes for expectations of short-run rates or long-run rates (Hicks 1939, 258-62). The direct effect of a rigid price structure is stabilizing, but the indirect effect, via substitution is destabilizing, and the direct effect is only certain to prevail in the case in which the rigid price structure concerns a factor of production. The existence of a pool of unemployed labour is a particular effective stabilizer (Hicks 1939, 265-9).

This line of thought was to evolve into "hydraulic Keynesianism". Hicks was surprised how influential his book was on those working on economics in America. 'Their achievements have been great; but they are not in my line.' (Hicks 1979b, 361). The culmination of this development resulted in a "neo-classical synthesis" which causes Kicks to remark that: 'Keynes had been pushed right over the edge.' (Hicks 1979a, 350). E.Weintraub aptly summarized what has already been stated here: 'The uncertainty theme somehow got lost in the successive refinements.' (Weintraub 1975, 157).

Hicks would later acknowledge that his approach to dynamics was not at all in accordance with Keynes's intentions (Hicks 1979a, 350). 'My own dynamic model .. owes much more to what I had got from the Swedes, from Myrdal and Lindahl.' (Hicks 1979b, 360). In fact, he tried to push general equilibrium forward into the dynamic field (Hicks 1979a, 350). Prices were determined in an equilibrium manner, i.e. "out" of time, while production was "in" time. However, because of '...the ridiculously instantaneous price-adjustment to which I had there committed myself' (Hicks 1979, 991), too much had to happen on Mondays. Furthermore, Hicks acknowledges his inability to link up the "weeks" and the following "Mondays" (Hicks 1982a, 290).

These statements reveal a wholly different approach towards economic activities. Since approximately 1956, Hicks was pushing on beyond both his IS/LM Keynesianism and the narrow flexprice approach. He came to regard cases in which price and marginal cost are equal as uncommon: To what extent the fixprice versus flexprice type of behaviour occurs is an empirical question. 'But in a world where the future is much more uncertain that it is in the textbooks, it must surely occur, not so infrequently.' (Hicks 1979, 994). Unfortunately, Hicks did not elaborate this latter statement.

5.4.2 Expectations and interdependent outcomes

George Shackle (1903-1992), '...the quintessential English Christian gentleman' (Harcourt 1990, xvii), is one of the prominent economists who pursued the ideas expounded in the writings of Keynes. As we will clarify in this and next section, Shackle remained true to most of the ideas he put forward during the 1940s, such as his views on uncertainty. 'My scheme of thought was enriched but not essentially changed.' (Shackle 1988, 233). A slight change in thought took place as a result of his growing dissatisfaction with the detailed mathematical representation of concepts.

In order to facilitate the comparison of Shackle with Keynes, and to establish that there is a bridge between Keynes and the Post-Keynesians, we intend to discuss Shackle's opinion on, and his restatement of, the *General Theory*. We go on to study the essentials behind Shackle's viewpoints; the framework consisting of time, uncertainty and expectations. These discussions are intended to put Shackle's central theme of economic decision-making under uncertainty into perspective.

As mentioned earlier in this chapter, Shackle's 1938 book was an attempt to extend the scope of Keynes's theory with the addition of the Swedish *ex ante/ex post* framework (Shackle 1938, xviii), since he felt that Keynes's theory was based on insufficiently elaborated ideas about the relation between expectations and investment. Shackle regarded the business cycle as being part of an evolving economic system. 'Indeed, I feel that the business cycle is much more akin to fatigue than to disease, in that it is not an exceptional and accidental occurrence, but part of the nature of a modern industrial economy.' (ibid., 5).

If a fully-fledged business cycle theory was to be developed, Shackle considered the use of sequential analysis unavoidable. In economic analysis there are essentially two stages; (1) showing what will manifest itself out of the decisions flowing from a given set of expectations. (2) showing how, after a short interval, decisions will be revised in the light of their composite consequences. A chain of related situations may thus be built up, representing a process in time. Keynes concentrated mainly on the first stage, and Hicks did so entirely (ibid., 1-2). Shackle however, is concerned to address both of the aforementioned stages. 'Before we can use Mr. Keynes's system to explain the economic pattern which emerges with the passage of time, we must release expectations from their status as a datum, and make them depend, at any moment, on the comparison which we may suppose businessmen to make between their expectations of a slightly earlier moment and what has actually happened in the interval.' (ibid., 2)

ex ante there is uncertainty as to the outcome of the interplay of investment decisions taken at any moment; at the beginning of an interval period. Investment decisions are mutually interdependent because prices for capital equipment, future supply-conditions, and future demand-conditions, although grounded in experience, are mere forecasts. For example, a widespread optimism/pessimism with regard to as yet unknowable future outcomes of present decisions will become something of a self-fulfilling prediction. Knowledge, which is necessarily *ex post*, may cause the vision of the expected future to be amended. When such an expectation hardens to a conviction, it will change investment plans, and the ensuing aggregate income is the next factor to change (Shackle 1938, 35, 80-1). Time lags are endemic to every change.

When applied to economics, we may distinguish between an improvement-phase, in which equipment is extended or replaced, the investment-flow therefore being at a high level, and a contiguous testing-phase in which the level of investment-flow is low (Shackle 1938, 3, 68). A higher than expected promptness of investment results in higher than expected aggregate income and thus unexpectedly improves the anticipated prospective yield of any kind of capital equipment. These expectations are taken seriously by the entrepreneur, and will thus induce a further rise in investments. The promptness of investment may alter with a change in the entrepreneur's expectation of future prices of his produce and/or inputs. The virtuous circle, i.e. the operation of the multiplier effect, will cease to exist, and may become vicious when the rise in aggregate income proves *ex post* to be less than, or equal to, that expected *ex ante* (ibid., 3, 4, 41). Such changes in expectations must arise from new knowledge derived *ex post* from preceding events, and will probably mean that for all future dates prices are expected to change once and for all, or up to a certain time-horizon. Causes of revision may be (1) external events, such as new governmental plans, or (2) a change in current prices which deviates from *ex ante* expectations (ibid., 68-70). Depending on their source, such changes will either be associated with a rise of a fall in the level of investments.

A fall in investments is associated with the growing number of manufactures who have arrived at a testing-phase (ibid., 3-4). Due to the long useful life which is largely typical of capital equipment, the anticipated value of a projected plant depends mainly on highly unstable expectations concerning the future. 'The greater the extent to which the scale or type of a businessman's operations (of making, carrying, or selling goods) have recently changed, the less confident and clearcut will be the expectations he can form on the basis of past experience as to the possibilities and the most profitable form of further extension and improvement.' (ibid., 3). It takes time to explore further possibilities, make plans, enhance efficiency, reorganize and test. In the interest of efficiency to take advantage of information about an extension of equipment, it will most probably first be studied extensively so as to optimize the evaluation of new plans. In other words, in order to reduce the uncertainty of estimates, entrepreneurs will invest in increments (ibid., 68, 100-3). 'The investment-fever comes to an end, in fact, for exactly the same reason that an influenza epidemic does: because everybody has had it, and has not yet lost a temporary immunity.' (ibid., 101)

Thus, the alternation of periods of boom and slump is caused by the clustering appearance of respectively rising and falling prospects of yields (Shackle 1938, 104). The interdependency of outcomes of decisions arrived at individually, and thus *ex ante*, may cause the collective outcome to differ from what is warranted (ibid., 38). Due to this interdependency, upward and downward adjustment of plans may result in abrupt changes in trends. A slump will become a reality more readily than a boom, because (1) the postponement of intended investments is easier to effectuate than the stepping up of investments, and (2) abandoning an investment plan will often result in worse outcomes than completing and executing a plan in the face of input price rises. A recovery may start with the gradual shrugging off of prevarication, the return of ambition to an enterprise, natural or political events, or with the invention of a new consumer good or technique (ibid., 88-97).

If a belief in a future rise in interest rates suddenly spreads, this may induce cash holders not to buy long-term income-bearing assets, such as securities. The expected volatility of the price of securities is endemic, for no specific expectation about interest rate behaviour will cause it to remain constant (ibid., 50-1). For '...uncertainty about the future, expressed in the existence of a positive rate of interest, *is itself an autonomous cause of change.*' (ibid., 52). A speculator is not very much concerned with fundamentals or basic influences, but rather with the opinions of the "bears" and the "bulls" about a price in the immediate future. Those who find their opinion falsified will adjust it and thereby change the rate of interest. If a certain opinion spreads, and becomes prevalent, the rate of interest will change accordingly (ibid., 52-3).

In private correspondence, Keynes remarks that this distinction between the improvement-phase and testing-phase is a very useful one (Keynes, 1938). Townshend however, criticised Shackle for the use of the term "discounted subjective certainty-equivalents": 'I do not feel sure that the treatment of an economic expectation as uniquely correlated with a value will stand logical analysis without modification. ... The logical objections to this view have been pointed out by Mr. Keynes in his Treatise on Probability.' (Townshend 1938, 523). This criticism was not unimportant to Shackle, for he considered Townshend as the person who knew Keynes's work better than Keynes himself (Shackle 1938, xvii, xxx), and Shackle was later to state that he had acknowledged the problem at that time. He was soon to reject the position, which was adopted by Keynes and Myrdal (Shackle 1988, 121), i.e. that of regarding with single-valued expectations as meaningful analytical tools.

To sum up, by 1938 Shackle had not yet systematically formalized his theoretical conception of uncertainty and the formation of expectations, and it was to take him ten years of hard work to do so. In order to fully come to grips with Shackle's eventual representation of uncertainty, we should first discuss an aspect common to uncertainty and the formation of expectations, namely: the concept of time.

5.5 After mature consideration

In his later publications, Shackle makes a habit of referring to Keynes's triad, by which he means: his *Treatise on Money* (1931), the *General Theory* (1936), and the 1937 article in the Quarterly Journal of Economics (QJE). Shackle considers the *Treatise* to be '...genial and gently didactic, relaxed and assured' (Shackle 1988, 37), and the 1937 summary article "brilliant" (Shackle 1958, 100), and '...the apotheosis of his thought' (Shackle 1966, 33; Shackle 1967, 135). For Shackle, Keynes drove his message home in the QJE article (Shackle 1967, 112). In contrast, he is less enthusiastic about the second book in the triad, the *General Theory*. 'It is a detour from a path which might have led direct from the Treatise to the Q.J.E. article.' (Shackle 1973a, 2). What evidence supports this idiosyncratic classification?

According to Shackle, marginalist economics with its attendant theory of maximization was based upon the assumption of universal perfect relevant knowledge. 'There is in this world of the late-Victorian theory of value, no ignorance, doubt, or uncertainty.' (Shackle 1988, 43). In line with this way of thinking '...Keynes in the *Treatise* gives very little place to uncertainty.' (Shackle 1988, 40). However, by the early 1930s, Keynes saw that economic theory as it stood could not explain the dramatic economic developments of the era. 'In the early nineteen-thirties uncertainty spread blackly over the whole economic sky.' (Shackle 1988, 41). In view of the inability of his *Treatise* to explain the new situation, Keynes decided to rewrite it (Shackle 1974, 80). It could be argued that the resulting *General Theory* was to become a study of '...the consequences for economics of the uncertainty which attend investment and lending' (Shackle 1958, 74-5; cf. Shackle 1938, xvi). In both his 1936 book and the 1937 article, we find a characterization of to uncertainty as '...the origin of the difficulty of maintaining the flow of investment at a level which can engender full employment in face of a given and considerable propensity to save.' (Shackle 1974, 28).

For Shackle, it remains unclear whether Keynes had already fully emancipated himself from the confident *Treatise*, or whether he was still struggling to find the best way to describe his new ideas (Shackle 1990, 111; Shackle 1938, xvii, 68). The *General Theory* '...is a paradox, for its central concern is with uncertainty, decisions based on conjecture, and situations altogether lacking in objective stability, yet it uses an equilibrium method.'

(Shackle 1955, 222). It has been made clear, for example by Pasinetti (Pasinetti 1991), that Keynes's break with the Marshallian tradition of studying equilibria was effectively a reality in 1932. This complication was acknowledged by Shackle, who emphasized the common features of what he regarded as the Keynesian triad..

5.5.1 Time and uncertainty

The dimension of time was to remain of paramount importance in Shackle's work, since he regards uncertainty and expectations as being inseparably bound up with time (Shackle 1958, 93). 'There has been one economist, G.L.S. Shackle, whose professional career has been devoted to these crucial themes of economics and time, expectations, and uncertainty.' (Weintraub 1975, 165). Although time has many facets (Shackle 1972, 263), in Shackle's writings there are essentially two time concepts to be considered: (1) The concentration on moment-in-being or the unique present amounts to the '...rejection of the actuality of future and past.' (Shackle 1961, 16); (2) "Extended time", or time as an endless, linear sequence of *a priori* equal points in a (dimension of a) space, is the prevailing mental construct of time, using the calendar axis for reference (Shackle 1961, 15; Shackle 1966, 20, 71-6, 119; Shackle 1972, 277-9; Shackle 1979, 1-2; Shackle 1988, 25). The second concept of time is common to most economic writings, and accordingly, no difference between past, present and future is recognized. Future reality is in principle accessible and may be learned just as the past can be. The categorical distinction between risk and uncertainty, theory and reality, which Knight first introduced, is entirely absent. The first time concept relates to the uncertainty and the troublesome accessibility of the future.

According to Shackle, extended time is of passing interest only, and it is an moment-in-being which really deserves attention (Shackle 1958, 13). 'Present time is the transience of thought.' (Shackle 1988, 1). When viewed from the human standpoint time essentially delineates that one '...simply cannot know how things will go.' (Shackle 1990, 107). It is interesting to note that the Post-Keynesian, Shackle, would come to use the metaphor favoured by the Austrian Kirzner, and with the same intention, when he states that relevant data are '...in the mists of time to come.' (Shackle 1990, 108). In the experience of individuals, the time of awareness in which actions and perceptions occur, is a unique moment (Shackle 1988, 22).

A person may look back into the past or forwards into the future, but '...he contemplates it all in one thought occurring at one moment' (Shackle 1966, 23). 'Expectation and memory are part of the essence of the moment-in-being, they are in it and of it.' (Shackle 1958, 16). Paradoxically, the present moment exists by changing, by carrying one situation into another (Shackle 1958, 14; Shackle 1961, 14-7; Shackle 1972, 277-9). Logically speaking, there cannot be any real comparison of two present moments (Shackle 1958, 14). An intertemporal comparison consists of a single act, at a present moment, which involves contemplating imagined experiences rather than actual feelings (Shackle 1966, 23). Memory and records may only help to evaluate past actions (Shackle 1961, 19). They '...give the notion of the past a certain objective reality.' (Shackle 1961, 15).

Such a concept of time cannot be conceived of as a linear progression made up of discrete points. Nevertheless, the passage of time is neither contradictory nor incompatible, although it must be distinguished from the movement along the calendar axis. We must draw a distinction between the solitary present and the flow of actions. 'The moment-in-being rolls, as it were, along the calendar-axis, and thus ever transports us willy-nilly to fresh temporal viewpoints.' (Shackle 1958, 15). Time as succession, as an '...axis in a Cartesian reference-frame' (Shackle 1979, 1), is an artefact, and something inferred (Shackle 1979, 1).

It follows from these axioms that outside our minds there is no objective future. Thus, '...the future is not there to be discovered, but must be created.' (Shackle 1961, 16). Projections into the future are entirely personal. Imagination on this level is *ex nihilo* creation. Even an extra-temporal observer, for example a scientist, always stands in a certain moment in time. However, since his feelings and decisions are not bound up with his observations, such an outside observer is to work with a calendar interval. The elements in his study are public and objective observables, in particular the actions within society as a whole (Shackle 1961, 26-8).

We may sum up with the statement that, even though we may possess knowledge *ex post* and we may entertain ideas about developments in some future period, we do not possess knowledge *ex ante*. We are unable to know the future before its time. Having accepted such a position, what are the consequences of such a time concept for an analysis of economic behaviour? When and how do we decide? How do we arrive at economic actions? And how is uncertainty related to this concept of time?

According to Shackle, uncertainty is a prerequisite for creativity, imagination and decision-making. There would be no uncertainty if a question could be answered by seeking additional knowledge. Conversely, under conditions of uncertainty individual imagination is essentially free to conceive of, and fill in, the open future creatively time and time again (Shackle 1958, 34; Shackle 1966, 119-20). 'The contrast I ultimately wish to present is between those constructions that exhibit uncertainty as a difficulty that can be overcome by an exercise of reason, and a view, utterly alien to that conception of remediable uncertainty, that sees in the void of time the indispensable condition of human originative freedom.' (Shackle, 1979a, 27; cf. Shackle 1958, 34)

Shackle defines uncertainty not as being "out there", but rather as a state of someone's mind and thus as subjective (Shackle 1966, 86). Uncertainty is ignorance (Shackle 1949, 115-8; Shackle 1955, 73; Shackle 1966, 119-20) or "unknowledge" (Shackle 1974, 8, 28) about the outcome of available courses of action. It transpires that Shackle came to prefer the term unknowledge because the term uncertainty had been appropriated those who associate it with probability. Possibly due to this association, uncertainty and knowledge are conflated. By coining and employing the term unknowledge, Shackle stresses that the fundamental imperfection of knowledge is the essence of uncertainty. When there is uncertainty in one's thoughts, one entertains a plurality of rival, that is mutually exclusive, answers to a certain question (Shackle 1966, 81, 86; Shackle 1974, 14, 43; Shackle 1976, 23).

If the words actuality, imagination and decision-making have any meaning in economics, there must be a place to introduce '...an essentially new strand into the emerging pattern of history.' (Shackle 1961, 3). Actuality brings together subjective thoughts and feelings, and imagination may provide us with several ideas about how future developments may take place. Moreover, in decision-making there must be more than one alternative to choose from. Therefore, '...uncertainty is part of the essence of decision, and it is, indeed, in the strictest sense meaningless and self-contradictory to speak as though decisions could be both creative and free of uncertainty.' (Shackle 1966, 85).

To be able to alter the course of events, however, uncertainty must be bounded. On the one hand, if a choice between alternative actions is supposed to alter its course, history cannot be determinate. On the other, if a choice is supposed to be meaningful, history cannot be random. Uncertainty is bounded when the decision-maker, like the observer, is able to classify some imaginary situations as being possible and others as impossible (Shackle 1966, 86).

Expectations are those products of imagination '...constrained to congruity with what seems in some degree possible.' (Shackle 1961, 13; cf. Shackle 1949, 1, and Shackle 1966, 78). Expectations are concerned with situations or events at future dates. They are '...statements of possible outcomes of the act in question' (Shackle 1966, 78). A possible hypothesis is a supposition which is congruous with reality. The bounds are set by a given amount of knowledge, in particular general principles and present circumstances (Shackle 1979, 21). In other words, a supposition is excluded by the agents when it is incongruous with the individual conception of laws of nature; human nature, ambitions and affairs; and the speed, in relation to the amount of time available, at which situations can be transformed in considered or hoped for situations. What remains may be labelled the set of expectations.

5.5.2 Uncertainty or probability

In view of the above, the question arises as to what, according to Shackle, the formal representation of uncertainty is? Before we go on to discuss Shackle's own theory, we first intend to discuss Shackle's opinion of the most prominent alternative representations of uncertainty, i.e. those which concentrate on probability. The reason for taking this route is that it may enhance subsequent understanding and evaluation of Shackle's own representation of uncertainty. 'Probability is a mode of thought not necessarily a character of the natural world.' (Shackle 1972, 385). He schematizes the alternatives as (1) the axiomatic, (2A) the structural objective, (2B) the experimental objective, (3) the subjective and (4) the rational treatments of probability (Shackle 1972, 372). The rational theory will be dealt with later in this chapter. We will therefore concentrate on the first three theories.

(1) In pure mathematics or pure logic '...the meaning of probability is internal to the system of propositions.' (Shackle 1972, 372). The structure resulting from logical deductions from a set of axioms is not related to anything outside the mind. To Shackle a crucial feature is that logic does not start from the study of human nature, although logic is the only test. The reader may recall that L. von Mises tried to develop praxeology starting from the study of human nature.

(2) The theories of probability which may be labelled objective, regard probability as a '...means of describing aspects of portions of the observable world.' (Shackle 1972, 372):

(2A) One is entitled to call frequencies *a priori* probabilities when they are deduced from a list of proposed answers related to certain assumptions about the behaviour of a structured system (Shackle 1961, 53). The ultimate nature of the structural account of probability is equi-probability, which relates to the symmetry of the alternatives. This structural objective treatment of uncertainty is a static approach. In fact, behaviour can only bring about what is latent in the set-up of such a situation (Shackle 1972, 372-6; Shackle 1961, 52-5).

(2B) Frequencies obtained by observation of the behaviour of the system in practice may be called experimental or statistical probabilities (Shackle 1961, 53). The related frequency theories prove to be useful in many cases, as in the life insurance business. Nevertheless, there are often no probabilities available. Moreover, in many situations '...there can in the nature of things be no possible neutralizing, no pooling and no probability' (Shackle 1961, 55-6).

Both the *a priori* and frequency theory of probability may be confronted with the probability paradox: how can a system both vary and be unchanging? It requires variation on a specified dimension aspect and strict fixed boundaries on all other dimensions (Shackle 1972, 381). This characteristic of the system rules out certain features and the system may be neither self-reinforcing nor evolutionary. In other words, first and foremost there is no room for cumulative processes or inherent tendencies to manifest themselves, and secondly, inherent evolutionary tendencies are also ruled out. The two points may be summarized in the statement that a system must be stable (ibid., 381-2). 'The die in its box is in a sense a *stable* system. The human intellect and imagination, the power of one human to influence millions of others, to inject thoughts of his own into their minds, to set fire to the tinder of their needs and desires, does not constitute the material and basis of stability.' (ibid., 384).

(3) In principle, subjective probability theory is based upon the same feature as frequency theory and *a priori* probability theory. Thus it is the case that '...the numerical assessments of different answers to a given question are required, essentially, to be proper fractions summing to unity, that is, together representing the certainty that, between them, the answers include all possibilities.' (ibid., 399). Frequency theory provides us with a measure of

confidence or positive belief, for this theory supplies one with certainty as to the distribution of outcomes of future events (Shackle 1958, 38-44; Shackle 1966, 170). In a frequency distribution, the answers are not mutually exclusive. The distribution of answers is a unity with a character specifically belonging to a particular set of circumstances, and the frequencies disclose knowledge about this aggregate (Shackle 1972, 403). The more numerous the alternatives, the more thinly confidence must be spread over them (Shackle 1955, 68-9).

According to Shackle, the orthodox treatment of uncertainty substitutes uncertainty with actuarial principles, such as the mathematically expected value. Actuarial principles give meaning to measurable risk only, summing up to unity, and thus provide us with a distributive uncertainty variable (Shackle 1966, 89, 103). Such principles are means of reducing or eliminating uncertainty.

In frequency theory, objective probability is thought of as expressing knowledge as to what "will" come to pass, for it relates to the contingencies which come to be realized with certainty, although some more often than others (Shackle 1958, 43). Therefore, frequency-ratio probability is useful as knowledge about the classes defined (Shackle 1972, 393), i.e. relating to cases devoid of uncertainty (Shackle 1955, 69). Perhaps as a consequence of the prevalence of this theory in representing uncertainty, '...uncertainty conveys the suggestion that there is a determinate future preexisting choice and independent of it, needing only to be found out.' (Shackle 1979a, 27).

Frequency theories require divisible experiments or repeatable situations. A divisible experiment implies adding together the results of a series of performances, which are sufficiently uniform in their circumstances (Shackle 1955, 4-5). Due to the additivity of the fractions, these theories indicate a distribution of certainty. Related to this is the condition of seriable performance, which refers to the items contributing to the divisible experiment (Shackle 1955, 8). The list of items, i.e. the set of outcomes, must be complete.   Conversely, in many situations involving economic behaviour, such as enterprise and investment, well-founded probability data on the basis of experience, or deduction, cannot be established. This is partly due to the fact that conditions are not sufficiently uniform, and moreover, many types of decision are non-seriable, isolated, i.e. virtually unique, events (Shackle 1948, 110; Shackle 1955, 81).

The argument more characteristic of Shackle's position may be summarized as follows: firstly, probability cannot deal with what we might call *ex nihilo* origination, a cause uncaused, i.e. the product of imagination. Truly new elements are excluded from discussion. "Residual probability" is no more than a stopgap to justify the use of a particular probability distribution. The problem of changes in structure is submerged in the search for a stable underlying structure, or has disappeared behind the plaster and ornamentation. Secondly, knowledge for a decision-maker in the setting of real world business is, in the nature of things, always incomplete, '...because [it is; EW] necessarily always being increased at one edge and eroded at the other and always being transformed and re-interpreted.' (Shackle 1988, 113). Some of our knowledge loses relevance with fresh information making it obsolete via discovery and invention. Agents have to engage in economic behaviour while information and insights are constantly being transformed '...The situation is utterly different from that of a game with known rules' (Shackle 1988, 113). Thirdly, the idea that single-valued statements, such as mathematical expectations, may express uncertainty is an contradiction in terms (Shackle 1990, 109). These ratios or expected values cannot be calculated in the important class of decisions called investment-decisions. Their non-repetitive character makes them unique, while frequencies must necessarily be obtained from a great number of similar cases (Shackle 1955, 83-7). Fourthly, to be able to introduce the seriousness or realism of a hypothesis we must discard the notion of a closed set of observed outcomes. Although he acknowledges that subjective probabilities may be assigned to the inaccuracy of primary probabilities (Shackle 1961, 281), he prefers to adopt a different approach: 'Non-additivity is more incisive than the piling-up of probabilities of the erroneousness of probabilities.' (Shackle 1961, 281). Fifthly, where there is choice amongst courses of action, i.e. in situations of uncertainty, distributions are non-existent, and meaningless. 'Frequency-ratio probability has nothing to do with true uncertainty.' (Shackle 1955, 26).

The situation involving choice is analogous to that of a crucial experiment, i.e. '...one where the person concerned cannot exclude from his mind the possibility that the very act of performing the experiment may destroy for ever the circumstances in which it was performed.' (Shackle 1955, 6). At least some essential circumstances of a situation are irreversibly destroyed by the performance of the experiment, e.g. when moving a rook in a game of chess (Shackle 1955, 6; Shackle 1961, 56-7). Such a crucial experiment, also called a non-divisible non-seriable, or a self-destructive experiment must be treated as unique (Shackle 1955, 7, 71; Shackle 1961, 56-9). This crucialness is pervasive in any case of choice-making (Shackle 1955,

63), for every significant experiment changes men's ideas: one cannot unlearn new knowledge (Shackle 1961, 57). Some simple examples are: the case of an election; the launching of an upgraded airliner; the decision on which career to pursue. According to Shackle, the essence of frequency theory is the elimination of the possibility of decision-making (Shackle 1966, 103; Shackle 1958, 43).

5.5.3 Possibility, plausibility and disbelief

Clearly, Shackle is dissatisfied with the orthodox treatment of uncertainty. But what alternative is there to offer? What preoccupies us in cases of uncertainty is not what "will" happen, but what "can" happen (Shackle 1948, 110; Shackle 1958, 40; Shackle 1961, 67; Shackle 1979a, 28). Consequently, probability is to be abandoned in favour of possibility (Shackle 1966, 90, 104).

The adoption of an approach based on "possibility" would, according to Shackle, not be tainted with the pair of shortcomings inherent in the 'probability" approach which would be expected to provide a language of expectation. The deployment of the concept of possibility as a measure of uncertainty is advantageous in that: (1) it is non-distributive, and (2) it can be applied to self-destructive cases (Shackle 1966, 104; Shackle 1972, 403-4). In other words, the various scenarios for the future are not in competition with each other, and by virtue of their feasibility are non-additive (Shackle 1979a, 25).

By means of imagination, one may envisage various actions which may be taken in a decision-making situation. Experience, records and the memory of field-reports may be of help in suggesting what can come to pass (Shackle 1979, 59). The imagined mutually exclusive courses of history, all related to particular choosable actions, '...are each themselves composed of mutually rival hypotheses, and the plurality of these rivals within each skein [i.e. cluster; EW] is in principle infinite in some meaning of that word.' (Shackle 1979a, 24). Each bundle of mutually exclusive hypotheses contains both disadvantageous and advantageous elements, and there is no room for choosing the good possibilities without also accepting the bad possibilities (Shackle 1988, 237).

For the time being, for the sake of clarification, we restrict ourselves to one specific action, a single course of activities. For such a specific action one may envisage several mutually exclusive hypotheses, of which an unspecifiable number may be congruous with reality, bearing in mind all that is known at present about the relevant situation (Shackle 1955, 69). These suppositions are called possible hypotheses, or expectations. It is essential to understand that for each policy there are at least two such mutually exclusive possible hypotheses.

The boundaries of the range of epistemic standing, that is the seriousness or realism of a supposition for one specific action (Shackle 1961, 280), are not certainty and impossibility: '...the highest epistemic standing that is logically attainable by its envisaged sequels is that of perfect possibility.' (Shackle 1988, 61). The epistemic continuum in fact extends from perfect possibility to impossibility (Shackle 1974, 33; Shackle 1988, 67). Hence, one may also speak of hypotheses of less than perfect possibility. However, the degree of belief in a hypothesis or its epistemic standing, i.e. '...the strength of its claim *ex ante* facto to be able to come true' (Shackle 1972, 368), is a product of personal judgment (Shackle 1988, 112-7; Shackle 1966, 120, 170)

To facilitate a discussion on decision-making we first need a formal measure of a hypothesis's plausibility. The non-additive nature of possibility must be made explicit to invest possibility with a meaning as it is actually reflected in our feelings, and in order to resist the temptation of adding together degrees of possibility (Shackle 1990, 110).

One of Shackle's inventions is his proposal to measure possibility by the degree of disbelief in a hypothesis, a device which thwarts attempts to conflate a scale of belief with the most likely outcome, or even with a system for measuring certainty. The degree of disbelief in a hypothesis which might be verified in future is equal to the degree of potential surprise in its apparent validation (Shackle 1961, 112-3). Potential surprise, or disbelief, is '...an inverted expression of epistemic standing.' (Shackle 1988, 6). In this respect, we recall a parallel in Shackle's preference for substituting unknowledge for uncertainty. One may call a hypothesis perfectly possible when it '...has nothing known against it.' (Shackle 1955, 69). Similarly, the product of imagination may not find subjective acceptance due to disbelief in imagination's congruity with reality as one knows it (Shackle 1988, 63, 66; Shackle 1961, 113). Disbelief relates to the recognition of some impairing circumstance (Shackle 1955, 30).

The feeling of surprise links this formal notion of disbelief to emotional disbelief in a natural manner (Shackle 1988, 66). The absence of disbelief is characterized by the absence of mental discomfort or shock in the face of evidence. Zero disbelief is synonymous with perfect subjective possibility; the full acceptance of a hypothesis (Shackle 1955, 9, 71; Shackle 1966, 104). Such information carries the implication that there is no need to adjust one's projections. Whether a certain probable outcome is validated or not, tells the agent nothing about the need to adjust them. The evident meaninglessness of adding together the zeros of possible answers, tempers the temptation to resort to additivity. The difficulty in imagining the validation of an improbable hypothesis entails the high degree of surprise which such an event would actually inspire.

If we take an orthogonal matrix on which the valuation of outcomes and the positive dimension of disbelief are plotted, the number of the imagined perfectly plausible outcomes is not necessarily limited. On the contrary, each cluster must be treated as incomplete (Shackle 1979a, 24). The potential surprises associated with the various imagined suppositions may constitute a potential surprise curve. In an early trial Shackle depicted the curve without a limit on potential disbelief, but he was soon imposing limits on disbelief. An arbitrarily chosen absolute maximum of disbelief stands for a perfectly impossible, impracticable or implausible scheme (Shackle 1966, 111; Shackle 1955, 11, 30; Shackle 1979, 87). Although possibility may thus be thought of as a cardinal variable, as a scalar variable, Shackle uses possibility primarily as a qualitative notion (Shackle 1961, 135-6). To sum up, the notion of potential surprise provides a practical notion of possibility and enables the introduction of a mathematically-graduated scale for potential surprise.

A high level of potential surprise is associated with counter-intuitive events, that is events for which possibility was deemed negligible. To some extent, this class of situations merges with the class of unexpected events, but must be distinguished from it. The validation of events from these classes calls for some re-examination of one's knowledge and the structure of assumptions. However, only the validation of absolutely disbelieved outcomes reveals a fallacious conception of the nature of things (Shackle 1961, 282-5).

An assessment of the potential surprise is the actual mental act of judgment at the moment of deciding. The feeling of actual surprise cannot co-exist with an *ex ante* assessment of the potential surprise, for the feeling of experienced surprise is located at another point on the calender axis (Shackle 1961, 68-9). However, '...recorded statistical frequencies may provide part or the whole of the basis of a judgement of possibility.' (Shackle 1961, 113)

More recently, Shackle waters down the idea of regarding possibility as a scalar variable. He welcomes the use of a categorical approach towards potential surprise, '...do we imagine this to be possible, yes or no?', as adopted in scenario-writing, for example by the Shell Petroleum Company (Shackle 1990, 110). Apparently, he feels the need for supplying us with a proxy variable for potential surprise or possibility. This proxy variable, without an absolute limit, is the length of time the actor considers necessary to overcome the foreseeable difficulties arising before an outcome can become a reality. It is, however, begging the question of an infinite regress, because it takes time to think out some value of the variable time. Shackle acknowledges that the problem of measurement is not answerable in any exact terms at all; one has to stop somewhere. We live in a world of changeable intuitions and feelings, using rules of thumb, routines, and other institutions. 'We don't live by clearcut ideas and choices.' (Shackle 1990, 111).

Certainty, implying a single and valid answer on the one hand, and absence of disbelief, indicating perfect possibility of a single conjecture on the other, are categorically different ideas (Shackle 1955, 31). Moreover, there is no relation between a probability and the degree of potential surprise. Possibility has nothing to do with a body of evidence, but with the absence of obstructions (Shackle 1988, 64): 'any and every probability greater than zero can correspond to perfect possibility' (Shackle 1961, 113).

We have so far only discussed the dimension of (im-) possibility and (dis-) belief, whose boundaries are perfect impossibility and perfect possibility. However, there is also the dimension of the value, the relative desirability, of the mutually exclusive hypotheses. Conjectures are valued at the present moment, while referring to future sequels of events. By means of a chosen calculation-rule, the individual renders the cluster of imagined outcomes of the different hypotheses with regard to one action compatible. This is usually but not necessarily discussed in monetary terms, i.e. profit and loss. Other terms for this dimension of valuation are: pleasure and pain, enjoyment and distress, success and misfortune, etc.

When we restrict ourselves to the possible outcomes, the set of points on the axis of relative desiredness of outcomes, we can find a neutral element and two extreme elements. The "neutral" hypothesis serves as a bench-mark: 'the neutral outcome is one whose realisation would make him [the decision-maker; EW] neither better nor worse off.' (Shackle 1988, 68). This outcome would scarcely change the decision-maker's situation (Shackle 1958, 48). Conversely, a change in his set of hypotheses for a single action changes his assessment of the neutral position (Shackle 1961, 126). The neutrally desired outcome is meaningful for it is claimed that owing to this neutral outcome different sets of conjectures and thus different actions, can be compared (Shackle 1961, 124). The two extreme elements, that is the most desired and the most undesired outcome, the best and the worst consequences, are called "focus-points".

In a discussion of a cluster of conjectures as a whole, attention will be concentrated on the valuation-extremes, while the intermediate expectations will be neglected. If there are more than two mutually exclusive imagined sequels of events, i.e. conjectures, considered equally possible, then the less extreme outcomes will be eclipsed by more desired outcomes or the more undesired outcomes. As a consequence, '...the whole force and effect of the set of points belonging to the skein [cluster; EW] as a whole resides in the two extreme points.' (Shackle 1988, 64). This position would find support in Arrow and Hurwicz (1971) where it is maintained that rationally one can only take account of the best and worst consequences attached to each course of action (Elster 1983, 12).

Shackle elaborates on the relation between the two dimensions, by defining an "attention-arresting-function". The relevance of this concept may become apparent when we extend our case and introduce hypotheses valued as less than perfectly possible. Straying outside the "inner range" of perfectly possible outcomes, one may suppose that the power to arrest attention depends on the desiredness and the surprise value of a hypothesis (Shackle 1961, 144). 'Its power to arrest attention, .., will I think be an increasing function of its desiredness or counter-desiredness and a decreasing function of its potential surprise.' (Shackle 1988, 67). The focus values are the two maxima of this attention-arresting curve. The one is the "primary focus gain" amongst the desired outcomes, while the other is the "primary focus loss", amongst the undesired outcomes (Shackle 1949, 10-31; Shackle 1955, 17-55; Shackle 1961, 115-93). The pair of primary outcomes may be identical with the pair of focus values when the attention arresting value falls as the inner range is overstepped. Shackle's revealed preference for discussing pairs of focus outcomes in a decision-making situation without also referring to pairs of primary focus values indicates that he is unsure whether agents actually evaluate in that detailed matter.

This model may also be applied when discussing alternative actions under uncertainty. It will result in pairs of focus values; one pair for each action, i.e. constellation of conjectures. The focus-hypothesis solution solves the problem of reconciling uncertainty and creativity (Shackle 1966, 82). The (primary) focus outcomes represent the bounds of uncertainty (Shackle 1988, 114). This approach enables economic actors to use uncertainty instead of ignoring it altogether.

5.5.4 Decision-making

The manner in which decision-makers come to terms with uncertainty is intimately connected with the decision-making process, both in subjective terms (feelings) and in objective considerations (results) (Shackle 1955, 82). To use uncertainty is the essence of the role of the decision-maker (Shackle 1958, 42-3; Shackle 1979, 149). But what is a decision in this line of thought? A decision is real, and paradoxically also unpredictable, when it is non-illusory and non-impotent (Shackle 1961, 271-4; Shackle 1966, 71-84). A decision is a choice amongst mutually exclusive courses of conduct (Shackle 1988, 5, 106).

In a determinist view of the world, for example that prevalent in Knight (1921), decision-making relates to the discovery of preexistent elements. At the one extreme, if we assume perfect foresight in a world of certainty, any act is an item in a fixed sequence of stages, and any decision is devoid of meaning. There is more to decision-making then a mere automatic response, the application of logic, or the discovery of concealed preexistent elements (Shackle 1961, 296; Shackle 1979, 32; Shackle 1979a, 27). In contrast, the decision-maker is powerless if he can discern no pattern of association between acts and sequels of events (Shackle 1966, 73-4). According to Shackle, scientists must assume that history is neither determinate, certain, nor random, and understand decision-making in this perspective. It is only a bounded uncertainty that makes man's choice non-empty, and permits him to act creatively (Shackle 1966, 74-5, 86; Shackle 1961, 271). Choices must be made between alternative actions under bounded uncertainty, that is between alternative bundles of expectations (Shackle 1961, 51; Shackle 1988, 107).

Decision-making is a psychic aspect of the adoption of a new policy, a resolution, a commitment of behaviour to a specific line of activities, with the aim of realizing an imagined situation, deemed possible (Shackle 1958, 14; Shackle 1961, ix; Shackle 1979, 15, 30; Shackle 1979a, 21). The decision-maker must inevitably compare expected bundles of hypotheses as wholes, being selectable entities, by means of subjectively comparing the pairs of (primary) focus values in the perspective of knowledge stored in memory (Shackle 1979a, 26). 'If so, the ultimate phase in his business of choice is the comparison of the choosable actions as pairs of focus outcomes. This comparison will be an exercise of *taste*.' (Shackle 1979a, 29).

In the perspective of time, choice is the asymmetrical starting point of a sequel. Shackle uses the words "origin" and "beginning" so as to implicitly invoke this notion of temporal succession. 'Being themselves uncaused, they [decisions; EW] claim to be a cause, to make a difference to what comes after them in time.' (Shackle 1979a, 20). If then, a choice is an ex nihilo beginning, '...an uncaused cause' (Shackle 1988, 12), is there no possibility of foreknowledge? Can it be the case that viewpoints and expectations change overnight, as a consequence of changed thoughts about what is deemed possible? According to Shackle the answer is: Yes, in both cases. Not only is foreknowledge out of the question but situations may also change overnight (Shackle 1979, 30). 'What does not yet exist cannot now be known.' (Shackle 1972, 3). The present is unique, and our knowledge is about the present. The future is the void. Choice is therefore originative, is choosing for what we hope for, and is an endeavour to realize ambitions (Shackle 1972, 122; Shackle 1979a, 27).

Society consists of interacting individuals. We are unable to know their motives, but we are able to observe their actions. Their interactions have become '...canalized in institutions, a word which seems to embrace almost every formal system of society.' (Shackle 1988, 212). The market, together with money, is the most important institution in the economy. A universal web of communication, it enables the individual to adjust his own affairs to his circumstances. The market binds the interests of individuals, firms and states, via actions, which results in more or less coherent '...reconciled specialization.' (Shackle 1972, 33-4). However, '...the market cannot solve the problem of expectations.' (Shackle 1972, 83). The market can only bring about a price at which bulls and bears exchange a certain quantity of goods. It does not harmonize their ideas about future developments. Nevertheless, even the eradication of the market would not abolish uncertainty, for we cannot plan feelings, aspirations, fashions and inventions (Shackle 1955, 81).

We influence each other in the formation of expectations and decisions, if only because any man's beliefs and consequent intentions contribute to his fellow man's stock of data. There is no dividing line between what we are to construe, i.e. expectations, and the way we are to construe them. As a consequence, we may say that uncertainty is a unity with two facets which are two sides of the same coin. While, first and foremost, the *ex ante* basis of expectations is vague and fragmentary, the opposite side of the coin is that this illusory basis affords scope for abruptly changing interpretations (Shackle 1974, 42). Having discussed the first question at some length, we now turn to the second question, relating to changes in imagination and expectations. It brings us to the main theme in Shackle's writings of the 1970s, namely the economic consequences of discussing fallible expectations. This theme will prove to be closely related to his theory about decision-making and his radical subjectivist epistemological position.

5.5.5 Profit and money

Is profit the reward accruing to the entrepreneur for confronting uncertainty? This question is ambiguous. Bearing in mind the above-mentioned two facets of uncertainty we may say that the concept of profit can be applied in two quite distinct contexts (Shackle 1955, 93, 100-1; Shackle 1988, 106-9):

(1) A context in which profit is expectational subject, is hypothesis, is a conjectural picture *ex ante*. In the *ex ante* sense, profit by its nature involves uncertainty. It stands for something imagined, an idea, a hope of gain which can '...counteract in the enterpriser's mind the discouraging influence of the idea or fear of loss' (Shackle 1955, 98). This profit "in the first guise" is part of the incentive to act (Shackle 1974, 58).

(2) A context in which profit is fact, a unique, recorded outcome. The *ex post* conception of profit emerges as unforeseen or windfall profits. They result from the outstripping of the focus-value by recorded events. Such a realized outcome was excluded from *ex ante* consideration as being less than perfectly possible. Profit *ex post* is the indicator of the failure of the range of envisaged possibilities to be sufficiently capacious (Shackle 1988, 122-3). Therefore, profit is by definition surprising and apart from changing the fortunes of the entrepreneur, stimulates a reexamination of expectations (Shackle 1972, 417-9). 'Profit is that degree of success beyond expectation, or of disaster beyond what was reckoned possible, which can bring about such an upheaval.' (Shackle 1988, 115). In this "second guise", profit is an incentive to thought; to strategic re-thinking; or, in the terms used by Keynes (1936), to decisions about expanding or curtailing the scale of operation (Shackle 1974, 18). 'But realized and recorded profit is just one ingredient,

..out of which expectations of profit are cooked up.' (Shackle 1955, 93)

As a yardstick with which to judge past actions, profit, which is expressible in monetary terms, will always pose troublesome evaluation problems. The reason why is that the classification of the components into those due to ability, to luck, to wisdom or to fortune, relies entirely upon full information. Without perfect information, one cannot judge the degree to which a decision-maker enjoyed perfect knowledge (Shackle 1955, 100).

According to Shackle, a model in which time and uncertainty are essential elements, and thus where the distinction between past and future, *ex ante* and *ex post*, is present, is the only model with which we can usefully discuss profit (ibid., 93). Although Shackle does not dismiss Walras's general equilibrium model as nonsense (ibid., 91), he nevertheless points our that in the theory of general static equilibrium the discussion of human affairs is abstracted from time in all significant aspects. As a result, profit is absent in the equilibrium model (ibid., 92). Even the "timeless" technical concept of monopoly power, which does result in profits, is more usefully discussed in a model which explicitly incorporates time and uncertainty (ibid., 93).

If we accept profit as an incentive to action and as an incentive to re-think one's expectations, we arrive at the question of whether it is possible to postpone decisions? The answer would inevitably be yes, since holding money is a means of fragmenting a chain of decisions. We will now turn to this theme.

An economic actor may prefer to hold money in order to postpone a choice because money confers the convenience of liquidity (Shackle 1966, 129). Shackle points out that, early in this century.. 'Keynes showed the intimate connection between uncertainty and liquidity-preference, the latter as a reaction to the former.' (Shackle 1958, 99-100). Moreover, money and liquidity are only meaningful in a world of uncertainty (Shackle 1974, 4, 8, 14, 28, 61-2). Because liquidity is considered to be Keynes's most original concept (Shackle 1988, 88, 159), we have come full circle, to end with Shackle's opinion of Keynes's ideas about money.

According to Shackle, money and its liquidity are psychic phenomena (Shackle 1966, 129). Money as a stock may be defined as '...the total of all payments which could be simultaneously made at that moment by all individuals, firms, and corporate bodies outside the list of banks in the strict sense' (Shackle 1972, 203). Confidence in the exchangeability of money depends upon convention, a shared evolved pattern of behaviour. In the absence of a comprehensive settlement of choices, conventions enable the decision-maker to make successive choices (Shackle 1972, 160, 208, 234; Shackle 1988, 215). The value and acceptability of money depends '...on its holders *not* attempting to spend every shilling in their possession at the first moment they possess it' (Shackle 1972, 204).

Money serves two purposes: (1) It is a means of finding buyers and sellers; (2) Money is a means of deferring choice, of avoiding commitment, of putting off deciding what to buy (Shackle 1972, 160-4, 174, 206-8, 235; Shackle 1974, 27, 72; Shackle 1988, 227). The first purpose reflects step-by-step sequential decision-making. Money in this respect is a useful means of making it unnecessary to find '...parties to a suitable multi-lateral trade.' (Shackle 1972, 207). Money offers the seller time in which to acquire knowledge. The reason for its existence is not so much the "transaction motive", but in a sense the opposite: the postponement of decisions (Shackle 1972, 149). By using money persons may detach selling and purchasing (Shackle 1966, 34). In this context, money exists '...because we are not yet ready to spend it.' (Shackle 1972, 207).

The latter purpose of money, i.e. the avoidance of commitment, is important when the awareness of uncertainty suddenly rises. The uncertainty inherent in not knowing precisely what successes or disasters are looming is at times more or less oppressive (Shackle 1972, 208). This may well be the case when news is confusing, and the scene obscure (Shackle 1974, 27). 'The ultimate refuge from market uncertainty (...) is money.' (Shackle 1955, 121). In this role money is hazardous because it throws the burden of action upon others (Shackle 1958, 99-100). This produces a negative connotation of liquidity, i.e.: as a response to awareness of uncertainty, directed at keeping all options open (Shackle 1974, 27; Shackle 1988, 215). This is the precautionary motive for holding a stock of money.

However, these two motives for holding money can be resolved in a third, namely: the speculative motive. The transactions motive may be assimilated by the other two, because it is directed by not knowing what one is going to need at specific future dates (Shackle 1988, 87). If one holds money out of precautionary reasons, it is only because non-liquid assets are exposed to capital loss (Shackle 1972, 216). Hence, Shackle infers that the three motives for holding money coincide, rooted in uncertainty, in the absence of foreknowledge, in the absence of fixed points (Shackle 1974, 63; Shackle 1972, 216). 'It is a speculative world.' (Shackle 1972, 164). A speculative movement is brought to a standstill only by recalling historic turning-points (Shackle 1988, 20). In conclusion, the propensity to hold money, the latent power to decide, can be said to arise from a lack of knowledge, but it in turn transforms the situation, and brings about uncertainty of its own (Shackle 1974, 61; Shackle 1988, 216).

Not all decisions are readily postponed. On the one hand, the daily expenses of keeping oneself alive are '...extremely repetitive, highly divisible, made in small instalments, and ... unavoidable.' On the other hand, large-scale investments can be postponed or cancelled (Shackle 1983, 247). Consumption, in contrast to investment, does not involve a great degree of uncertainty. Investment is the most vulnerable element of the economy, since the Marginal Efficiency of Capital (MEC) is a convention founded on the vagaries of men's expectations (Shackle 1974, 81). Keynes does not suggest that the notion of the MEC incorporates the effects of uncertainty and therefore does not state how this might occur (Shackle 1988, 88). On the contrary, it is uncertainty that lends the MEC its strategic importance (Shackle, 1958, 66). In this respect, it is significant that Keynes hardly ever discussed the influence of output on investment. This is even more striking when we consider his extensive treatment of the converse influence of investment on output (Shackle 1974, 48).

An absolute preference for liquidity is tantamount to the negation of enterprise. The decision not to invest causes a falling off of activities and thus a decline in employment. 'What it [the General Theory; EW] enshrined was the brief theme that uncertainty, that inescapable condition of life, can in a money economy inhibit enterprise and destroy employment.' (Shackle 1968, xxxiii; cf. Shackle 1984, 391). Uncertainty is important in Keynes's theory of employment (Shackle 1967, 112). Although *ex post* realised saving and investment are necessarily equal, expected or intended amounts of saving and investment are not necessarily equal. Shackle summarizes Keynes's position with regard to employment as follows: 'he ascribes the possibility of involuntary general unemployment to the existence of a liquid asset in a world of uncertainty.' (Shackle 1974, 28).

5.5.6 Kaleidoscopic expectations in Keynesianism

We trust that we have established that, according to Shackle, economic activities take place on speculative markets simply because the prime mover of the market process is "unknowledge", or to use the more orthodox term: uncertainty (Shackle 1988, 20). It does not seem foolish to go along with

Shackle in assuming that men are both reasonable and creative (Shackle 1961, 22). The market is envisaged as constantly evolving in new directions, generating an endogenous perpetual dynamic in the economy, regardless of whether exogenous influences play a role. Reason and imagination, therefore, operate via judgment and understanding to form expectations, although the inclusion of creativity in expectations means that decisions are no longer predictable (Shackle 1961, 22). Any decision which has some element of novelty precludes the logical possibility of prediction (Shackle 1966, 116). What then, if this line of thought is to be followed, is left intact in economics? Are models, statistics and econometric exercises totally useless? Shackle's answer to these questions sounds remarkably modern. He first wanders into the maze of so-called chaos theory, and then goes on to plead for an eclectic application of the various theories available. We will now examine both of these responses in turn, but concentrate on the latter response.

As early as 1966, Shackle examined the example of the absence of a split-pin which may cause the crash of an aeroplane (Shackle 1966, 112-8). 'For the central notion is the self-reinforcing process, where every stage generates a sequel larger than itself.' (Shackle 1966, 115). This mechanism of circular reinforcing causation is characteristic for chaos theory. However, Shackle did not elaborate systematically upon this mechanism.

Economic conduct is the result of decision-making, is a response to scarcity and ubiquitous uncertainty (Shackle 1966, 22). This implies that virtually unpredictable decisions are part of this field of research. In this domain of meaningful choice, inspiration and vision may generate something yet unforeseen. Shackle calls this world, in which a person's images are haphazard, the kaleidic world (Shackle 1979a, 31). The kaleidoscope '...seems to epitomize in some sense the limitless richness of mutations and the incalculable instability of the task of expectation-forming. The economic society whose affairs depend on its valuations of desirable equipment can perhaps be suggestively labelled *kaleidic*.' (Shackle 1972, 428). According to Shackle, uncertainty is the kaleidic element, and thus expectations are, in principle, kaleidic, haphazard (Shackle 1972, 428, 183; Shackle 1974, 42).

How is Shackle's idea of a kaleidic world linked to economics? The answer lies in the fact that economics may be regarded as the study of the operation and implications of exchange (Shackle 1972, 445); the study of economic conduct. The speculative market is the business aspect of such a world (Shackle 1988, 22; Shackle 1984, 393). Mutually exclusive orientations and ambitions create a society in which a natural social response to uncertainty is the interspersing of intervals of ostensible stability and confidence with abrupt shifts, disintegration and a spontaneous creation of a new institutions. Such a process may take a few years, a decade or several decades (Shackle 1972, 76-9).

In a society, one finds events involving objects and related thoughts assigning uses and valuations to these objects (Shackle 1972, 77), whereby the rules and mechanisms of the game actually constitute the social space (Shackle 1966, 112). The fact that the various orientations in the economic aspect of affairs are only partially successful creates situations in which decisions result in either (1) a course of events within the inner range of possible situations, and thus the confirmation of the orientation, or (2) in unexpected or counter-intuitive events, producing a temporary loss of a sense of direction (Shackle 1972, 76). Given the possibility of this effect, thoughts and opinions may change suddenly, or, in other words, the objects do not need to change much for thoughts to change abruptly. The disintegration of social life '...can happen abruptly in a manner unforeseen, unplanned and perhaps almost universally undesired.' (Shackle 1966, 113). Such a loss of direction might take the form of a serious depression or runaway inflation with the depreciation of the currency and the erosion of society's confidence (Shackle 1972, 77). 'The deformation of the social space is an event which renders the subject's world-picture obsolete in some vital respect, and thus destroys the basis or meaning of his plan.' (Shackle 1966, 112).

Where there is a prevailing sense of uncertainty, when expectations are mutably suggested by the stream of news (Shackle 1974, 42), one may believe that perhaps far more is to be lost than gained. The revision of images of the larger elements in the business scene, the policies of governments, and of the greater commercial concerns, may be momentous and dominating. Although, there will be widespread hesitation, there will also be a desire to uphold the general order of things. Meanwhile, activities planned on a smaller scale will continue. The smaller pieces will constitute stability, '...until a clear advantage for ...one or other party to the large-scale game appears.' (Shackle 1972, 78)

The kaleidic model is claimed to be realistic. The crux of the kaleidic theory is the opinion that expectations '...can undergo complete transformation in a hour or even a moment, as the patterns in the kaleidoscope dissolve at a touch.' (Shackle 1974, 42). By starting from notions such as uncertainty, the imagined clusters of mutually exclusive sequels, and degrees of possibility, the analyst may in some degree conform himself to this viewpoint. He may recognize the rig of a society, that is '...the tensions or pressures existing at some moment in that society' (Shackle 1966, 113), but does not acquire foresight about the course of history, if only (1) because it may even take generations before the tension experienced by a great number of people bursts out, and (2) because one cannot divine the track in which it will burst out. The tension arises from a discrepancy between the image held by someone of what is and his image of what could be (ibid., 113-4). Statistical regularities which may be found may help to reveal, not the crucial event, the catalyst, but the character of the rig (ibid., 115). 'We may, that is, be able to guess what sort of thing can happen, we cannot guess when it will happen.' (ibid., 114). Facts gleaned from the present are merely sources of suggestion (Shackle 1967, 246). The most useful thing we can do, for it may temper surprise, is to anticipate and prepare for the mutually exclusive possibilities implicit in the rig (Shackle 1966, 114).

In Shackle's view, Keynes himself assembled the components of a kaleidic method, but his assembly was incomplete and awkward (Shackle 1974, 83). 'No doubt the kaleidic method, if I may be allowed so to call it, was invented and used unconsciously and by accident, and exists in the *General Theory* as a mute, unformulated possibility.' (Shackle 1972, 441). Moreover, in his *Treatise on Money* Keynes uses the metaphor of the kaleidoscope to clarify the influence of monetary changes on price levels (Shackle 1974, 76). Shackle maintains that in his 1937 article Keynes made it clear that men consciously bind themselves in the face of the unforeseeable future, and that they do so by means of conventions; (1) we fall back on the judgements of others; (2) we assume we are in possession of a correct summing up of future prospects in current prices and output; (3) we overvalue the present as a guide for the future. These three ploys are subject to violent changes as fears and hopes may suddenly break through the surface (Shackle 1974, 38). It was Keynes who first showed governments how to prolong the suspension of disbelief (Shackle 1967, 247).

We can now usefully turn to Shackle's "definition" of the term kaleidic economics: 'Only by the method of studying the abstract adjustments which the expectations and beliefs (..) prevailing at some moment would lead to, given a breathing-space or moratorium to work out their logical inter-active consequences, and then of imagining, so far as possible, the cascade of real events which must flow from the inevitable upset of any such state of rest accidentally attained.' (Shackle 1972, 435).

Having discussed what Shackle means by kaleidics, we must now face the problem of accurateness versus simplicity, reality versus theory. Science is abstraction, the search for permanent and unchanging elements (Shackle 1972, 287): 'Science aims to *skeletize* phenomena.' (Shackle 1972, 116; cf. Shackle 1979, 148). But how should economic theorizing take place when it is continually outpaced by the velocity of change which its object of study exhibits? In the first place, time itself is a theme which ultimately eludes the grasp of the economic theorist. 'Time is a denial of the omnipotence of reason.' (Shackle 1972, 27). In the second place, the part about which we cannot reason exerts an influence on the part about which we can reason. To acknowledge that novelty can exist, in the sense of fundamentally undeducible things, is to accept that we cannot build comprehensive models which elucidate the course of a society's history. However, the scientist is only able to reason about what is closed and complete. Therefore, the '...analyst is obliged to practise, in effect, a denial of the nature of time.' (Shackle 1972, 27)

Economic reasoning is never conclusive. Economics may provide us with insights and be of help in small-scale cases, but in more important situations the gap between logic and experience cannot be bridged by logic alone (Shackle 1979, 148). Ergo, we need various models based on different premises, depending on our analytical interests. For Shackle, models are tools: 'A model is an abstraction, a map, an idealization, a dramatic heightening of supposed essentials.' (Shackle 1966, 117). No modern work on the principles of economics could be written as a unified coherent system of ideas. They would have to be embodied in a collection of models or a scheme of theories. For example, we may use an equilibrium model, which abstracts from uncertainty, because it provides us with some vital insights. We do not subscribe to some ultimate philosophy, but rather put our faith in diverse, though not unrelated, tools (Shackle 1966, 19; Shackle 1988, 214).

Thus, Shackle regards the constructs of economic theory as being idealized models, which may be applied in '... whatever rough and ready way' (Shackle 1990, 106). Without a model, we cannot even discern or classify a fact (Shackle 1966, 117-8). He is in favour of the use of sequence analysis, and although sequence analysis or period analysis is artificial, it nevertheless best represents the pattern or sequence of phases in a decision-making process (Shackle 1988, 109-10). 'All we can do is to draw a sort of sketch map of how we think, how we feel, how we decide.' (Shackle 1990, 111)

It comes as no surprise that Shackle rejects the mechanistic viewpoint in which the future and the past are merely distinguished by the fact that we are now, at present, discussing them. But when he states that a decision is not merely a step in a mechanical chain of reactions, he also rules out the logical possibility of prediction (Shackle 1958, 104). 'Economics is not physics, it is psychics, the study of men with all their capacity for learning and experimenting and inventing and imagining.' (Shackle 1955, 235). Economics ought not to be turned into a quasi-psychology, but economics may use psychology in order to better understand how people think (Shackle 1990, 111-2).

Economics cannot dispense with ordinary language for the expression of its ideas (Shackle 1988, 217). Furthermore, while Shackle takes the usefulness of mathematics to economics for granted, he warns against the possible pitfalls of trying to fuse that mathematical system with human freedom and originality (Shackle 1972, 26-7; Shackle 1988, 231). 'I do not believe that human affairs can be exhibited as the infallible and invariable working of a closed and permanent system.' (Shackle 1988, 239)

Furthermore, empirical work must be carried out, even if it may obscure the simplicity and sharpness of the outline of a model, and perhaps even entail its abandonment (Shackle 1974, 27). Although, in the best cases, we can observe some stability of the manifest aspects of the behaviour of a system (Shackle 1972, 386), our conception of the future will necessarily remain a figment (Shackle 1974, 27). 'I conclude, in an expression of mere personal conviction, that man in his true humanity can neither predict nor be predicted.' (Shackle 1958, 105)

We may conclude this summary with a short comment on Shackle's ontological and epistemological viewpoint. Shackle adopts a subjectivist approach towards economic actions and a realist perspective with regard to the scientific knowledge about those economic actions. He rejects the subjectivism in which uncertainty corresponds to probability and information is merely incomplete. Subjectivism to him is closely related to the active economic person who discerns unexpected ideas, who somehow processes external information, and whose opinions may, in principle, change overnight. Shackle's understanding of knowledge as having potential for change despite an unchanging object of research makes him a scientific realist. He explicitly takes public and objective observables, memory and records as useful elements and real in their own domain. Scientists may try to understand the complex of economic activities by looking for underlying structures and mechanisms, for example, in economic decision-making.

5.5.7 Criticism

Shackle's view of uncertainty certainly makes him a radical subjectivist (Lachmann 1990, 1-8), but does it make him a nihilist (Coddington 1983, 61)? Is his message one of radical subversion (Littlechild 1979, 47)? Lachmann and Shackle judged this annoying charge of nihilism as odd if not grotesque (Lachmann 1989). In response to the accusation that the exponents of Post-Keynesian economics, of which Shackle is a representative, are nihilists, Shackle concedes to those who call his mode of thought nihilistic, but also retorts that then '...Keynes also was nihilistic.' (Shackle 1984, 391). Keynes's final position, presented in the QJE article (Keynes 1937), was that the rate of interest, and thus the rest of the economy, is expectational and subjective. 'The stability of the system, while it lasts, rests upon a convention: the tacit general agreement to *suppose* it stable.' (Shackle 1967, 247). Although Shackle does not believe in grandiose constructions, such as general equilibrium, he considers ideas such as the marginalistic calculus to be illuminating (Shackle 1990, 105-6). We have sought to establish that Shackle is not entirely negative about theorizing, but prefers to use different models for different purposes. We live by vague intuitions and ideas, fluid thoughts and feelings. Therefore, ideas and choices are not clearcut. Judgment must somewhere break the infinite regress of levels of uncertainty involved in a choice process: 'We have to be practical.' (Shackle 1990, 111)

'But is Shackle *too* subjectivist even for Austrians?' (Littlechild 1979, 37). Lachmann placed him in the camp of Mises and Menger, and several authors in the Austrian School, especially from the "pro-subjectivist" group such as O'Driscoll and Lachmann, borrow elements from Shackle. An important bone of contention seems to be the relegation of the theory of imaginative creation to psychology (Littlechild 1979, 46). Shackle extended the principle of subjective valuation to a point where its connection with objective knowledge becomes problematic. For example, in the present moment, the clusters of possible sequels, and choices, are crucial in discussing economic developments which are to be expected. But Shackle leaves little room for informational leads and lags. The role of governmental institutions seems thus to have been neglected.

An ambition connected with this point is the wish to create a closed theory, a desire which is clearly present in Austrian economics. Shackle, however, is not searching for any such "Holy Grail". While he does cherish his favourite theories, he is nevertheless positive about the partial usefulness of other theories.

With regard to the "positivistic versus normative" discussion, Shackle leaves us in the dark. On the one hand, he states that when he provides us with his ideas about how the world works, leaving out qualifying remarks, he is not supplying us with the sole correct description, but merely offering suggestions. On the other hand, he freely admits that his theory of decision-making, of choice under uncertainty, is normative in character. 'Although, it is one that makes sense.' (Shackle 1990, 109). Bearing in mind that it will always be difficult to separate the two, it is now left to the reader to decide where Shackle seems to be giving us his positivistic account, and where he is offering normative recommendations. In fact, he hardly tested his theories.

Another problem is the absence of a clear distinction between various forms of decision-making: by the entrepreneur, by the consumer, decision-making by a board of directors, political decision-making, etc. In effect Shackle lumps the first three groups together, while ignoring other decision-making mechanisms (Shackle 1988, 115; Shackle 1990, 109).

A related problem is that of classifying decisions into those for which a non-distributional uncertainty variable is required, and those for which a distributional variable may be used. Where does the one group start and where does the other begin? In any case it is evident that the class of investment-decisions cannot meaningfully be appraised by the calculation of the mathematical expectation (Shackle 1955, 87). Shackle, however, does not appear to see any clearcut distinction between uncertainty faced by the businessman, and uncertainty experienced by the consumer (Shackle 1990, 109). Where may the concept of probability be used and where should one refrain from doing so and use the concept of possibility?

Empirical research does not seen to help us much in deciding on the best representation of uncertainty. John D. Hey has performed an experiment to discover whether probability or possibility are concepts actually operationalized by individuals. Alas, '...the experiment casts doubt on both the conventional wisdom and on Professor Shackle's position' (Hey 1990, 185).

In the planning processes, Shackle's theory of uncertainty, together with related ideas, is associated with the scenario, the use and proliferation of which has been significant. However, no standard procedure for developing scenarios has been established. Since the early 1970s, the use of scenarios in companies like Reed International and Shell has yielded promising results. The approach adopted by Shell closely resembles Shackle's view of decision-making (Loasby 1990).

5.6 Post-Keynesian economics

Since the 1970s, a number of lines in economic thought have been lumped together under the heading Post-Keynesian Economics. These lines of thought were attempts to fill the gap which resulted from the widespread disenchantment with the Neoclassical synthesis. Before we proceed to discuss theses lines of thought in relation to their introduction of uncertainty into economic theories, we offer some remarks on the term Post-Keynesian Economics as such. What unites the Neo-Ricardians with so-called "chapter 12 fundamentalists"?

In 1975, Eichner and Kregel published a thorough overview (Eichner and Kregel 1975). In their opinion, Post-Keynesian Economics has the following four characteristics: (1) growth dynamics; (2) distributional effects; (3) Keynesian constraints; and (4) a micro-economic base. Different Post-Keynesian models incorporate these characteristics in differing combinations. For Joan Robinson, the term Post-Keynesian '...applies to an economic theory or method of analysis which takes account of the difference between the future and the past.' (Robinson 1978, 12). Such an emphasis on the role of time links Shackle directly to Post-Keynesian Economics. What is usually regarded as the main problem of Post-Keynesian Economics, i.e. the lack of a set of first principles, is considered to be an advantage by others (Nentjes 1991, 73; Sawyer 1991, 32-3, 50; Carvalho 1984, 214): Post-Keynesian economics '...incorporates a "horses for courses" type of methodological approach.' (Sawyer 1991, 32).

In this section, and thus under the heading Post-Keynesian Economics, we propose to discuss the lines of thought which must be distinguished with regard to the (non)introduction of uncertainty into Post-Keynesian Economics. Three lines of thought are discussed: (1) The line followed by S. Weintraub, P. Davidson, and B. Loasby, drawing on Shackle; (2) The line first followed by Sraffa, and subsequently pursued by eminent economists such as Pasinetti, Kaldor, and Harcourt; (3) An intermediate line of thought subscribed to by Kalecki, J. Robinson, Eichner, and Kregel.

According to Paul Davidson, the following three elements are the characteristics of Post-Keynesian Economics: a) The economy is a process in historical time; b) In such a world of uncertainty, expectations have an unavoidable and significant effect on economic outcomes; c) Economic and political institutions play an important role in determining economic outcomes (Davidson 1980, 158-64). S. Weintraub became a forerunner in this line of thought, stressing as he did the imperfect adaptations, and the guidance which estimates about the future provide to decisions and actions (Davidson 1985, 534). Reminiscent of Shackle, we find an elaboration of the role of time and uncertainty in the direction of monetary institutions. In particular, economists working along this line of thought concentrate on the reasons why people should choose to hold money (Kregel 1980, 39n7).

To enable himself to make his point about the short-run and long-run non-neutrality of money, Davidson discusses the definition of uncertainty. Economists usually assume that economic situations evolve as the product of ergodic stochastic processes (Davidson 1988; Davidson 1990). 'If the stochastic process which generates the realisations is *ergodic*, then, for infinite realisations, the space average and the time average will coincide.' (Davidson 1988, 331). Statistical or space averages are estimates from a universe of cross-sectional data at a fixed point in time, while time or phase averages refer to averages over an infinite time horizon from a fixed realization. In the case of finite realizations, the two averages will tend to converge as the number of observations increases. Consequently, the probability distribution of past outcomes (time series), and the distribution at the present (cross-sectional data), may provide an estimate for the probability function that will govern future outcomes (Davidson 1983, 185; Davidson 1988, 331). 'In an ergodic environment, knowledge about the future involves the projecting of statistical averages based on past and/or current realizations to forthcoming events.' (Davidson 1988, 332).

Uncertainty about the future implies a non-ergodic decision-maker's environment. 'Uncertainty about future relationships can be defined in terms of the absence of governing ergodic processes.' (Davidson 1988, 332). The existence of crucial decisions, as Shackle defined them, are a sufficient condition for the existence of a non-ergodic world (Davidson 1983, 192-6). Important choices change the existing distribution functions, and entrepreneurship inevitably features such crucial decisions. In a non-ergodic world, past and present events cannot supply statistical guidance to the acquisition of knowledge about future events; 'there is no basis whatever upon which to form any calculable probability.' (Lawson 1985, 914).

In such a non-ergodic world, the existence of explicit money contracts provides a means of creating some assurance as to the possible future outcomes. It creates a kind of stability, a viscosity, in a market economy. Furthermore, money itself opens up the possibility of a flexible response, whether this involves taking advantage of yet unforeseeable future opportunities, or protecting oneself against misfortune (Davidson 1988, 333-5). Money and real forces are intimately connected (Davidson 1980, 184). Essential properties of liquid assets are a zero or very low production elasticity and substitution elasticity. As a consequence of a very low production elasticity, an increased demand for liquidity will not cause the re-employment of workers laid-off in industries which produce liquid assets. The low substitution elasticity inhibits or precludes the shift of a part of the rising demand for liquidity to goods and services which have not risen in price and are readily produced by workers. Thus, the existence of money can throw light on the problem of unemployment (Davidson 1980, 167-9).

However, money cannot be discussed independently of institutional usages. Specific money instruments for different purposes usually exist. There is heterogeneity of capital assets and financing terms (Minsky 1986, 228). Nowadays, the first role of banking is guaranteeing that some party is creditworthy (ibid., 229). 'But the risks bankers carry are not objective probability phenomena; instead they are uncertainty relations that are subjective values.'(ibid., 239). The "amount of risk" for the banker is related to the bundle of assets, and liabilities, which constitute commitments to pay cash on demand (Minsky 1982, 185), and the leverage, i.e. the ratio of assets to equity (Minsky 1986, 239). The bankers' profit drive manifests itself in different policy decisions at different times. The economy is considered to be liable to inherent and inescapable instability (Minsky 1980; Minsky 1986). 'Capitalism is unstable because it is a financial and accumulating system with yesterdays, todays, and tomorrows.' (Minsky 1986, 294). Criteria for "acceptable risks" predominantly reflect recent experience.

Bankers and borrowers know that their decisions are taken in the face of a highly conjectural future (Minsky 1986, 118), and uncertainty manifests itself in margins of safety (ibid., 184). Tranquillity, a term to be preferred to equilibrium (ibid., 176), attenuates the uncertainty of future developments. During a tranquil period, a positive yield curve will prevail, and realized events provide us with data which indicate stable risks. As a consequence, financing policy and portfolio preferences of banks may be adjusted in the direction of lowering the margins of safety, increasing short-term financing of long positions, and innovations in financing techniques (ibid., 213, 274). Hence, the initially robust financial structure will in time evolve into a more fragile structure.

This fragility will not become apparent immediately, among other things because of at least the following four reasons: (1) the banker may be reluctant to believe optimistic forecasts about recovering potential borrowers; (2) time is needed for financial innovations to spread throughout the financial market; (3) borrowers adopt conservative attitudes to financial-market innovations; and, (4) during an investment boom, rising profits and corporate funds are directly available for investments or indirectly available for raising extra funds (ibid., 210-3). Financial fragility is a prerequisite for financial instability (ibid., 250-1).

Shifts from favourable to unfavourable views about the future take place in response to economic phenomena. Such shifts create uneasiness as to possible future developments, and doubts about the future creditworthiness of borrowers (Minsky 1986, 118). They increase the feeling of uncertainty and exacerbate the difficulties inherent in decision-making. Businessmen and bankers live in same expectational climate, and thus '...the governor mechanism by way of financing terms is often dominated by positive, disequilibrating feedbacks.' (ibid., 228). Rising doubts as to the continuation of certain observed trends, may cause borrowing and investment to be delayed or cancelled. A negative or inverted yield curve most likely prevails, and business confidence is lacking. Such an increase in uncertainty '...is a damper on economic activity, especially long-lived investment.' (ibid., 17). A crisis may thus result.

In the final analysis, what is acceptable as a financing technique is not technologically constrained but rather depends upon the changeable feelings of borrowers and controlling institutions as to what an acceptable means of financing might be. The liability structure which is regarded as appropriate is determined on the basis of history and conventions; it can only be known with the benefit of hindsight, but it can never be known in advance, *ex ante* (Minsky 1986, 184).

Institutions and policy '...can contain the thrust of instability.' (Minsky 1986, 10). We must constrain uncertainty so that expectations may reflect a vision of tranquil progress. The bank's exposure to uncertainty has traditionally been constrained by customer and collegiate surveillance. Customer surveillance diminished as the view that protection from the regulatory authorities would make it redundant gained adherents. Collegiate surveillance takes place in terms of differential interbank lending rates. Reserve deficiencies are handled via the lender-of-last-resort, i.e. the central bank.

The function of central banks as lenders-of-last-resort will concern them with guiding the evolution of financial practices along non-disruptive routes. As a result, central bank interventions must be possible so as to prevent or, if necessary, contain and offset financial disruption (Minsky 1982, 185-90; Minsky 1986, 38-67, 322; Davidson 1990, 72). Profit-seeking innovators will always outpace regulators, but the latter may constrain banks by keeping their asset-equity ratios within certain bounds (Minsky 1986, 250-2, 314).

Government intervention in markets may be needed to curb potentially destabilizing market forces, to help in cases of market failures, to contain fluctuations in aggregate profits, and to manage externalities. Industrial behaviour must promote competitive industry. A sufficiently strong government is also necessary to ensure minimum standards of living, guarding against the deterioration of working conditions. Aggregate interventions in the economy are to be preferred to detailed interventions; programmes for full employment, price stability and greater equity are to be preferred to an emphasis on investment and economic growth if only because the latter results in unstable performance (Minsky 1986, 292-3). It is even doubtful whether governmental and monetary policies can be considered neutral or ineffective in economic affairs, if one way or the other they affect economic institutions, i.e. the accepted behaviour of individuals. We must opt for a theoretically based system of changes not for isolated changes. There are no simple and final answers to the problems of our capitalism. 'Instability, put to rest by one set of reforms will, after a time, emerge in a new guise.' (Minsky 1986, 333).

Having presented the first line of thought, which stresses time and uncertainty, we now turn to another line of thought within Post-Keynesian Economics. This line of reasoning is the one which has been developed by various economists, notably Sraffa, Pasinetti, Garegnani, Eatwell, Harcourt and Kaldor, all of whom investigate the long-term evolution of an economic system. For example, Luigi L. Pasinetti places the emphasis on detecting '...the "permanent" causes moving an economic system, irrespective of any accidental or transitory deviation which may temporarily occur.' (Pasinetti 1983, 127). From the three "natural" forces, namely (1) an evolving technology, (2) a growing population, and (3) an evolving pattern of consumers's preferences, the features of a growing economic system have been derived (ibid., 80-3, 127-8). Given a chosen trend in working hours, a central organisation must move the long-run trend in capital accumulation to the desired level, and influence the short-run effective demand so as to maintain full employment (ibid., 85-91).

The model is developed independently of the institutional set-up of society, and disregards short-run considerations. The problems that relate to the institutional mechanisms of any society are considered, at least conceptually, to be subsidiary to problems related to the logical relations in an evolving economic system. Institutions have an instrumental role, and come into play as means to achieve efficient structures of process and outputs; to ensure tendencies towards agreed ends (ibid., 153-5). Short-run influences such as weather conditions and market fluctuations, are not regarded as influencing long-run developments. They are temporary, that is, reversible, influences. Accordingly, the uncertainty of outcomes is confined to the short-run, without influence on systematic forces.

The emphasis placed on external direction of the economy to curb undesired macro-economic developments in an evolving economic system is present in both lines of reasoning already discussed, as it is in the third line of thought, which is now to be examined. The focus of this intermediate line of thought, pursued for example by J. Robinson and Kregel, is on the effects of responses to uncertainty on employment and income distribution.

Keynes analysed the uncertain world not in terms of the absence or presence of uncertainty, but rather in terms of alternative speculations about the effects of uncertainty and disappointment. As we mentioned in our introduction, Kregel distinguishes three models in the work of Keynes (1936) and in his 1937-lectures, '...each depicting different assumptions about the effect of uncertainty and disappointment.' (Kregel 1976, 222). These are: (1) the model of static equilibrium, in which short-term expectations are by definition always realized; (2) the model of stationary equilibrium, in which disappointed entrepreneurs may find the point of intersection of the stationary demand and supply curves, by means of trial and error; and, (3) the model of shifting equilibrium, in which disappointed short-term expectations may affect long-term expectations and thus shift the curves of the system (Kregel 1976, 214-7). Models of static or stationary equilibrium, i.e. the long-run steady-state growth models, such as Pasinetti's, are considered useful for focusing on the warranted growth rate, and its determinants. This research provides the means by which to put actual problems in growth rates, long-term capacity and short-term utilization of this capacity into perspective, as it does for unemployment and income distribution in an expanding economy (Eichner and Kregel 1975, 1294-6). J. Robinson on the one hand considered it the task of Post-Keynesians to reconcile Keynes and Sraffa (Robinson 1978, 14), but on the other, criticized the stress on the notion of stable equilibrium positions, and the inadmissibility of long-term comparisons for describing processes (Harcourt 1986, 93-6, 105).

The Post-Keynesian approach modifies the Harrod-Domar growth model to allow for two groups with a different propensity to save out of different sources of income. A higher (lower) level of investment, and thus a higher (lower) growth rate, *ceteris paribus*, implies that a higher (lower) share of national income is residual income. The derived conclusions '...apply to any economic system in which some one group, private or public, receives a residual share depending on the level of economic activity.' (Eichner and Kregel 1975, 1299). The groups distinguished are usually workers and non-workers, the latter representing the capitalist class, or the sector of large industrial corporations, with respectively primarily wages and profits as income categories. Furthermore, the boldly simplifying Kalecki (-Kaldor-Robinson) hypothesis is commonly used to state that '...wage earners spend all while capitalists save all income.' (Weintraub 1979, 101).

Ex ante, but not *ex post*, investments may deviate from savings. If consumers do not know what they will buy in the future, investors cannot know future demand either. This is no case of market failure because there is no information to be transmitted. 'The consequences of past events can, in principle, be known, .., while the consequences of a present event can, at best, be predicted with a range of possibilities which may turn out not to have been correctly anticipated.' (Robinson 1980, 219). There is no market capable of linking future consumption decisions to present expenditure decisions determined by the expectation of future income (Kregel 1980). 'In the capitalist production system, the information needed today for rational decision-making does not *exist* today, it is only available tomorrow, while current income is determined by decisions to produce for future consumption.' (Kregel 1980, 45).

National expenditures may be divided into non-discretionary and discretionary expenditures, i.e. consumption and investments. The discretionary incomes, or savings, are reflected in the monetary flows of the national accounts (Eichner and Kregel 1975). Investments are the primary factor determining the level of economic activity and thus savings must necessarily adjust. Due to the aggregate condition of aggregate equilibrium, there is necessarily *ex post* equality between the two. It is an empirical problem to find out whether the resulting macrodynamic situation, in which the *ex ante* rate of growth of investments diverges from the rate of growth of savings, is unstable or stable when compared to the long-term warranted growth rate (Eichner and Kregel 1975, 1300-4).

Although money may provide the most certain link between the present and the future, this is independent of short-term behavioral reactions in the face of uncertainty. Money allows consumers to postpone decisions about future consumption, to prefer liquidity, in response to the existence of uncertainty. Although it offers a store of wealth, money does not predict the future, and neither could its price, the interest rate, provide pointers to the correct actions.

The economic system copes with ignorance and uncertainty by means of economic actors agreeing on certain regulations, contracts, agreements, and standardized prices. Their value is denominated in the most value-stable unit, which is usually money. As a consequence, in order to stabilize the economic system it is important to keep the value of money stable, i.e. prices in general. The largely exogenously determined nominal wage in combination with the widespread use of mark-up pricing together offer such an instrumental variable for influencing the aggregate price level (Eichner and Kregel 1975, 1305; Kregel 1980, 46-7).

5.7 Continuity or Change

Post-Keynesian economists have returned to Keynes's writings, firstly re-reading and elaborating upon his economic writings, and secondly clarifying the relationship between his economic writings and his early philosophical writing. On the one hand, their exegesis of the *General Theory* (GT) itself and, by then published, related correspondence and papers, supplied ammunition for a critique of the dominant formalistic Keynesian economics. On the other hand, Post-Keynesians endeavoured to support their own viewpoints by establishing links between the GT and other work by Keynes, especially his philosophical writings, i.e. by trying to understand Keynes as a philosopher-economist. A possible motivation for this research into Keynes's writings in general may be the search for an objective test with which to assess rival interpretations (Gerrard 1992).

The view that Keynes's philosophical work *The Treatise on Probability* (TP) had little to do with his economic writings is put forward in Harrod (1951) and in the Collected Writings of J.M. Keynes (1973). In an appendix to his biography on Keynes, Harrod refers to the TP and qualifies this work as '...an appendix to the monumental work of Whitehead and Russell' (Harrod 1951, 654), i.e. their *Principia Mathematica*. With regard to Keynes's Collected Writings, it may suffice to note that the editors gave the TP a volume number out of chronological order, a volume introduced by a philosopher which remained unrelated to Keynes's economic writings. Finally, we should note that, although the TP was published in the very year when Knight published his views on risk and uncertainty, there are neither referential connections between the two publications, nor is there a personal relationship between the authors. Knight (1921) was clearly working in the field of economics, while the Keynes who was writing the TP was mainly preoccupied with philosophy.

With respect to the treatment of uncertainty in economics, there are clearly reasons for trying to understand Keynes as a philosopher-economist. He first develops ideas on probability in the absence of demonstrative argument in his philosophical writing *The Treatise on Probability*. The direct link between the GT and the TP is the well-known quotation, already referred to, from the GT: 'By "very uncertain" I do not mean the same thing as "very improbable". Cf. my Treatise on Probability, chap.6, on "The Weight of Arguments".' (Keynes 1936, 148n). The TP at least seems to hint at ideas on uncertainty and expectations as present in his later writings in economics. The writing of the TP, under the influence of Johnson, Moore and Russell (Keynes 1921, v), was Keynes's prime activity in the period 1906-1911, and again in 1920 when he prepared the final version of the TP for its publication in 1921.

We now turn to advance our opinion on the (dis-) continuity stance, being forewarned by a remark made by Moggridge, who concluded from Keynes's habits of thought and methods of exposition: 'This plainly left his work open to a wide number of interpretations.' (Moggridge 1975, 75).

At least there appears to be widespread agreement on Keynes's life-long practical orientation. Due to his '...passionate concern for the world and its ills' (Moggridge 1975, 76), Keynes was relentlessly working on getting across certain fundamental opinions with the aim of pursuing certain practical policies. This practical orientation also explains his constant emphasis on argument rather than theory (Skidelsky 1975, 94).

Furthermore, we may state that there is continuity on the level of Keynes's metaphysical vision (Fitzgibbons 1988, 195-8). Under the influence of G.E. Moore (1873-1958), Keynes distinguished between the ideal and reality; 'between the mental sphere of pure ideas and the real world of fluctuation and change.' (Fitzgibbons, 1991, 130). In the TP, Keynes relies on pure ideas founded on logical intuition. In this work, he distinguishes between *causa essendi*, the true causes of things, and the *causa cogniscendi* (Keynes 1921, 5, 308), the grounds for believing something, the cause according to our theories and common knowledge (Carabelli 1985, 153-5; Fitzgibbons 1988, 18). The former is supposed to reign in the TP, the latter in the GT. In the TP, Keynes discusses probabilities as objective logical relations, as degrees of rational belief, based on logical intuitions of the mind, but does not discuss probabilities as psychological orientations or empirical observations. In the GT, the state is presumed to be wiser than the investors who act on precarious conventions (Keynes 1936, 153). Here, and in related papers, irrational behaviour is discussed at length. Such behaviour may occur because the rate of interest is primarily determined by underlying conventions, hopes and fears, and only secondarily by savings and investment schedules (Keynes 1936, 162). Clearly, this discussion could not have had a place in the TP. Although one may point to continuity on the metaphysical level, there seems to be no escape from a disconcerting conclusion: the belief in logical intuitions, clearly present in the TP, does not seem to add much to our understanding of Keynes as a pragmatic economist, passionately concerned for the world and its problems, nor as the author of the GT.

5.7.1 Weight and probability

In the GT, Keynes refers to the concept of weight found in his TP, a reference which seems to promise some clarification of his understanding of uncertainty. However, this does not appear to be quite as straightforward. Firstly, Keynes fails to elaborate on the relation between uncertainty and weight. In fact, the word uncertainty is not even mentioned at all in the TP. Secondly, in the TP there are several concepts of probability and weight, which may be of interest for an understanding of uncertainty, but their relative importance is unclear. Finally, in response to criticism levelled at him by Ramsey, Keynes abandoned the objective epistemic theory of probability in favour of a subjective epistemic theory of probability. The question of whether uncertainty is dealt with in the TP, or not, revolves around the link with weight. Since an understanding of the concept of weight may teach us about uncertainty, let us concentrate on the latter two points.

In his exploration of the logical relation between two sets of propositions in the absence of a demonstrative argument, Keynes defines probability, denoted as p, as '...the degree of our *rational belief* in the conclusion, or the relation or argument between two sets of propositions, knowledge of which would afford grounds for a corresponding degree of rational belief.' (Keynes 1921, 4). This implies, among other things, that two persons in possession of the same evidence cannot but arrive at the same conclusion on the probability of a specific conclusion. Certainty may be regarded as being the maximum probability, or the highest degree of rational belief. This is the well known limit relation 'b implies c' or 'if b then c'. But Keynes is interested in partial implications, "b partially implies c".

Probability (p) and weight (v) are the two objective and independent properties of an argument (Keynes 1921, 76). When we state that a proposition 'a' is probable, '...this expresses strictly a relationship in which they stand to a *corpus* of knowledge, actual or hypothetical, and not a characteristic of the propositions in themselves... so that it is without significance to call a proposition probable unless we specify the knowledge to which we are relating.' (Keynes 1921, 3-4). When 'h' stands for the corpus of knowledge, i.e. the evidence, we may state: $p = a|h$. Probability refers to the, potentially variable portion of relevant evidence which confirms our statement. When 'h' rises 'p' may rise, fall or remain equal.

Weight is a measure of the completeness, or of the sum, of relevant evidence, that is, the corpus of knowledge h: $v = v(a|h)$ (Gerrard 1993, 2). 'New evidence will sometimes decrease the probability of an argument, but it will always increase its "weight".' (Keynes 1921, 77). In principle, however, sub-divisions are possible, first, by stressing absolute versus relative completeness of evidence, and second, by establishing different orders of knowledge of the relevance of evidence. As a consequence, when weight is considered to indicate the relative completeness of evidence, it may transpire that with the finding of additional evidence 'h', one may also find out that the knowledge is less complete than assessed before, and thus the weight of the proposition falls: $v(a|hh') < v(a|h)$. This is the case when additional evidence sufficiently raises the assessment of relative ignorance. At the limit there is zero knowledge and full ignorance of the relevance of information (Dow 1993). Orders of probabilities may exist in relation to the various routes in the rise of completeness of evidence.

In the TP, there is at least a three-fold conception of probability: (1) Measurable and cardinally comparable probabilities. In this case, the range of outcomes and the data generating process must be known. (2) Ordinally comparable probabilities. Different evidence-related orders of probabilities are comparable, because there is at least one set of evidence where these orders are equally favourable. (3) Probabilities which cannot be compared: (a) there is not a single point of indifference between different orders; or, (b) there is no ordering possible because the weight is not a continuous variable; or, (c) both probability and weight are to be judged.

Uncertainty as it is used by Keynes has been related to weight, to the absence of logical insights, and to non-comparable probabilities. Firstly, in the GT, Keynes refers to low weight uncertainty, indicating the actuality of situations of incomplete relevant information (Stohs 1980; Weintraub 1975). Keynes did not deny the usefulness of any sort of calculation, but states that there is no scientific basis to the Benthamite calculus when applied to long-run prospective yields (Stohs 1980, 379). With regard to this position we would object that it does not pay due attention to the probability property of an argument, which is of prime importance in the TP. In the GT, the known probabilities play a subsidiary role. Secondly, Keynes (1937) stresses the irreducibility of uncertainty: agents lack the logical insight to perceive the probability relation.

This stress on the irreducibility of uncertainty is the centrepiece of the continuity thesis submitted by Carabelli. The logic of probability must be understood as the logic of rationality, connected to the notion of limited knowledge, not as a logic of truth (Carabelli 1988, 21-2). Carabelli thus interprets the TP as an anti-rationalist and anti-empiricist tract (Carabelli 1988, 1-13; Dimand 1989, 890-1). This second stance is troublesome, because the conceptions of probability used in the TP differ from the meaning of uncertainty as presented in the GT. The rational intuitions and technical solutions which occupy a place of importance in the TP, are allowed no scope whatsoever in the GT's treatment of uncertainty.

Thirdly, in 1938, in his correspondence with Townshend, Keynes discusses unrankable uncertainty. This term alludes to the impossibility of generating cardinal or ordinal orderings of alternative courses of action. Both Lawson and O'Donnell emphasise this understanding of uncertainty as arising

'...when the probability relation is numerically indeterminate and non-comparable, .., to other probability relations.' (Lawson 1985, 914; see also, O'Donnell 1989, 77-8; O'Donnell 1990, 258-9). According to Lawson, Keynes's theory of uncertainty is about logical probabilities. Hence, although knowledge of the future outcomes of all present actions is unobtainable, rational behaviour is still possible. We acquire knowledge of the ways of doing things by participating in society. Not conventions or numbers but logical intuitions, pure ideas, take priority in social actions. Lawson claims that Keynes holds this idea both in his TP and in his GT (Lawson 1985).

We may criticise the third stance for leaving out irrationality. Irrationality is entirely absent in the TP, but is at least relevant to several of the arguments present in the GT. The alternative view presented by O'Donnell has it that Keynes works along two lines; strong rationality rules in the determinate domain, where probabilities and weights are known, while weak rationality is supposed to be dominant in the indeterminate domain, in which weight and probability are non-comparable among themselves. The strategies and responses developed in this domain are practical but imprecise. Examples are the acceptance and following of conventions and customs, and the use of rules of thumb. The rationality-concept involved boils down to having good reasons. It is true that the indeterminate domain was assigned a subordinate position in the TP (O'Donnell 1990, 257-8), but we may question, however, the claim that, next to the prevalent rational theory of probability, Keynes developed a theory of "weak rationality" in the TP. In any case, the second theory of rationality is never explicitly mentioned in the TP. Furthermore, there is no place in the TP for socially-founded behaviour next to the logical intuitions of the mind. Finally, to discuss a weak rationality concept in relation to the GT is somewhat at odds with Keynes's presentation of the speculative and economically damaging acts of persons (Bateman 1991, 108-9).

Keynes's openness to objective aleatory theories of probability may be traced back to his 1921-publication. In fact, he was not dismissive of quantitative analysis based upon statistical data, although he was somewhat sceptical about its applicability. As a social scientist he was sceptical on this point because he considered the related atomic hypothesis to be of limited value to the social sciences (Hamouda and Smithin 1988; Rotheim 1988; Davis 1989; Winslow 1989). Keynes seems to believe that as long as we have not found long-run stable distributions of variables, objective aleatory theories of probability are not yet applicable. We are thus vindicated in concluding that it is correct to represent Keynes's views by means of an epistemic theory of probability (Bateman 1987; Bateman 1990; Pesaran and Smith 1985). The position taken by Keynes on the best probability theory filtered through in the famous debates which Keynes held with Harrod and Tinbergen (Keynes 1973, 277-320; Lawson 1985a; Bateman 1990).

As we stated above, it is widely acknowledged that Keynes's switch from an objective to a subjective epistemic theory of probability took place in reaction to Ramsey's criticism. Thus, Shackle, Stohs and Loasby are correct as to his later advocacy of a subjective epistemic theory of probability (Bateman 1987, 117). There is certainly something in the following statement made by Shackle: 'It is a clear-cut mistake, .. to identify the Keynes of the TP with the Keynes of the GT.' (Shackle 1988, 238). However, Shackle's opposition to the logical thrust behind decision-making is not reinforced by the proposal to extend Keynes's conception of probable inference by adding subjectivism. Indeed, as Shackle himself acknowledges, such an extension '...would no doubt have been *unacceptable to him.*' (Shackle 1972, 388). This suggestion is as radical as the proposal to drop Keynes's claims for objective logical entities and thereby safeguard the continuity within Keynes's work (Runde 1993, 16). Clearly, one may advance economic thought by adapting and modifying theories, but such a rewriting of the TP is unjustified within the field of the history of economic thought. When Keynes abandoned an objective epistemic theory of probability, he conceded to Ramsey's criticism, and in 1931 he states:

> 'But the basis of our degrees of belief - or the *a priori* probabilities, as they used to be called - is part of our human outfit, perhaps given us merely by natural selection, analogous to our perceptions and our memories rather than to formal logic. So far I yield to Ramsey - I think he is right.'
>
> Source: Keynes 1972, 338-9.

He was willing to accept that we make decisions based on subjective probabilities, but he did not accept Ramsey's attempt to call these probabilities rational, i.e. objective (Keynes 1972, 339). Moreover, Keynes did not mention Ramsey's novel method for measuring subjective probability on which subjective expected utility models would soon be developed (Bateman 1991a, 60-1). In fact Keynes was unwilling to discuss the role of uncertainty in economics for several years, until external influences finally made him change his mind in 1933 (Bateman 1992), when preparing the GT. As we were discussing the GT and the role of uncertainty within it at length at the beginning of this chapter, we have now effectively come full circle.

To sum up, during the 1980s, something known as "das Maynard Keynes Problem" emerged: how does one reconcile the early advocate of probability as the guide for life with the late theorist who said that people follow conventions, not probabilities, in making decisions about the future? (Bateman 1991, 102). The consensus between the various commentators on the (dis-) continuity in Keynes's thought is found in their ability to give a positive answer to the following question: 'Are not all saying that Keynes needed to go beyond TP's theory of rationality to make it more practical?' (Gerrard 1992). Furthermore, one is nowadays justified in stating that uncertainty is more important in Keynes's writings than was acknowledged before this aspect of his work was investigated, and he certainly did not introduce it into the GT as a mere ornament. However, when one examines the details of the controversy, one finds a range of widely differing opinions. For example, in the GT, uncertainty relates to the sudden shifts in opinion, given evidence, while it seems impossible to draw such a conclusion from the TP. Moreover the (dis-) continuity debate has so many dimensions that it is hard to envisage a single interpretation that will finally satisfy all involved. "Das Maynard Keynes Problem" looks like being here to stay.

5.8 Conclusions

The closing section of a chapter is generally used to provide kind of overview as to the main lines of thought discussed in it. With regard to the introduction of uncertainty into Keynesian economics it must, first of all, be concluded that Keynes had a vague and imprecise conception of uncertainty. With regard to the main current in Keynesianism, the one which has its roots in the work of Hicks, we witness the submergence of uncertainty in line with Hicks (1931), as presented in chapter two of our study. Uncertainty was encapsulated in the Hicksian week. In the other main current in Keynesianism, i.e. that actually founded by Shackle, uncertainty is ubiquitous.

Shackle considers uncertainty to be an implication of time, and crucial to decision-making. Uncertainty involves the open future, not a future which is given and needs only to be discovered, but rather a future which is still to be created by the actions of men. When discussing the contrast between his theory of uncertainty and probability theories, Shackle stresses the mutual exclusiveness of the alternative outcomes of an action. Uncertainty relates to the "un-knowledge" about the outcome of available courses of action. When there is uncertainty in one's thoughts, one entertains a plurality of mutually-exclusive answers to a certain question. Uncertainty can be transformed or reduced, but it cannot be eliminated by seeking additional knowledge. It enables individual imagination to conceive of, and fill up, the open future time and time again. Uncertainty is bounded when the decision-maker is able to classify some imaginary situations as possible and some as impossible. He is then left with a cluster of manifold, mutually exclusive possibilities in the face of a given amount of knowledge.

From the growth of the style of theorizing known as Post-Keynesian Economics, with its strong emphasis on analysing the influence of uncertainty on economic behaviour, we may conclude that uncertainty can be and has been introduced into economics and thus recognized as a pervasive element of human life. Uncertainty is sometimes characterized as the propensity to countenance multiple possible outcomes for each deliberated action, and is sometimes equated with macro-economic instability. But paradoxically, Shackle concentrates research on the individual agent, while Austrians referring to him, expand their analysis to the layers of the market and the economy. A large number of Post-Keynesians, however, did concentrate on the macro-economy.

Additional definitions of uncertainty have emerged out of new research into Keynes's collected work. In particular, his *Treatise on Probability* contains ample material to fuel the dispute about what Keynes really meant by the term uncertainty. However, although it is doubtful whether an authoritative definition of uncertainty as derived from the Collected Writings of Keynes will ever emerge, his writings on this theme prove at least that the complexity of economic life informed his view of the world. Post-Keynesian work on this dis-continuity in Keynes' work shows that entertaining various ideas of uncertainty may ultimately yield fruitful insights into the complex economic reality. The key to this complexity can only be fashioned out of a metal tempered by uncertainty.

6: ECONOMIC GAME THEORY: ACKNOWLEDGEMENT OF UNCERTAINTY?

'Institutions ...affect individuals and emerge from, or are
created by, human action.'

(Frey 1989, 3)

'Instead, it will be necessary to classify the environments
to which game theoretic ideas are to be applied much
more closely than is attempted at present.'

(Binmore 1992, 1, 26)

6.1 Introduction

So far we have presented and discussed the contributions which several
schools of economic thought brought to the discussion of uncertainty,
especially in relation to independent individual decision-making. The
evolution of the argument from Knight (1921) to New Classical Economics
was traced in the chapters two and three. From a view of uncertainty linked
to a vision of a dynamic, but itself stable economy, we came to understand
the economy as a probability-related exhaustive group of projections into the
future. In chapter three, a discussion on how to arrive at decisions on the
basis of subjective ideas concerning the environment and how to learn the
given objective probability-distributions, was succeeded by a review of the
rationality of decisions based on the "right" probability distributions of
outcomes. The future environment is considered to be stationary and
uncertainty is totally excluded from economics. In sharp contrast to this
tendency to exclude uncertainty is the discussion of uncertainty in Austrian
Economics, presented in chapter four. Austrians linked uncertainty to
entrepreneurial actions and to the dispersion and the interpretation of the
information created by such actions. The complexity of the economy, the
uniqueness of situations, precludes exact predictions and finally the uncertain
expectations about future developments raises problems relating to the
predictability and stability of economic developments. These problems were
again taken up in chapter five, on Post-Keynesianism. They concentrated on
the changeable, evolving macro-economy which is the result of actions taken
by the individuals who create it in the light of their expectations. All these
views as discussed in those chapters focus on independent decision-making.

A somewhat underdeveloped and troublesome element in the aforementioned approaches is the uncertainty caused by handling interdependent decision-making itself, that is where strategic behaviour is exhibited in the presence of dominant positions. Let us elucidate this point, which was already made by Morgenstern (1935). The exchange relationships we have or create constitute economic activities. In an economy, individuals do not act "in vacuo" like so many Robinson Crusoes, but in relation with others, i.e. within a specific social and institutional environment. No one person determines all the variables which affect his or her interests (Neumann and Morgenstern 1944, 11). The related choice problems concern the simultaneous determination of all the relevant variables. In economic terms, can a single optimal economic equilibrium really exist, and can it prevail, even under conditions of perfect foresight? For a start, is it not true that the possible use of premiums and rebates already obliterates the uniqueness of such deduced outcomes (Neumann and Morgenstern 1944, 564). 'Always, there is exhibited an endless chain of reciprocally conjectural reactions and counter-reactions. This chain can never be broken by an act of knowledge but always only through an arbitrary act- a resolution.' (Morgenstern 1935, 174). Interactive decision theory addresses such behavioural situations all of which are characterized by reciprocal dependencies (Morgenstern 1935, 174; Neumann and Morgenstern 1944, 87; Schelling 1960, 86).

This chapter discusses uncertainty from the perspective of this currently important approach to the problem of choice under uncertainty: the game theory approach. How have game theorists discussed uncertainty and choice under uncertainty? What forms of games have been developed to represent specific decision-making situations? Contrary to most economic approaches towards institutions, the game-theoretic approach addresses problems such as how institutions, e.g. stable market prices, cartels, and vigorous competition, come about. Institutions are not taken as given, but are rather the outcome of formal analysis (Aumann 1987, 17-8). Game theory may expand economic analyses so as to include the behavioural inclinations of the individuals involved together with the specific problem situation (Bianchi and Moulin 1991, 179-80). At the time of writing, there is no consensus about the historical line of development which game theory has followed. Engaging in historiographic polemics would distract from the theme of this thesis and probably be hopelessly inconclusive. This chapter is therefore constructed thematically rather than historically. Furthermore, if we may distinguish between the formal logical context, intuitive background and applications of a theory (Brams, Schotter and Schwödiauer (eds.) 1979, 5), we then intend to put the emphasis on the latter two aspects, so as to avoid entanglement in logical and mathematical complications. However, a number of basic principles and distinctions will first need to be discussed, because different authors sometimes use similar terms while advocating essentially different interpretations.

In this chapter, we will argue that situations of decision-making under uncertainty may be understood better when related to the following two distinctions; first, a distinction based on the relative coincidence of interests; second, a distinction based on the possibility of correlating strategies. Furthermore, several of the positions presented in earlier chapters will surface again in these elaborations. Of central importance to this chapter are the relations between the structural elements involved in interactions and the economic behaviour to be expected. The rationality and knowledge assumptions are discussed in this context. These discussions will reinforce the need for widening the scope so as to introduce institutions, that is social practices, to solve certain problems of choice under uncertainty.

6.2 Some basics

A game-theory model is a configuration of a possible social or economic order (Neumann and Morgenstern 1944, 436). Understood from the perspective of the philosophy of science, game theory '...develops methodologies that apply in principle to all interactive situations, then sees where these methodologies lead in each specific application.' (Aumann 1987, 2).

Historically, game theorists built on the theorems provided primarily in Von Neumann (1928), von Neumann and Morgenstern (1944) and Nash (1951), i.e. on notions devised during and around the 1940s. During the fifties and sixties, game theory grew steadily, but remained an "in" group concern, with few or delayed publications. In the 1970s, however, game theory took off with a rapidly growing output of game-theory articles, resulting in the present mature "roaring flood" (Eatwell, Milgate and Newman (eds.) 1989, xii), featuring elaborate applications in economics, biology, computer science, cost allocation, and moral philosophy. However, the field has become so broad that the present state-of-the-art is reminiscent of a meadow with numerous molehills, whereby it remains unclear whether they are interlinked via a hidden network. Economists attempt to take account of the prevalence of interactive economic decision-making by employing various game-theoretic techniques.

Formally-speaking, a "game" may be defined as '...a set of rules for a particular situation that delimits the actions available to the players (the agents engaged in the situation) and awards payoffs to them on the basis of the actions chosen.' (Schotter 1981, 15). The "players", often referred to as "agents", are the decision-making persons involved. There is usually no distinction drawn between the substantial result of interdependent decisions, e.g. building a railway, and the monetary or utility index appraising these results, i.e. the payoffs. The "payoffs" are either the monetary or the utility outcomes, from the agents' point of view, of combinations of choices. Of course, the unit of calculation is not unimportant as the various marginal utilities of a unit of money may be relevant to the decisions taken. A "payoff-profile", also termed a payoff n-tuple, is a list of the outcomes for the (n) agents involved, related to a list of (n) chosen strategies. Nearly all game theorists postulate *homo economicus*, i.e. *homo sapiens* who optimises personal benefit in a mathematically rational manner. A "strategy", or a decision rule, is '...a plan which specifies what choices he will make in every possible situation, for every possible actual information which he may possess at that moment in conformity with the pattern of information which the rules of the game provide for him for that case.' (Neumann and Morgenstern 1944, 79). We may distinguish between pure, mixed and behavioural randomized strategies. A "pure strategy" signifies to an agent detailed prescribed courses of action for each eventuality, in a specified game (Luce and Raiffa 1957, 55). When the choice between pure strategies is delegated to random device, we say that a "mixed strategy" is being used; or, reversing our perspective, regard the pure strategy as a special case of a mixed strategy. To complete the list, a "behavioural strategy" prescribes, for each local information set, a probability distribution for selection among the alternatives available. If nobody forgets anything, i.e. if there is "perfect recall", then the behavioural strategies may be understood as decentralised mixed strategies (Van Damme 1987, 140-1; Luce and Raiffa 1957, 159; Binmore 158-9).

A number of game theorists study repeated games, suspecting that the reproduction of a situation may finally create cooperation; since ongoing relationships create types of enforcement mechanism, altruism, revenge, and signalling of information may thus be analysed. A "supergame" is defined as the same game played repetitively, whereby agents are mainly interested in their long-run average payoff. Supergames have become widely known since Axelrod experimented with them, primarily in order to address the problem of the relative effectiveness of alternative strategies (Mertens 1987a, 238-9). A "repeated game" is a generic name for any model in which agents make their moves in turn, whereupon in an independent environment, or unknown "state of nature", current payoffs and information signals are selected, e.g, by means of a lottery. In economics, such models apply to fields like insurance, industrial organization and agency theory. In this respect, incomplete information is said to reflect uncertainty about the true setting, and is introduced by adding an initial stage to the game with a lottery selecting the relevant rules of the game and the agents' information sets (Mertens 1987, 205-6).

To enhance understanding of the discussion in this chapter we already need to consider another distinction, namely that between extensive form games and normal form games. "Extensive" or "tree form games" consist of a complete formal description of how the game is played, including the sequence of decisions, the information at each moment of the game, including possible chances, and the resulting payoffs at the end of the game (Aumann 1987, 2-3). The term extensive form game was coined by Neumann and Morgenstern, who also thought that these games could be reduced to "normal form games" without a loss of generality. The normal or "strategic form game" presents a list of all possible combinations of pure strategies and the outcomes resulting from them. It reduces a game to simultaneous decision-making. The two-person strategic form game often appears as a "matrix form game", with rows and columns representing pure strategies of the respective agents. The entries in the matrix depict the related payoff-profiles. Von Neumann and Morgenstern's confidence in the reduction of all extensive games to normal form games is misplaced insofar as agents may commit themselves in advance, that is before playing the game. "Dynamic games" and "static games" are alternative terms for extensive form games and normal form games respectively. Although interest in the promising-looking evolutionary game theory, which is based on the former, is increasing dramatically (Mailath 1992, 259), such elaborations on dynamic games are only of relatively recent vintage (Hirshleifer 1982). Therefore, we propose to concentrate on the mature static, rather than the juvenile dynamic game.

Finally, once a game has been described, what do we know about the final situation, i.e. what payoffs will actually be realised? A function that associates such resulting payoff-profiles with a specific game is called a "solution concept" (Aumann 1987, 11). Von Neumann and Morgenstern used the following definition of a solution set V of payoff-profiles: solutions conform to the requirements of Pareto-optimality (group rationality) and individual rationality. The elements of the solution set V are precisely those payoff-profiles which are not dominated by any other payoff-profile in V (Neumann and Morgenstern 1944, 264, 39-40). They tried to translate this solution set back to social phenomena by calling the elements of V the accepted standards of behaviour; no accepted standard of behaviour can be occluded by another accepted standard of behaviour (Neumann and Morgenstern 1944, 41). The best known solution concept is the "core": and the core consists of those situations which no (coalition of) agent(s) can improve upon (Hildenbrand 1987, 108). However, since every coalition or subset of agents is required to be instrumentally rational (Luce and Raiffa 1957, 197-8), the existence of this solution concept entails fierce and enduring competition (Aumann 1987, 17). The simple example of 2-person coalitions in the 3-person voting game immediately indicates that many games have empty cores: there are always opportunities for (other) coalitions offering better results for the partners involved (Neumann and Morgenstern 1944, 35-6). A major problem for game theory is the creation of an abundance of often mutually-unconnected solution concepts, representing different points of view or different approaches. A, to some extent related, problem associated with solution concepts concerns the existence and the uniqueness of a solution: it is hard to find solution concepts presenting an existing and unique solution.

6.3 Uncertainty, decision-making and game theory

Choice in game-theoretic decision theory is commonly classified into the following three categories; (1) choice under certainty; (2) choice under risk; and, (3) choice under uncertainty (Luce and Raiffa 1957 13; Fishburn 1987, 303). This classification focuses not on the alternative strategies, but rather on the different strategy-outcome relations. A decision is made under conditions of certainty if each alternative action or strategy will lead to a specific outcome or prospect. It is possible to choose a mixed strategy under certainty. We are in the field of decision-making under risk when an action will not lead invariably, but with a known probability, to a specific outcome. With regard to each alternative action both the set of alternative prospects and the related probabilities, summing up to unity, are assumed to be known to the decision-making agent. The realm of decision-making under uncertainty (dmuu) encompasses all those situations which, for each alternative action, comprise '...a set of possible specific outcomes, but where the probabilities of these outcomes are completely unknown or are not even meaningful.' (Luce and Raiffa 1957, 13). We will discuss the first two groups only to aid the comparison with game-theoretical choice under uncertainty, which is central to this chapter.

Well-known examples of decision-making problems under certainty are linear programming problems and the travelling salesman problem. When we restrict ourselves to problems relating to a finite set of feasible actions, the decision-making problem may be stated as follows: from a given set F of feasible actions, find action(s) x' which yield(s) the maximum (or minimum) index, i.e. $f(x') \geq f(x)$, for all x in F (Luce and Raiffa 1957, 15).

Decision-making under risk boils down to the following problem: from a given finite set F of feasible actions, find those actions x' which yield the maximum (or minimum) expected value of an index over the n discrete alternative outcomes a; $f(x') \geq f(x)$ for all x in F, with $f(x') = \Sigma^n p(a)f(a)$. Or, described in game-theoretical terms, choose from the set of alternative strategies the one with the highest expected value, which is calculated from the related payoff values multiplied by their respective probabilities. If the index is utility, then the agent is assumed to maximise expected utility.

Expected utility theory, based on an axiomatic system, which was presented in Neumann-Morgenstern (1944), and featured properties which remained unproven until the 1947-edition, has become the major paradigm in choice under risk (Schoemaker 1982, 529; Hey 1982, 130). According to Von Neumann and Morgenstern, the utility function is cardinally unique up to a positive linear transformation, '...leaving the zero and the unit scale open.' (Morgenstern 1979, 176). Probabilities are considered to be fundamentals or primitives, with objectively given values (Neumann and Morgenstern 1944, 26; Schoemaker 1982, 532, 535-6; Luce and Raiffa 1957, 304). 'We have practically defined numerical utility as being that thing for which the calculus of mathematical expectations is legitimate.' (Neumann and Morgenstern 1944, 28). The values of utility combine with probabilities like mathematical expectations. Note that utility usually represents preferences, whereas in neoclassical theory it determines or precedes preference (Schoemaker 1982, 532). Furthermore, for this normative variant of expected utility theory they assume that an agent knows, and knows for certain, the set of possible states of nature, the set of choices open to the individual, and the outcomes related to the combination of the aforementioned sets (Hey 1982, 130-131).

Uncertainty in game theory primarily relates to the spectrum of possible discrete outcomes for each alternative strategy. This spectrum of outcomes itself originates from the interdependence of outcomes in the yet unknown future environment, i.e. a state of "nature", or results from the diverse strategies open to other participants. 'Game situations may be considered to represent a special case of uncertainty, since in general none of the agents will be able to predict the outcome, or even the probabilities associated with different possible outcomes. This is so because no agent will not be able to predict the (chosen) strategies of the other players, or even the probabilities associated with their various possible strategies.' (Harsanyi 1986, 88). Analysis of decision-making under uncertainty has for a large part evolved from the understanding of experimental evidence. Conceptually, this uncertainty amounts to a state of affairs in which participants in a social exchange economy are obliged to seek to obtain an optimum result despite the fact that nobody controls all of the variables which influence his own result.

As a result of the above, a distinction between independent decision-making under interdependent results and interdependent decision-making has emerged. The distinction is, in fact, between (1) evaluations by a single (group of) person(s) given a set of mutually-exclusive alternative future states of the environment, and (2) decision-making among a relatively small number, mostly two groups, of decision-making agents. In the second set of games, individual decisions may affect the other agents' decision-making processes, which may be incorporated in the agent's private evaluation of alternatives. The decision-making individual may learn from actions performed, inform after the decisions made, infer decision-making procedures and introduce all of the information thus gleaned into his own evaluation of alternative strategies. In the first set of games, interaction is indirect and parametric; indirect, because the agent does not think of the environment as responding agents; parametric, because the agent perceives magnitudes, e.g. a market price, as given facts external to himself but internal to the system as a whole (Johansen 1981, 231-2). The research problem takes the form of choosing some best action given an independent nature (Luce and Raiffa 1957, 306). If a person decides in the (perceived) environment of a non-reacting large group of individuals to which he does not belong, we may regard such a group as constituting the independent nature.

In these "games against nature" we find interdependence of outcomes, but not of decision-making: for an act chosen will not affect its own realization (Fishburn 1987, 309). The limiting cases with respect to these games of dmuu against nature are the situations of decision-making under complete ignorance and decision-making under risk respectively.

6.4 Choice criteria for dmuu against nature

If it is not reasonable to assume an *a priori* distribution over the alternative future states of nature, then the scientist must find a choice criterion without having recourse to the element of probabilities. Agents are supposed to be ignorant with regard to probabilities. A well-defined criterion prescribes a precise algorithm which unambiguously selects, for any decision problem under uncertainty against nature, the optimal act(s) (Luce and Raiffa 1957, 278). Complete ignorance as to which state of nature, i.e. the setting, will eventually obtain may be characterized in game-theoretical terms by the following two axioms: (1) the set of best actions should be invariant under labellings of the different possible states of nature; thus, apart from the related payoffs, it should not matter whether, for example, you will become a cleaner in a rundown hotel or in a prestigious bank; (2) the optimal set is not altered by the deletion of repetitious columns. For example, essentially it should not make a difference whether you are evaluating the list of payoffs correlated with the rundown hotel once, or twice (Luce and Raiffa 1957, 294-295).

In order to facilitate the explanation, take F as a finite set of alternative acts f, and S as a finite set of n alternative states s of nature, with the consequences f(s) in a set X. Furthermore, assume that the use of utilities is numerical up to a monotone transformation function, and a utility function u on X. Now we can present the four dominant choice criteria which have been proposed as rules of thumb to resolve the problem of dmuu against nature.

I. The maximin criterion: choose act f which maximizes the $\min_S u[f(s)]$.

This "conservative" criterion amounts to finding the highest security level. This is realized by first tracing the minimum payoff for each alternative act. Next, the optimal choice is the act promising the highest payoff among these worst cases. Although its safety-first conservatism is considered to be the advantage of this criterion, it may produce counter-intuitive results. For example in figure 1.a., with two alternative states of nature, i.e. s^1 or s^2, the maximin criterion selects act f^2 instead of f^1 in the given utility payoff constellation: security level 1 ranks above security level 0.

Table 2: Alternative payoffs given independent decision-making

Figure 1.a: Utility Payoffs.

	s^1	s^2
f^1	0	100
f^2	1	1

Figure 1.b: Loss Payoffs

	s^1	s^2
f^1	1	0
f^2	0	99

Where f^i is a strategy or act; s^i is a state of nature; and, the numbers, or entries, are the results.
Source: Luce and Raiffa 1957, 280

II: Von Neumann's minimax loss criterion: choose f to minimize $\max_S$ $\{\max_F u[f(s)] - u[f(s)]\}$

This criterion, also known as the minimax risk criterion, transforms the utility payoff matrix into a loss or regret payoff matrix. As presented in figure 1.b. above, each single entry shows us the utility foregone for act f^i when the state of nature s^i will obtain. In figure 1.b., act f^1 may result in a maximum regret of 1. Act f^2 may, as the case may be, result in maximum regret or a risk value of 99. Here risk is defined as the utility which might be foregone. What action will be taken? The selected action is f^1, because it minimizes the maximum difference between what could happen and what actually happens. Thus, should the least desired state of nature manifest itself, the agent knows that at least that the disappointment will be as slight as it could be. Again we witness a highly cautious approach towards the indeterminate nature of the future state of affairs. Minimax is applied in, for example, worst case analysis and linear programming (Aumann 1987, 7).

III: Hurwicz's pessimism-optimism index criterion: given $0 \leq \alpha \leq 1$, choose f to maximize $\alpha \min_s u[f(s)] + (1-\alpha) \max_s u[f(s)]$.

This alternative combines the evaluation of the best and worst case situations. If $\alpha = 0$, the procedure is the maximax (utility) criterion, whereas if $\alpha = 1$, it is the maximin (utility) criterion. The maximax criterion reflects the use of the most optimistic, that is best-best, approach possible towards the indeterminism of the future state of affairs. The prescribed action is that action promising the highest of the best case payoffs. Where, in particular, entrepreneurial activities are concerned, there is no substantive reason why maximin, or "best-worst", should be a better criterion than maximax, the option with best-best consequences (Elster 1989, 12).

IV: The insufficient reason criterion: choose f to max $1/n \; \Sigma^s u[f(s)]$.

This criterion, first formulated by J.Bernoulli (1654-1705), states that, given ignorance with respect to the probabilities of alternative states of nature actually being realized, each state of nature should be judged as being equally probable: the agent maximizes the average of utilities over s. This criterion is not equivalent to asserting the aforementioned axiom number (1) (Luce and Raiffa 1957, 278-86). Asserting the equivalence of axiom (1) and the assumption that each state of nature is equally likely is only justified when the other desiderata underpinning decision criteria hinge on a unique *a priori* probability distribution over the states of nature (ibid., 294).

This principle of insufficient reason carries us back to the other limit of problems of dmuu, i.e. decision-making problems under risk. To recap, with choice under risk the best strategy is the action with the highest expected value.

All four of the above decision-making criteria under ignorance are open to criticism. When we concentrate on an axiomatic evaluation, we may then assert as true that the four criteria satisfy several of the elements on the list of reasonable desiderata, e.g. the invariance under labelling of acts, as proposed by Luce and Raiffa (ibid., 288-95). However, the maximin utility criterion is not consistent with the axiom of irrelevance of a constant: the optimal set may change if a constant is added to a column. All of the Hurwicz α-criteria similarly fail to fulfil this axiom and all but one of these α-criteria are ruled out by the requirement that a probability mixture of two optimal acts should also be optimal. Using the minimax risk principle it is possible to demonstrate unwanted dependence on irrelevant alternatives. Finally, under application of the insufficient reason criterion, the optimal set may be altered by the deletion of repetitious columns. This is in violation of the second axiom which characterizes the complete ignorance case (ibid., 288-97, 325).

6.5 Subjective expected utility theory

So far, we have been discussing decision-making under certainty, under risk, and under complete ignorance of the probabilities linked to the various states of nature. However, we may observe that probabilities may be used, even when the imperfectness of our *a priori* knowledge concerning the true state of nature is acknowledged. The decision-making hiatus in those intermediate situations between complete ignorance and complete knowledge with regard to the appropriate probability distribution over the alternative states of nature has been filled by the subjective probability approach. In line with this approach, we state that the probabilities related to the alternative possible situations are subjective, simply because they are specific to the individual. These probabilities are expressions of relative degrees of belief and quantify our partial beliefs, our intuitive judgments (Fishburn 1987, 309).

This line of thought has been pursued within the (Savage) subjectivist school, which is built upon de Finetti's calculus of subjective probability and von Neumann and Morgenstern's theory of expected utility. The central concepts have been primarily elaborated by Savage himself (Luce and Raiffa 1957, 300-4). When, for each strategy, an *a priori* probability distribution over the possible future states of nature is considered meaningful by the decision-maker, then the decision-making problem is relegated to evaluating the subjective expected utility values for the alternative strategies, and thereafter making a choice (Luce and Raiffa 1957, 276-7).

One can apply subjective expected utility theory in dynamic problems through the use of backward induction. Moreover, we may incorporate the learning of endogenous information, i.e. information that is generated within the choice problem itself (Hey 1982, 134). Experimental evidence may subsequently be allowed to alter the subjective probability assessment pertaining to the states of nature if the Bayesian decision rule, called "Bayes's theorem", is applied to the subjective *a priori* probability distribution (Luce and Raiffa 1957, 312-3, 326). After the revision of the subjective probabilities pertaining to the alternative states of nature, the choice problem is again one of choice under risk. Some scientists even proclaim this theorem to stand '...with Einstein's E= mc² as one of the great, simple truths.' (Lindley 1987, 11).

This standpoint is highly dubious, however, as long as the question of the origination of consistent *a priori* probabilities is left unanswered. Let us elaborate upon this assertion. The Bayesian updating of *a priori* probabilities, the "priors", hinges on the formation of *a priori* probabilities and the decision-makers' wish to be consistent. Nevertheless, genuine learning, which involves responding to surprises, may reasonably prompt the probing of a new theory which is inconsistent with current theories. It is foolish to be consistent, when consistency proves itself to be consistent only in error. *A priori* probability distributions are based upon intuitive judgments and it is in the formation of these consistent, massaged partial beliefs that actual learning takes place. To borrow an analogy from Binmore (1990), it is in the assembling and the labelling of the books for the library that surprises are incorporated, not in the subsequent ability to find a specific book in that library (Binmore 1990, 143-4). Only with an all-inclusive set of future courses of action at one's disposal can the scientist exclude the chance of unexpected data being stumbled upon. However, in a practical sense, how inclusive are the sets of states of nature? Are all conceivable future histories taken into account? Bayes's theorem excludes real decision-making. It is only in a closed universe of small-world problems that Bayesian theory applies (Binmore 1990, 144).

We now propose to end our discussion of Bayes's theorem as such, because it is time to turn attention to its core principle, i.e. the maximization of subjective expected utility, which has already been introduced in chapter three of this study. Because (subjective) expected utility theory (SEU) underpins Bayesian decision theory, the criticism raised against it is relevant to game theory as well. First of all, the technical complexity of EUT is already immense, but is likely to become still greater in the future. The reason for making this observation is the need to elaborate the theory in the direction of exogenous information, dealing with such problems as price-setting (Hey 1982, 135). Secondly, and possibly more importantly, there is a huge problem lurking in linking this normative theory with descriptive data. A large number of experiments on expected utility axioms, field studies on descriptive usefulness, information process research and context effect, and research on the predictive value of the theory, inspire serious doubts as to the usefulness of EUT (Schoemaker 1982; Fishburn 1987, 308-310).

Expected utility theory seems to be feeble when it comes to describing actual decision-making processes, possibly except when applied to well-structured repetitive tasks featuring important stakes and trained decision-makers. For example, with regard to the principle of independence, i.e. the absence of the certainty-effect, the so-called "Allais Paradox" and its generalization by Kahneman and Tversky (1979) offer falsifications. Although these falsifications may not involve a paradox at all, they are no less than a fundamental claim to take account not only of the mathematical expectation of cardinal utility, but also its (perceived) dispersion about the average (Allais 1987, 6-8). This dispersal term characterizes the propensity to avoid or take risks, i.e. the '...preference for security in the neighbourhood of certainty.' (Allais 1979, 441). During the 1970s, Allais was finally able to analyse, and find support, in empirical research related to his original 1952 statement of the paradox (Allais 1979, 445-55). Proposed alternatives, such as Prospect theory (Kahneman and Tversky 1979), and Regret theory (Loomes and Sudgen 1982), still incorporate subjective expected utility theory as a special case (Hey 1982, 137). Moreover, the real-world structuring of problems does not accord with the theory. People are not inclined to the once-and-for-all calculation of the optimal strategy, but instead tend to simplify problems and adapt their information processing strategy to the specific task. Thirdly, research on context effects gives rise to serious doubts as to the predictive value of expected utility theory with regard to choice behaviour. 'The failure of EU theory as both a descriptive and predictive model stems from an inadequate recognition of various psychological principles of judgment and choice.' (Schoemaker 1982, 548). Neumann and Morgenstern had already anticipated the possibility of the notion of gambling generating flak (Neumann and Morgenstern 1944, 28). By 1979, Morgenstern was waiting for an better alternative. 'What the ultimate theory of utility will look like is hard to imagine even after so many works have been published on the basis of the von Neumann-Morgenstern theory.' (Morgenstern 1979, 182).

When we broaden our attention to take in game theory as discussed so far, we see that similar lines of thought have been pursued and similar conclusions drawn. What all of the variations on EUT take as given can, in game-theoretic terms, be stated as follows: (1) the set of possible choices, (2) the set of possible "states of nature", and (3) the set of payoffs, are all certain and known. While discussion often focuses on the status of probabilities and on choice criteria, important decision-making problems may very well relate to one of these three given sets. For example, a decision-making problem may be due to not knowing the alternative choices open to the individual. Differences in the lists of the possible strategies may be secondary consequences of entrepreneurial behaviour. Furthermore, as discussed in relation, for example, to Shackle and Lachmann, the absence of any surprise is imperative, and highly problematic, when a person is supposed to list all possible states of nature that may occur. Does an agent really know all the alternative market constellations? Moreover, although the final consequences and utilities related to today's options and the possible states of nature may extend far into the future, the agent is supposed to use backward induction, starting with these final consequences. Decision-makers obviously often do not, and cannot, adopt this procedure (Hey 1982, 137-138). Often, the "decision tree" just cannot effectively be generated because the number of alternative paths may be too large or it may prove to be burdensome to estimate the results of various alternatives (Williamson 1975, 22). A moderately complex decision-making problem may already extend beyond the boundary of available calculation capacity. Neither the proposed device of maximizing expected utility, nor the minimax-strategy, '...simplifies the computational problem that faces the decision maker.' (Simon 1957, 203).

6.6 Interdependent decision-making

So far, we have emphasized decision-making in the context of a set of alternative "states of nature"; a single-person game against an environment-generating processor. Uncertainty relates primarily to the spectrum of possible outcomes for each alternative strategy. Given the agent's ignorance of any probability distribution of outcomes, he may choose a strategy according to the insufficient reason criterion, the pessimism-optimism index criterion of Hurwicz, the minimax loss criterion, or the maximin criterion. An alternative open to the agent is the subjective probability approach which we have discussed, since it stresses the quantification of partial beliefs. This approach is relevant when the decision-maker considers an *a priori* probability distribution over the future states of nature to be meaningful. Thus, the decision-making process is reduced to choice under risk.

These techniques have the following element in common: the agent's preference for a specific strategy does not affect the choice of actions among others. Such theories on dmuu examine independent decision-making with interdependent results, but there is no substantive elaboration of the possibility of interdependent decision-making.

In many economic situations, atomistic perfect competition is dominated by another transaction facilitating mechanism. In the computer market, for example, fierce, if not cut-throat, competition reigns, but Apple mangers know that their strategy affects the choice of strategies made by their competitors. In theory, a decision-maker may try to learn from actions performed, inform after the decisions made, and try to anticipate the strategies likely to be chosen by others involved. He may weigh all this information, incorporate it in his own decision-making procedure, design the best course of behaviour given the constellation of the relevant situations, and act accordingly. It is assumed that each agent rationally selects a particular strategy that maximizes his payoffs in a given strategy space.

The incorporation of the decision-making procedures of others may not, however, be that simple. Of course, when the best solutions for two competitors harmonise there is a simple solution to their game. However, in situations in which defection is instrumentally rational, it is important for the agents to know what the inclinations of the other agents, within the set of behavioural rules of the game, are. Do they yield to the dominant, or "rational", strategy or do they forego a direct and certain increase in profit and try to build up a reputation for loyalty? Are contacts and contracts integral parts of the constellation? Likewise, one should already know whether defection is actually the individually rational strategy or not. In other words, an agent needs to know the payoff-profiles of the game. And how would we find a solution in a game featuring several stable Nash-equilibria but lacking any means of communication? We may conclude that the establishment of both the particular payoff-profiles and the set of available behavioural patterns, are of prime importance in any discussion of interdependent decision-making.

Although the importance of distinguishing situations according to both behavioural patterns and payoff constellations for establishing the result of a game has been recognized within game theory, there is nevertheless no integration of the two distinctions. In fact, they may be regarded as two dimensions in a 2x2 classification: we may distinguish between (1) a game-theory literature emphasizing the constellation of conceivable behavioural patterns, and (2) a literature with an emphasis on the constellation of the payoffs. Before the twofold distinctions, and their consequences for decision-making under uncertainty, can be integrated, we first need to discuss the two distinctions separately.

6.6.1 (Non-) Cooperative Games

With the publication of the pioneering paper by Nash, entitled *Non-cooperative games* (Nash 1951), and the enormously influential *Games and decisions* (Luce and Raiffa 1957), game theory became the theory of small number interdependent decision-making, with an emphasis on the set of conceivable behavioural patterns of the agents. These scientists take as the basic distinction that between cooperative and non-cooperative behaviour. In line with this approach, research has been carried out on (a) cooperative games, and (b) non-cooperative games. The terms cooperative and non-cooperative "contexts" are also used (Binmore 1990, 32, 43).

In cooperative games, agents may (1) engage in direct contact, this in order (2) to make "binding", i.e. enforceable, commitments, and thereby (3) synchronize strategies. The result may be a stable outcome with or without compensatory side payments or transferable utility (Luce and Raiffa 1957, 89, 152). Although, in formal terms, the cooperative game is a special case of non-cooperative games, it has its own impetus. Cooperative games concentrate on the likelihood of coalition forming, on opportunities for reaching enforceable agreements. While the presence of free communication is not seen as problematic but rather taken for granted, the design and creation of (optimal) rules of the game is an integral part of the study. Examples of cooperative games are constitution creation games (Schotter 1981, 28) and insurance games.

In contrast, the preplay communication which is a feature of cooperative games is considered to be impossible in non-cooperative games. Moreover, as a consequence no preplay agreement can be established. However, in contrast to the condition of parametric indirect interaction in independent decision-making, the non-cooperative environment may now be perceived as being pervaded by behavioural patterns, and not merely by certain values of parameters. The interaction is thus functionally indirect (Johansen 1981, 231-3). Examples of non-cooperative games are the traffic game, the telephone game (Schotter 1981, 8-10, 28-30), and atomistic market competition.

The basic solution concept of non-cooperative theory dates back to Cournot (1838), but was formalized by Nash, around 1950; it is usually called a (Cournot-) Nash-equilibrium (Nash 1951; Radner 1980; Kreps 1987, 167; Shubik 1987). The emphasis is on the (reacting) individual and his strategy. In a finite group, each agent adopts the strategy that is the instrumentally rational reaction to the strategies chosen by the other agents. In a specific game there may be a number of such n-tuples of optimal strategies, which are called "equilibrium points" (Harsanyi 1982, 217). Although an equilibrium point is self-enforcing, and is itself a necessary condition for self-enforcing agreements, further necessary stability conditions are required. One of these is 'trembling hand perfection', a term which refers to modifying the agent's estimation of the best response, by introducing the possibility of minor perturbations in the strategies of the agent's opponents (Kreps 1987, 173; Binmore 1990, 161). In a non-cooperative situation, it seems reasonable if the agent reflects upon the consequences of the imperfect realisation of chosen strategies by the other agents involved. This condition of robustness excludes saddle point Nash-equilibria, because they are unstable. But even under these conditions games may still present agents with more than one Nash-equilibrium, and thus create an equilibrium selection problem to be solved (Binmore 1990, 72).

6.6.2 (Non-) Coordination Games

By limiting their scope of discussion to the potential behavioural tendencies of the agents involved, scientists render their analyses one-dimensional in what is, at least, a two-dimensional world. It is more than a trivial affair to choose some payoff-constellation by assumption. What agents perceive or know about the payoffs resulting from a specific constellation of relations may be difficult to find out, but is crucially important for the interdependent choices under uncertainty. Assessments of future results may change overnight or over years. The preceding chapters on Austrian and Post-Keynesian Economics have made it clear that the agent's expectations about economic results are often far from self-evident, stable and unique.

The importance of the specific constellation of payoff-profiles is stressed by those writers who concentrate on the distinction between coordination and non-coordination games. Their approach gained momentum within game theory in the 1970s, thereby securing a niche which was consolidated during the 1980s. The theorist's attention is here concentrated on the form of the payoff matrix as well as the origin, operation, and persistence of, and changes in, economic and social institutions (Schotter and Schwödiauer 1980, 480; Field 1984). This line of research has been pursued by writers such as Schelling, Lewis, Aumann, Ullmann-Margalit, and Schotter. A consequence of this approach was that emphasis shifted to the difference between (I) Prisoner's Dilemma games, and (II) coordination games. The terms PD-situations and coordination "situations" (Ullmann-Margalit 1978, 9), and PD-problems and coordination "problems" (Vanberg 1986, 90-93; Schotter 1981, 22-23) are also found in the literature. Some of them also discuss a third group, called zero-sum games (Ullmann-Margalit 1978). For all combinations of strategies in such a zero-sum game the interests are in absolute opposition. Although, for example, Neumann and Morgenstern (1944) are very much concerned with such games, zero-sum games in fact represent exclusively perfect-redistribution situations, which seem to be rare in economic affairs. We will, therefore, concentrate on the other more realistic games. The following illustration may serve to bring the differences between a PD-game and a coordination game into relief.

We may define coordination games as situations in which interdependent decision-making by at least two agents occurs, whereby '...coincidence of interest predominates and in which there are two or more proper coordination equilibria.' (Lewis 1969, 24). A combination of strategies results in a proper coordination equilibrium if each agent involved prefers this payoff-profile to any other combination of strategies, given the other agent's strategies (Lewis 1969, 22). In the first place, we have pure coordination games, i.e. games featuring perfect coincidence of the agents' interests: the motives of these agents, who may suitably be called partners, are perfectly positively related (Schelling 1960, 89). The agents' payoffs are equal in every square. Matrix I in figure 2 offers an example using the entries between brackets. In such a game there are '...several mutually beneficial states, none of which is strictly preferred to the others.' (Ullmann-Margalit 1978, 10). Secondly, in certain other coordination games, preferences are locally parallel, although globally divergent: there is both opposition and coincidence of interests (Lewis 1969, 14). In matrix I of figure 2 the first row of entries shows us that b prefers strategy pair ß,ß, with payoff-profile 3,7, to strategy pair α,α, with payoff-profile 6,4. In contrast with agent b, agent a prefers α,α, to ß,ß, although both a and b prefer the diagonal entries to the cross-diagonal entries. The diagonal payoff-profiles are, in fact, proper coordination equilibria in the two examples, and are also Nash equilibria. Real life examples of coordination games would be: choosing whether to drive on the right or on the left; selecting a computer network communication system; selecting a location for retail trading; agreeing on a medium of exchange and a language for communication.

A situation poses a coordination problem '...if the payoff space of the game it defines is such that at any equilibrium point, not only does no player have any incentive to change his behaviour, given the behaviour of the other players, but no player wishes that any other player would change either.' (Schotter 1981, 22). At the heart of the problem of coordination lies the fundamental (non-probabilistic) uncertainty with regard to the choice among equally-preferred alternative actions (Ullmann-Margalit 1978, 80).

Table 3: Payoff-profiles and (non-) coordination games

matrix I: Coordination game (Schotter 1981, 23), or Schelling's (1960) mixed motive game:

		b: α	β
a:	α	6, 4 (4, 4)	0, 0
	β	0, 0	3, 7 (4, 4)

matrix II: Non-coordination game or PD-game (Rapoport 1987, 199; Schotter 1981, 24):

		b: α not confess	β confess
a:	α not confess	0.5, 0.5	5, 0
	β confess	0, 5	2, 2

Prisoner's Dilemma (PD) games focus on interdependent decision-making problems in which the best outcome for the agents considered collectively is not the best, but in fact second-best, for each agent individually (Field 1984, 696). We can speak of a PD-problem if the payoff space of the game it defines is such that at a Nash equilibrium point, no agent has any incentive to change his behaviour, but each would prefer the other agent(s) to have chosen another strategy (Schotter 1981, 23). When all agents defect, that is betray the others, the result will be collectively and individually suboptimal: each suspect is worse off than alternatively possible. However, there seems to be no individually rational alternative: individually aiming for the common best outcome may result in the individually worst outcome, namely when all of the others opt for their individual best outcome. Each agent has an impetus to defect, when he weighs the collective optimum of strategies.

Consider matrix II in figure 2, which is based upon an example presented by Rapoport (Rapoport 1987). Two persons, caught in possession of goods which have definitely been stolen, are suspected of burglary. If only one person confesses, plea-bargaining means that the first to confess will be dealt with leniently, to the detriment of the other suspect. If both suspects independently confess, they each face two-years' imprisonment. If neither confesses, each suspect receives six months, since the charge is receiving stolen goods, and the burglary charge is dropped. When '.>.' stands for '.. is preferred to ..', then the ranking adopted by a is the following: $(ß,α) > (α,α) > (ß,ß) > (α,ß)$. Thus, if b chooses strategy ß, and confesses, ß dominates α for a. Alternatively, if b chooses strategy α, i.e. b does not confess, again ß predominates over α in the eyes of a. Ergo, for a the dominant strategy is to confess. The ranking for b is $(α,ß) > (α,α) > (ß,ß) > (ß,α)$. Again strategy ß is preferable to α, but now for b, this is irrespectively of whether a chooses strategy α or ß. To conclude, in this PD-constellation strategy ß, i.e. 'to confess', is the dominating strategy for both a and b.

Ullmann-Margalit (1978) offers an excellent formal exposition of the four characteristics inherent in the PD-game. The case under consideration is that of at least two agents each of which is faced with the mutually exclusive choice between A and not-A:

> '(i) If, in any occurrence of the dilemma among them, most of them do A, the outcome is (and is known to them to be) mutually harmful; (ii) If, in any occurrence of the dilemma among them, most of them do non-A, the outcome is (and is known to them to be) mutually beneficial- or at any rate better than the outcome produced when most of them do A; (iii) Each of the persons involved obtains, at least in some occurrences of the dilemma among them, the highest payoffs in the situation when he himself does A while most of the others do non-A; (iv) If, in any occurrence of the dilemma among them, some do A, the outcome to the non-A doers is less beneficial than it would have been had everyone done non-A.'
>
> Source: Ullmann-Margalit 1978, 25-26.

PD and its n-person generalization, dubbed the "Tragedy of the Commons" (Hardin 1968; Rapoport 1987, 199, 204), is prevalent in situations in which it is impossible or inefficient to exclude others from 'consumption', e.g. as is the case where public goods are involved (Mueller 1979, 15-16). The following examples may serve to convey the importance of past and existent Prisoner's Dilemmas: An example of exhaustion of resources would be the competitive exploitation of oil reservoirs in America just after the turn of the twentieth century (Eggertsson 1990, 268-271) and overfishing of fishing-grounds such as the North Sea. Under the heading of '...fouling our own nest' (Hardin 1968, 1245), there are the harmful emissions into the atmosphere, soil, rivers and oceans, but also the 19th century pollution of inner cities. Generally-speaking, moral hazard problems and free rider behaviour can be modelled as PD-games. 'Ruin is the destination toward which all men rush, each pursuing his own best interest in a society that believes in the freedom of the commons.' (ibid., 1244).

The distinction which is most discussed in game-theory literature is the distinction between cooperative and non-cooperative games. Moreover, many game-theorists regard questions about the payoff constellation, as being external to game theory: the payoffs are simply considered as given (Harsanyi 1986, 95). Such writers concern themselves with finding complex mathematical means by which to arrive at equilibrium concepts. Notwithstanding the numerous merits of the results, in terms of clarification, the following important argument weighs against focusing too strongly on the set of conceivable behavioural patterns, and on contract-enforcing elements: 'In practice we lack a systematic[al; EW] method for testing the behavioral mood of our players' (Bianchi and Moulin 1991, 185), independently from testing the pay-offs. We cannot test them independently of actual strategic interactions, i.e. without introducing the particular payoff matrix. Therefore, at least we need to have a listing of alternative strategies, the resulting payoff-profiles, and the information at the agents's disposal.

A step towards enhancing our understanding of interdependent decision-making in an environment of uncertainty will certainly be the integration of the two clusters of writings, which have just been discussed. It is important to be precise in designing suitable classificatory schemes, because the subsequent analysing and classifying of observed behaviour is already difficult enough. Consider the case of a pedestrian who crosses a street and notices money lying on the sidewalk. If he does not stop to pick up all the money, is he after a larger sum of money, is he signalling behavioural inclination for future plays, is he contractually forbidden to stop, is he ill-informed, or is he irrational? The combination of the two distinctions may enhance cross-fertilisation and provide additional insights.

6.7 A game-theory matrix

In this section, the usefulness of elaborating on the combination of the two angles of incidence will be clarified by discussing the dominant matrix-outcomes for the resulting four types of games, both for single play and for supergames. The dimensions of cooperation and coordination may be integrated in a 2x2 classification. The matrix is depicted in figure 3, with some illustrations. For example, the dynamics of the "invisible hand" fit the non-cooperation-coordination game: by trying to advance their individual interests the agents in fact promote the public interest. The emergence of bank-crises may serve as an example. The publicly-financed common infrastructure features a cooperative Prisoner's Dilemma. However, when food extraction from the common land is greater than its carrying capacity, there may be a persistent non-cooperative Prisoner's Dilemma situation. The examples count for nothing more than mere illustrations to the use of game theory as a tool for cataloguing certain interactive situations.

To facilitate the comparison between Economic Game-Theory, the Austrian School of Economics and Post-Keynesian Economics we may pinpoint their respective accents in a Game-Theoretical setting. Austrian economists stress the heterogeneity of situations, and thus concentrate on the entries of a game. Because Post-Keynesians are inclined to stress the heterogeneity of decisions, they may be understood as concentrating on the strategies available. Another contrast can best be presented as follows: the viewpoints presented by adherents of the Austrian School of economics often involve a non-cooperation-coordination game. In contrast, Post-Keynesian economics may be linked to cooperative-PD games, which may sometimes even break down to non-cooperative PD-situations.

Table 4: An integration of two dimensions

	I. Prisoner's Dilemma/ non-coordination	II. coordination
a. non-cooperative	competition pollution Software piracy overfishing free riding	personal appointments use of money emergence of the week 'invisible hand'
b. cooperative	cartels co-makership negotiation games public infrastructure	networking standardization

What are the dominant equilibrium outcomes of these different games under instrumental rationality? Note, firstly, that the outcomes depend on interdependent decisions made by individuals pursuing individual objectives and, secondly, that the fringe games discussing zero-sum payoff-profiles in economic constellations are excluded from discussion. Given instrumental rationality in a game-theoretical context there is no place for evoking collective rationality or imputing some collective goal (March 1978, 148). Does this apply to all games, even supergames? We will first survey the outcomes of the different games.

Group (a,I): In PD-non-cooperative single play (n=1) games, the dominant matrix-outcome will be realized. This outcome will be the worst result collectively-speaking and individually the third-best outcome. The reason for this unpleasantly surprising outcome is the absence of collective rationality in an agent's individual calculations of self-interest. Furthermore, there are no economic means to commit individuals to the common good and thereby prevent free riding. 'It pays to "let George do it".' (Olson 1982, 18). Partial analysis will induce each agent to adopt a non-cooperative attitude irrespective of the attitude of the others involved, because no contract can be agreed upon which forces all parties to be loyal. In situations that do not permit enforceable agreements, game theorists may consider changing the circumstances into a PD-cooperative-type situation, for example, by introducing enforceable agreements. Alternatively, positive or negative selective incentives may be introduced to change the matrix in order to realise collective actions (Olson, 1965; Olson 1982, 21-35).

In the multi-play (n>1) PD-non-cooperative games, i.e. supergames, it seems fruitful to express behavioural (reaction-) rules via moves in the games. Other agents may learn from these behavioural (reaction)-rules by incorporating them in their own calculations about the optimal behavioural attitude. The outcomes will probably be better than the single play dominant result. However, this statement about expressing behavioural rules can only be fruitful under the following restrictions: firstly, those involved must presume that the game is still to be played a substantial, finite but unknown number of times: there is uncertainty as to the number of games. If the number of games were infinite, the problem of how to understand immortality would arise. However, if the agents think that the number of games will be a large finite albeit unknown number, is this not tantamount to an infinite number of games? The problem of immortality persists under this alternative supposition that agents believe positively in the probability that the game will be repeated in the next time period (Hargreaves Heap 1989, 46-50). Alternatively, if the residual length of the supergame is known, all of the agents will play the individually dominant strategy in the last game, for it is a one play game in itself. Consequently, instrumental rationality prevails in the last game, and there is therefore no need to carry over some magnanimous behavioural rule from the penultimate game. In consequence, backward induction will result in the dominance of the instrumentally dominant strategy in all games of the supergame. In the contrasting intermediate case of an unknown but bounded number of games, there is definitely a last game of the supergame. This case, however, contains a contradiction similar to the one inherent in the statement that there will be an exam someday this week but it will certainly take place unexpectedly. Secondly, agents can grasp expressed behavioural rules only under some common culture of signalling via interdependent decision-making. For example, if A expresses a tit-for-tat rule with a friendly start, B may deduce from A's behaviour that A is dumb, because A's play is not instrumentally rational in the first game. You need to know the available alternative behavioural rules and the particular signals associated with them. A common understanding of market signals is imperative if learning from market signals is to occur. We thus conclude that in the case of a PD-non-cooperative supergame, the scientist must face both the conceptual problems related to an unknown number of games, and the need for a common understanding of sufficiently discriminatory learning procedures.

Group (b,1): In PD-cooperative games, e.g. negotiation games, communication and enforceable contracts are feasible. In the single play (n=1) constellation, the agent may neutralize the otherwise destructive instrumental rationality by introducing the element of writing a contract with compensatory payments due after each violation of the deal. As Nash has made clear, a problem has already arisen as soon as the decision to enter the cooperative context has been taken. Why would you join a group to share the costs of providing or preserving public goods if you cannot be excluded from using these goods anyway? Thus, the first decision is whether to join in a cooperative game or not. A second point, which gives the lie to Aumann (1987, 21), is that any idea about the principle of PD relating only to situations in which people fail to cooperate is erroneous. Possible disputes over who gets what (compensatory) share may lead to negotiations which in turn produce a contract fostering a collectively sub-optimal combination of strategies. The relative bargaining powers are especially important in the case of PD-games, because none of the agents have stakes in the collective best outcome. Finally, since a problem arises concerning the uncertainty associated with the costs of writing, signing and enforcing a contract, contracts cannot supply perfect certainty on the results to be expected. Although the matrix payoffs may net of contracting and enforcement costs, Prisoner's Dilemmas always offer the agents the temptation of opportunistic behaviour, and thus leave the agents involved without knowledge of enforcement costs in each particular instance of recurring situations. Consequently, agents do not know the true payoff vectors (Field 1984, 701).

In PD-cooperative supergames (n>1), the repetition of games requires the presence of some stable jurisdiction. Otherwise, contracts would have to be written for each game separately, leaving us with a number of isolated plays. For agents interested primarily in their long-run average payoff *ex ante* knowledge of the enforcement costs is important. Although in rare situations compensatory payments may exactly compensate the shortfall in the expected average payoff, the distribution of outcomes may not be irrelevant in general, as we pointed out earlier. However, this knowledge can only exist *ex post*. Apart from this effect, the writing of a contract seems to have the same consequences for the outcomes of a single-play game as for a multiple play game. Further communication may distract attention from opportunistic behaviour and disputes about who gets what, thus ensuring the collective best outcome; nevertheless, in principle the game does not change. However, standards of behaviour, such as norms and fairness rules, may emerge and these may influence an agent's value system, thus changing the payoff matrix and thereby the choice of strategies. This would also be the result of changes in externally imposed rules and laws. In fact, such a game is encompassed in another game.

Group (a,II): When scientists concentrate on coordination problems in the absence of means of direct communication, the scientist may assume that one is dealing with a non-cooperative-coordination constellation. Given a single play (n=1), the problem finding an equilibrium is easily solved, provided that the dominant outcome is both individually as well as collectively the best outcome. In contrast, all strategy pairs will suffice if all payoff-profiles are individual best outcomes. However, when the agent is indifferent to several, but not all, payoff-profiles, finding an equilibrium proves to be a problematic task. If those involved do not subscribe to a common interpretation of the situation, they may evaluate the decision-making problem differently from at the outset, and/or they may evaluate the matrix entries differently. In that case, luck alone will result in the collective and individual best outcome. However, even if the agents share a common understanding of the problem situation, economic man cannot choose from among the remaining subset of alternatives in an instrumentally rational manner (see figure 4 for an illustration of this fact). The subset of collective best payoff-profiles is (4,4) resulting either from the equilibrium strategy pair (1,1) or from (2,2). However, given the problem of coordination under non-cooperation, agent A may choose strategy 1 while agent B chooses strategy 2, with the inferior outcome (0,0). Find a subset of coordination equilibria, is therefore no solution in itself. In fact, economic man needs social man to arrive at such an equilibrium. If the agents share a cultural background and subscribe to a common interpretation of their problem situation, they may prefer a salient equilibrium: 'One that stands out from the rest by uniqueness in some conspicuous respect.' (Lewis 1969, 35). Thus, the labelling of the alternative strategies becomes relevant, and this uniqueness of the salient outcome, e.g. meeting each other in the lobby of the Royal Opera instead of in one of the pubs nearby, must, in principle, be independent of the payoffs associated with this equilibrium.

Table 5: Uniqueness problem in (n=1) non-cooperative-coordination games

		B:	
		1	2
A:	1	4, 4	0, 0
	2	0, 0	4, 4

Recurrent (n>1) non-cooperative-coordination problem situations may be solved as in the single play game. Again the act of choosing from a subset of individual best outcomes proves to be problematic for economic man. The problem may be solved by recalling solutions to previous instances of the coordination problem in hand. In fact, because the agent cannot do exactly what he did before, the present game and its commonly-known precedent are effectively linked by means of analogies. Furthermore, it does not really matter whether the coordination in the previous game(s) was born of luck or preference for salience (Lewis 1969, 39).

Group (b,II): The case of single play cooperative-coordination situations is essentially equivalent to recurrent (n>1) cooperative-coordination situations (b, II). Agents can communicate directly and at negligible costs and at least one coordination equilibrium is available. If there is only one collectively and individually rational best equilibrium, the agents involved will rationally agree to choose those strategies that result in this unique payoff-profile. A game with a number of collective and individual best equilibria will result in a more or less arbitrary choice among these payoff-profiles by means of agreement. Communication promotes the formation of a common understanding of the situation and enables agreement on a cooperative-coordination equilibrium. However, such an agreement may be either explicit or tacit or even simply amount to an exchange of declarations of present intentions. The writing and enforcing of a contract is superfluous.

Let us summarize the results so far. In the n=1 PD-non-cooperative game the dominant outcome is neither individually nor collectively the best outcome. In recurrent situations it may result in collectively better outcomes, by means of learning. However, this is possible only where the agents share a common culture, which facilitates a common system of signalling via interdependent decision-making. The problem resembles that of signalling superior quality by some sort of discriminatory pricing policy. In PD-cooperative games the collective best outcome may certainly be arrived at, since its realization is fostered by the characteristic elements of communication, and the possibility of writing an effective contract, in these games.

In non-cooperative-coordination games agents may reach an equilibrium if the subset of equilibrium outcomes covers only one of or, paradoxically, all of the possible matrix entries. Instrumental rationality is otherwise insufficient for reaching a best outcome. This shortcoming of rationality will induce economic man to seek some social means of reaching a salient equilibrium. In cooperative-coordination situations agents can communicate directly, and thus arrive at an agreement regarding a collective best outcome. In contrast with cooperative situations of the PD-form, which depend on the element of writing contracts, this element is superfluous in coordination-type cooperative situations.

6.8 Problematic game theory?

Can the uncertainty regarding the outcomes of games characterized by interdependent decision-making be reduced by addressing the tenuousness of results due to the assumptions taken by game theorists? After all, game theory has been attacked for its faith in the element of presumed knowledge and in the rationality concept. We therefore intend to introduce a number of problems related to the predominant rationality concept, whereupon we discuss the problematic knowledge requirements.

The concept of instrumental rationality has not only been criticised for being thin, dealing merely with consistency (Elster 1983, 1), but also for demanding too much of the interpretative and calculative capacities of individuals (Simon 1955). In view of the destructive influence of instrumental rationality in PD-games, some theorists have concluded that the dominant solution demonstrates irrational or even perverse behaviour, for the result will be both collectively and individually suboptimal (Aumann 1987, 21). As most economic practices which can be captured in such games are thought of as being arenas of rational behaviour, instrumental rationality is rejected. Rejection on these grounds is, however, unjustified insofar as there is hardly anything more to be discussed save the isolated functioning of a meagre rationality concept. Instrumental rationality is more fruitfully questioned for the following reasons.

In the first place, during the 1950s, there seemed to be hardly any dispute regarding the problem of rational choice dealt with within the theory of games. However, by now we have all become aware of the leader of a small group of early dissidents, namely Herbert Simon, who advanced '...very nearly the judgment of a minority of two.' He stated that the approach taken in the theory of games is fundamentally wrongheaded: 'It is wrong, .. in seeking to erect a theory of human choice on the unrealistic assumptions of virtual omniscience and unlimited computational power.' (Simon 1957, 202). This group, whose roots are in the Carnegie-Mellon school, posited that while agents are rational, their rationality is bounded. From casual empiricism and psychological research on perception and cognition, e.g. learning theories, Simon learned that although people pursue satisfaction, they do not, in general, optimize (Simon 1955; Simon 1956). 'The capacity of the human mind for formulating and solving complex problems is very small compared with the size of the problems whose solution is required for objectively rational behaviour in the real world- or even for a reasonable approximation to such objective rationality.' (Simon 1957, 198). Nowadays, many economists at least respect the opinion that the instrumental rationality concept entails '...an extremely severe strain on information-gathering and computing abilities.' (Arrow 1987, 35).

Having rejected instrumental rationality, Simon substituted the principle of bounded or procedural rationality for it (Simon 1976). Agents know that they cannot perform all calculations in the time available. They, therefore "satisfice" and use decision-making heuristics such as rules of thumb. A problem involved is the counter-argument that Simon only adds extra constraints to the deployment of instrumental rationality; optimising man is bounded by memory capacity and computation time (Halpern 1986, 5, 7). Concise means thus aid the achievement of given ends (Hargreaves-Heap 1989, 212). Another argument in defence of a maximization theory refers to Occam's razor in order to recommend the use of the simplest assumptions available. However, the "strength" of assumptions must be considered before the succinctness of statement. Thus, these two edges of Occam's razor cut in different directions (Simon 1978, 8; Simon 1979, 495). Another difference hinted at by Simon is that theories of bounded rationality must be derived from laboratory and real-world empirical study of human decision-making (Simon 1987a, 18).

A second argument for rejecting instrumental rationality concerns the unjustified manner in which other influences which direct human activities, such as the evidence available to the agent, are simply ignored. The reduction of uncertainty, which itself is due to the entrance of multiple equilibria, especially necessitates the introduction of historical or social evidence, so as to enable an equilibrium to be singled out. Historical information might make us aware of former idiosyncrasies and peculiarities in decision-making. Institutions, that is formalized or non-formalized shared standards of behaviour, bring about predictability because structures constrain and enable actions (Hargreaves Heap 1989, 88-90)

Furthermore, the instrumental rationality concept might be supplemented with other rationality concepts so as to substantiate the psychological, philosophical and social connotations of rationality, as expressed in economic behaviour. Instrumental rationality cannot deal with group-related consumption effects. Positional goods, i.e. goods which derive their value from the fact that others do not possess them, reveal group-related effects. Other group-effects are bandwagon effects, i.e. demand is positively related to total expected consumption, and Veblen effects, i.e. positive price-demand relations within a certain range informative about social status, evince "conspicuous" consumption (ibid., 96-98). These effects '...make(s) the problem of multiple equilibria a real one for instrumental rationality.' (ibid., 103). However, when consumers buy famous brands of clothing, replace a year old tie with one more recently designed, and give leading brands as gifts, they are complying with cultural conventions, and this enables a decoding of choices into group-related preferences based on non-verbal communication, the creation of a personal identity and the fostering of self-esteem (ibid., 99-103, 163, 166). The equilibrium facilitating function of conventions and norms will be discussed later in this chapter.

The idea that human motivation is more sophisticated than instrumental rationality may be supported by the concepts of procedural rationality and expressive rationality. The former is about guidelines which govern "doing" and the latter is about what we are "doing" (ibid., 174). Procedural rationality is action which stems from the use of procedures or rules of thumb (ibid., 116). When in doubt, agents may rely on shared norms or conventions, a tactic which is socially conformist and may also imply an effort to '...fix meanings through appeals to numbers' (ibid., 157). Conventions create conditions, facilitating the formation of expectations in situations of uncertainty (ibid., 119). Not only inertia, but also vicious and virtuous circles driven by cumulative causation, as well as hysteresis effects and emergent properties may thus be discussed in relation to interdependent decision-making in a game-theoretic context. The second concept, i.e. expressive rationality, pertains to the propensity of the agent to evaluate the execution of certain activities rather than the accomplishment of certain goals (ibid., 173-4).

A final reason for rejecting the concept of instrumental rationality is that there are many highly desirable states that cannot be intentionally brought about by the exercise of intelligence, and evidently because such states are unintended, but hoped for, by-products (Elster 1983, 56). A person cannot pursue love, happiness, admiration, or an ability to sleep well any more than one can plan to be spontaneous, pious, courageous, or able to exercise will in the absence of will. Such conditions may be the unforeseen by-products of an action undertaken for some other end, or they may come about by fortunate accident, i.e. intended and hoped for outcomes which are not the product of intelligent deliberation (Elster 1983, ch.3).

Advanced discussions on the adequate rationality concept are to be found in numerous writings. It hardly makes sense for us to survey the game-theory literature on this discussion here, partly because only a handful of economists writings about game theory have seriously tried to work out its implications, and partly because others have reviewed this part of the literature lucidly and satisfactorily (e.g. Hargreaves Heap 1989; Elster 1983; and March 1978). For example, regarding the problem inherent in the existence of numerous and extremely disparate equilibrium points, the problem of uncertainty has refused to disappear despite further research on non-cooperative games (Harsanyi 1986, 100, 102). 'The main product of the very elegant apparatus of game theory has been to demonstrate quite clearly that it is virtually impossible to define an unambiguous criterion of rationality for this class of situations (or, what amounts to the same thing, a definitive definition of the "solution" of a game).' (Simon 1979, 505). We will return to several rationality-related elements in our discussion on conventions and knowledge concepts.

6.9 What price knowledge?

As soon as scientists start to discuss the assumption of knowledge, they open another Pandora's box full of problems which are to some extent related to those which have been discussed above. With regard to knowledge, the scientist must first of all beware of simply equating knowledge with information, because there are numerous intricacies involved. It is possible to distinguish between private information, (in-)complete information, (im-)perfect information, differential or asymmetric information, and common information (Smith, McCabe and Rassenti 1991, 203-204; Harsanyi 1986, 90). Furthermore, the categories of (common) information must be distinguished from (common) knowledge. Evidently, the category of knowledge also differs from common knowledge, beliefs and expectations, and some analysts even discuss explicit knowledge separately, while many scientists have heard of tacit knowledge. Moreover, common knowledge is not the same as common expectations. Finally, this listing will surely be far from exhaustive, and several concepts are defined or used differently by different persons. Before switching the focus to the informational element in relation to uncertainty in interdependent decision-making, let us first try to circumscribe some of these concepts and related problems. This approach will bring us straight to the former topic, and provide background knowledge on the way.

The term private information stands for the idea that the only information exclusively available to each agent concerns his own message-contingent utility functions. We may speak of a game featuring incomplete information if, at pre-play stage, at least some of the agents lack at least some information about the following three parameters defining the game: (a) the agents' utility (payoff) functions; (b) the rules of the game, i.e. the identity of the agents, the strategies available to each agent, and the outcome generation function (Binmore 1990, 122; Harsanyi 1982, 123): and (c) the amount of information others possess about (a) and (b). If complete information is assumed, as it frequently is, all agents are deemed to possess full pre-play information about (a), (b), and (c). Game theorists have indeed long since been concentrating on complete knowledge models. One reason may be that incomplete knowledge games appear to give rise to an inconvenient '...infinite regress in reciprocal expectations on the part of the player.' (Harsanyi 1982, 119).

The concept of perfect information supplements the concept of complete information with the assumption that all agents possess all of the relevant information about the actions which have already been taken in the game, i.e. they are cognizant with the history of the game. Under imperfect information all of the agents are aware of the nature of the game, i.e. the three parameters just mentioned, but at least some of the agents have less than full information about previous moves, which have been decided either by the agents or by chance. These two concepts are usually introduced when there are no simultaneous moves (Luce and Raiffa 1957, 68; Harsanyi 1982, 119n2, 214-215; Harsanyi 1986, 90). In a game featuring asymmetric information the agents have dissimilar information sets. The scientist may use the term common information, when in addition to possessing complete information the agents are collectively informed that all agents have complete information. For example, the instructions and payoff tables are read aloud and are audible for the whole group of agents (Smith, McCabe, Rassenti 1991, 203).

6.9.1 Common knowledge

The use of the term common information introduces a field of research which took off during the 1970s following the publication of Lewis's work on common knowledge and conventions. Game theory had previously merely discussed consequences of differences in perfectness of complete or perfect information. It turned out that the complete information assumption in itself is both rather demanding and insufficiently elaborated. Luce and Raiffa considered the complete information assumption to be '...a serious idealization which only rarely is met in actual situations.' (Luce and Raiffa 1957, 49). Moreover, this idealization is, in any case, deficient: not only must each agent be aware of x, but all agents must also be aware that all agents are aware of x, must all be aware that all are aware that all are aware of x, and so on ad infinitum (Aumann 1987, 31). For example, if I do not know that you also appraise a situation as a PD-non-cooperative game, I cannot readily incorporate your decision-making evaluations into my own evaluations. Incorporating such an element into economics is more than writing a mere appendix, as became apparent with New Classical Economics. 'The common knowledge assumption underlies all of game theory and much of economic theory.' (Aumann 1987, 31).

Let us now, for the following four reasons, introduce the logical propositional language, which we intend to refer to subsequently. We may use this language (1) to describe some of the common threads in insights into human knowledge and the agent's use of it as found in such fields as philosophy, economics, and linguistics; (2) to clarify the relations between such concepts as (common) knowledge, beliefs and expectations; (3) to distil a practical, and concise method from a range of approaches in order to define (common) knowledge (Halpern 1986, 9); and, (4) to aid the subsequent discussion of conventions and norms.

Let δ be a formula within the logical propositional language T. For example δ may stand for the fact that 'Lex invests in project a.' Agent i who knows that δ holds, is denoted as $K_i\delta$. Alternatively, agent i who believes that δ holds, is denoted as $B_i\delta$. In more general terms, a formula δ is known to agent i, $K_i\delta$, only if δ is true in all worlds deemed possible by i, given his knowledge in his present situation. 'Not true' is denoted as $\neg$.

The following complete axiom system (Halpern 1986, 4-5), characterizes the notion of knowledge comprehensively:

A1: All instances of propositional tautologies.
A2: $K_i\delta$ & $K_i(\delta\rightarrow\tau) \rightarrow K_i\tau$
A3: $K_i\delta \rightarrow \delta$
A4: $K_i\delta \rightarrow K_iK_i\delta$
A5: $\neg K_i\delta \rightarrow K_i\neg K_i\delta$
R1: If δ and if $\delta\rightarrow\tau$ then agent i may conclude τ. (modus ponens)
R2: If δ then $K_i\delta$

A1 and R1 are well-known elements from propositional logic. A2 states that agents know all of the logical consequences of their knowledge. A3 states that an agent knows only things that are true, while R2 states that agents know all valid formulas. The axioms of introspection are A4 and A5: an agent can examine his knowledge base and will then be aware both of what he knows and of what he does not know.

Scientists should distinguish between explicit knowledge and implicit knowledge. The much-criticised logical omniscience implied by this axiom system for knowledge is less problematic when the characterized notion of knowledge is understood as implicit knowledge, as opposed to when it is understood as explicit knowledge. Implicit knowledge satisfies the given knowledge axioms (Halpern 1986, 8). The explicit knowledge in the possession of agent i consists of that part of his implicit knowledge which agent i is aware of. In a closed system, a cooperative group of agents can only learn the facts which are already available among them as (implicit) knowledge (Meyer 1990, 36).

Agent i believes that δ holds, if it is not the case that he knows that not-δ is true, given his knowledge in his present situation:

$$B_i \delta = \neg K_i \neg \delta$$

In other words, it is not true that agent i knows that 'Lex will not invest in project a.' Lex may hold false beliefs, but he cannot have false knowledge (Halpern 1986, 5; Da Costa Werlang 1987).

Eδ stands for complete knowledge. In the case of Eδ states is stated that every agent knows that δ holds, i.e. that everybody knows that 'Lex invests in project a.' In the case of many (say m) agents, then:

$$E\delta = K_1 \delta \ \& \ K_2 \delta \ \& \ K_3 \delta \ \& \ .. \ \& \ K_m \delta.$$

An example of complete knowledge is found where it is assumed that '...each player ... is fully aware of the rules of the game and the utility functions of each of the players.' (Luce and Raiffa 1957 49). Complete knowledge has also been called mutual knowledge (Brandenburger 1992, 89).

Alternatively, Cδ states that it is common knowledge that δ holds. When the fact that δ holds is common knowledge, all agents are aware that δ holds, and all agents know that all agents know that δ holds, and so on ad infinitum. We may express common knowledge in formal terms as:

$$C\delta = E\delta \ \& \ EE\delta \ \& \ EEE\delta \ \& \ EEEE\delta \ \& \ ... \ \text{(Mutsaers 1992, 22;}$$
$$\text{Meyer 1990, 29)}$$

This "formula" only contains some intuitive content: although the spiral of conjectures and counter-conjectures is in principle without an end, the agent cannot reasonably be supposed to engage in infinite conjectures (Meyer 1990, 29). In order to elucidate the content of the common knowledge concept our best course may be to seek illustration outside economics. The case of the passive telephone answering machines makes it clear that common knowledge problems can occur in the most innocuous cooperative-coordination games. If persons A and B wish to confirm a 1 million dollar transaction they may call each other only to find an answering machine running. Suppose that in this particular cooperative-coordination game, the information to be exchanged is the agreement by both A and B on the deal.

If A rings B and records his agreement with the deal on B's tape-recorder, there is no guarantee of a successful information transfer. On the one hand, A does not know whether B will soon be aware of that the message has been put through. This may be because B has a malfunctioning telephone, is unwilling or unable to listen to the taped messages, or may not understand, or be dissatisfied with, the message. On the other hand, B has no way of knowing whether A will be confident that B has received the message.

Furthermore, B will want to inform A both of receiving the message and of his reciprocal approval, and will thus phone A, and record his message on A's tape-recorder. The shoe is on the other foot, and it is now B who does not know whether A will both receive and perfectly understand this message. A understands that B is not necessarily aware that A has received both the confirmation of the receipt of the message which was originally conveyed by A to B. A is also aware that the original information from B may also have gone astray. Therefore, A calls B again and puts a message on B's taperecorder confirming that he (A) has received the message from B confirming the initial message from A to B, B's approval on the deal, and informing B that A has received B's approval. This telephone-bill nightmare and time consuming activity, may, in principle, continue ad infinitum. We may at least conclude that the answering machine is no substitute for direct contact. This calling back and forth can, in any run of protocols, in principle, and over and above reactions and bargaining arguments, never result in mutual agreement. In general it may be concluded that we cannot transmit information without there being some essential underlying common knowledge: common knowledge of the logic of the market system to facilitate the signalling of information via prices; common knowledge of a language for the communication of information; and common knowledge of the model to enable the simulation of a game.

9.9.2 Common Information or Common Knowledge?

The relationships between common information, common expectations and common knowledge are problematic. Common information is the shared set of information; provided that in addition to possessing complete information, the agents are collectively informed that all agents have complete information. The common expectations concept is different from the concept of common knowledge, although the two are widely interpreted as being equivalent (Smith, McCabe, and Rassenti 1991, 203-204). The concept of common beliefs provides a key to elucidating the difference.

Let Sδ stand for complete beliefs. Sδ implies that every agent believes that δ holds, i.e. that it is not the case that every agent is aware of the fact that 'Lex will not invest in project a.' Given a number of agents, designated as m:

$$S\delta = \neg K_1 \neg \delta \ \& \ \neg K_2 \neg \delta \ \& \ \neg K_3 \neg \delta \ \& \ ... \ \& \ \neg K_m \neg \delta.$$

Let Rδ stand for it is common belief that δ holds. When the conviction that δ holds is common belief, all agents belief that this is the case, and all agents believe that all agents believe that δ holds, and so on, ad infinitum. A formal expression of common belief would be:

$$R\delta = S\delta \ \& \ SS\delta \ \& \ SSS\delta \ \& \ SSSS\delta \ \& \ ...$$

Most game theorists assume that the situation of common knowledge is associated with common expectations (ibid., 203-4, 214). However, expectations may be better discussed as being the content of a set of common beliefs, rather than as being directly related to common knowledge. With the previously-discussed multiple equilibria problems in mind, we feel justified in stating that is not true that agent i knows that not-δ is true, but we can hardly feel secure in asserting that agent i knows that δ is true. It therefore follows that expectations are in principle only indirectly dependent upon common knowledge.

In the experimental context, the scientist cannot guarantee common knowledge in principle. Laboratory tests can only establish that common information may, or may not, be shared by the experimental subjects before the experiments starts. The state of knowledge, of expectations, and of the reduction of uncertainty, depends to a large extent upon individual information-processing parameters. 'Behavioral or strategic uncertainty is not eliminated by common information.' (ibid., 216). It is tempered by experience, because agents may learn what to expect from other subjects (Smith 1991, 886-887). A total of 78 laboratory stock market experiments featuring common information on dividend value yielded no evidence which could contradict the observation that common information is not sufficient to induce common expectations (Smith, McCabe, and Rassenti 1991, 214-218). If a share is ultimately to sell at dividend value, then it must do so in all trading periods. In point of fact, that sustainable capital gains cannot be realized by selling below, or buying above, dividend value agents learn first of all from experience. When subjects are inexperienced, i.e. at the beginning of a series of trading periods, '...the data under certain and uncertain dividend structures are indistinguishable from each other.' (ibid., 216). The results of the stock market experiments confirm the results of other research which have shown that participants in an independent decision-making game fail to apply backward induction logic to common expectations. This failure is neither a failure of rationality nor of logic, but rather a consequence of a lack of expectations: at the outset, agents do not have concrete expectations about the strategies which other agents are likely to adopt. Futures markets offer an institutional tool which does not provide knowledge of the "future" so much as '... provide data that enables the formation of common expectations.' (ibid., 218). This is discussed in other terms by reference to Lachmann in our chapter on the Austrian School of economics.

It is often stated that common knowledge refers to the fact that agents know that their fellow agents know that they know that their fellow agents know that.. etc. (viz: Fudenberg and Tirole 1991, 541). Such approaches are erroneous, or at least incomplete. They refer to only one of many layers just referred to, that is the case of EEEE...Eδ. In fact, there is a requirement that the model itself must be assumed to be common knowledge, otherwise the model is insufficiently specified, and the analysis is consequently rendered incoherent. For example, all agents must be aware that they are involved in a single play PD-non-cooperative game, characterized by incomplete information. Moreover, all agents must be aware that all of their fellow agents are familiar with this constellation; and so on, ad infinitum. In more general terms, the model itself must be assumed to be common knowledge among the agents acting in all of the models under discussion.

While the philosopher D.K. Lewis was the first to discuss this notion of common knowledge, it was R.J. Aumann who introduced the notion into economics. The concept of common knowledge has since become '...a persistent theme in almost every discipline that has considered knowledge at all.' (Halpern 1986, 9). For example, in order to derive their conclusions, New Classical Economics must assume the predictions of the future to be common knowledge. The future is assumed to be a function of interdependent individual actions, which depend on individual predictions, which are themselves the outcomes of the model and its information input. However, if in interdependent decision-making situations agents arrive at dissimilar predictions, as a consequence of assuming different models to be valid, no individual prediction may be borne out. Thus, not only is the basic knowledge of these predictions important, but also that (almost) all agents are aware of these predictions, that all agents know that all agents are aware of these predictions, and so on, ad infinitum.

We have already discussed the fact that instrumental rationality is insufficiently discriminative. As a consequence of that theoretical consideration in addition to real life social influences, such as bandwagon effects, multiple equilibrium problems will result. Moreover, the requirements of common knowledge add another problem which is fundamental. The rules of the game and the rationality concept must be assumed to be common knowledge. The problem of explaining how common knowledge arises is usually side-stepped (viz: Brandenburger and Dekel 1989, 61). But how far-fetched are such assumptions? 'Common knowledge assumptions are a way of telling the questioner to go away.' (Hahn 1989b, 122). Will pre-play contacts alleviate this bothersome requirement? Certainly not in the case of non-cooperative games, since preplay contacts as means of exchanging knowledge are assumed to be impossible in such games. Common knowledge is also unattainable in cooperative games when message delivery time or the languages used may cause communication problems. But even the cooperative-coordination games contain important common knowledge-assumptions, because '...agreement implies common knowledge.' (Halpern 1986, 11). If decision-makers presume dissimilar rules of the game and/or dissimilar rationality concepts, or if they presume that others presume different rules of the game and/or different rationality concepts, etcetera, then the model is insufficiently specified, which renders the analysis incoherent. In this respect (instrumental) rationality is a social phenomenon (Arrow 1987, 33).

Having established the importance of common knowledge, we would like to stress that a momentous, though subtle, variation in viewpoints exists among authors who emphasize that agents have the possibility of agreeing to disagree, for example, on what they assume as their *a priori* knowledge of the evaluation the alternative strategies, i.e. the knowledge "priors". The relevance of this argument is to be found in the requirement of some level of agreement among the agents: it surely makes a difference whether agents are obliged to agree *a priori* on the beliefs upon which the interaction will be based. Aumann has stated that, in order to facilitate Bayesian updating in interdependent decision-making, there is virtually no choice open to us but to assume that all *a priori* subjective probability distributions on the possible states of the world, or payoff-profiles, are common knowledge. In fact, there should be common knowledge of common priors (Aumann 1976, 1236-9; Binmore 1990, 134). Binmore, however, modelled agent's thinking and learning by adopting a '...constructive rather than axiomatic view of rationality.' (Bianchi and Moulin 1991, 192-193). He maintains that our priors must be common knowledge, but our beliefs about the states of the world need not necessary be identical, that is, they are not necessarily common priors. Experimentation can enable us to arrive at Bayesian correct posteriors, and subjective correlated equilibria. Thus, although our posterior, or retrospective, beliefs about our fellow agents' choice of strategy are common knowledge, we may nevertheless entertain dissimilar prior beliefs (Binmore 1990, 134-137). Although this understanding of the role of knowledge in interactions is still highly abstract, it would make game-theory somewhat more realistic.

We may close this paragraph by stating that this discussion on the assumptions of knowledge and rationality suffices to illustrate the '...overload of knowledge and information which is required that agents possess in order to make a rational decision' (Bianchi and Moulin 1991, 191). Placing the stress on interdependent decision-making hardly helps us to arrive at more realistic descriptions of economic practices. 'The failure to optimize appears to be cognitive (i.e., related to the way problems are structured and what decision strategies are used) rather than motivational (i.e., the amount of mental effort expended).' (Schoemaker 1982, 554). The troublesome relation between common knowledge and common information strengthens the need '...to distinguish between the real world and the actor's perception of it and reasoning about it.' (Simon 1987, 27). Although Simon is convinced that uncertainty only exists in the eye and mind of the beholder and not in the outside world, he realizes that there is no justification for ignoring it: 'If economics is to deal with uncertainty, it will have to understand how human beings in fact behave in the face of uncertainty.' (Simon 1976, 82). Introducing social man into the picture may help to arrive at more realistic descriptions of people's behaviour.

In different categories of games different social-economic practices may be apparent, practices used by agents to solve a number of game-theoretical problems. In the multiple outcome case which is found in non-cooperative-coordination games, preferences are locally parallel, although globally divergent. Even when we permit contracting and side payments in coordination games it is still unclear which outcome will result. Why should instrumentally rational agents prefer an equitable division of the proceeds to an unequal division in their own advantage? Scientists need to study the role of institutions in order to solve the problem. For example, in coordination games one may find a pacifying external procedure, and as soon as such a procedure has become a widely-accepted, i.e. standardized, mode of behaviour, it has in fact become a convention. In situations presenting the non-cooperative-Prisoners' Dilemma we may call such a standardized mode of behaviour a norm. Standardized behaviour induced and bounded by consistent rules may help to facilitate improvements in cooperative-coordination situations.

6.10 Conventions and norms

In the case of incidental non-cooperative-coordination situations a solution is possible if salient outcomes or precedents are available. In the case of cooperative-coordination problems solutions depend upon agreement. Agreement, salience or precedent, can solve a coordination problem by creating a complex of mutual expectations (Lewis 1969, 52, 57). That the atypical, salient, strategy will attract attention is something that Schelling discussed early on (Schelling 1960). An explicit agreement is not a necessary condition for the growth of a convention. Furthermore, where conventions are operative, no explicit cooperation is needed in order to solve a coordination problem in recurrent situations of interdependent decision-making (Lewis 1969, 42). In such repetitive situations conventions may flourish.

Lewis's analysis of convention was to some extent a breakthrough in that the account of the concept was couched in terms of tacit rather than explicit agreement (Ullmann-Margalit 1978, 75-6). However, he still needed the common knowledge concept to clarify his own idea of a convention. The defining conditions for the existence of a convention are: (1) regularity in behaviour, (2) a system of mutual expectations, (3) a system of preferences, and (4) state of affairs in which conditions 1,2, and 3 are common knowledge (ibid., 58). He provides us with the following definition of a convention:

'A regularity R in the behaviour of members of a population P when they are agents in a recurrent situation S is a *convention* if and only if it is true that, and it is common knowledge in P that, in almost any instance S among members of P:

(1) - almost everyone conforms to R;

(2) - almost everyone expects almost everyone else to conform to R;

(3) - almost everyone has approximately the same preferences regarding all possible combinations of actions;

(4) - almost everyone prefers that any more conform to R, on the condition that almost everyone conforms to R;

(5) - almost everyone would prefer that any more conform to R', on the condition that almost everyone conforms to R',

where R' is a possible regularity in the behaviour of members of P in S, such that almost no one in almost any instance of S among the members of P could conform both to R' and R.'

Source: Lewis 1969, 78.

Conventions confirm themselves because nobody is motivated to exhibit anomalous behaviour. Once a convention has become established from an in principle arbitrary outcome, it will be upheld until the situation is perceived as having changed. As a consequence, conventions will govern the pattern of mutual expectations.

All conventions are arbitrary, in the sense that an alternative regularity in behaviour may exists which could have been our convention instead. In this context, we may refer to Austrian economists, who, as stated before, stress non-cooperative-coordination situations: a regularity in behaviour is the result of human actions but not of human design (Schotter 1983, 684). Conventions are impossible to predict, because: 'There is no such thing as the only possible convention.' (Lewis 1969, 70). Where there is no alternative regularity R' possible in behaviour, R is not a convention but the strategic best outcome. A social contract is therefore not necessarily a convention. The maxim which inspires agents to choose the salient outcome is itself a convention.

We need to draw a distinction between conventions and norms. Conventions are hypothetical imperatives, rather than iron rules (Ullmann-Margalit 1978, 4). The norm is the suitable counterpart for conventions in Prisoners' Dilemma situations. Where a convention is being observed, agents have no reason to for ignoring it. Under a (social) norm, however, individual agents may be tempted to adapt their behaviour in an instrumentally rational manner. If the norm is to be observed, there must be countervailing moral pressure which obliges agents to resist the temptation. A norm is a pattern of obligations between members of a group, and as such is a collectivist concept. Social norms can be identified in the contexts of money transactions, exchange of information, and in making commitments and promises (Hartogh 1985, 7).

The initial motive of the agents to adhere to such a norm must be the possible consequences, but in order to sustain the norm, agents must develop a deontological disposition: they must wish to react in the right manner to behaviour displayed by fellow agents (Ullmann-Margalit 1978, 12). A similar state of affairs may emerge where a convention is in force. Agents learn that norms and conventions are effective.

Our 2x2 game-theoretic matrix of (non-) cooperative and (non-) coordination games in section seven of this chapter, enables us to relate norms to cooperative-coordination games. Since contingent contracting is very rare, there is a need for more than merely two communicative parties and an enforceable contract. Norms are needed to sustain the relationship in a "proper" manner. Gauthier (1986) elaborates this point by developing a theory of morality based upon rationality. It is not self-interest, but rather reason which prevails; not instrumental rationality, but rather procedural rationality inspires agents to accept the moral principle of their collective interests (Gauthier 1986; Pellikaan 1988, 291-294). For example, norms help the market to evolve gradually; they enable competitors to concentrate on ordinary business; and, in several markets, may well protect the parties involved from the injurious effects of cut-throat competition.

When we are discussing the predominant institutions directing economic behaviour in non-cooperative Prisoners' Dilemma games, we may thus conclude that the enforceable external rules are the crucial ones. For example, financial markets are stable as long as the rules of the game can be enforced.

6.11 Conclusions

In this chapter we have made an effort to chart the role and influence of uncertainty in economic game theories. Perhaps the most important structural contrast with the other chapters of this thesis is the absence of a core of economic thought, as opposed to the tool itself. The history of economic game theory is still too short to warrant its writing. This lack of an integral historical account, combined with the fact that the most impressive output has been of recent origin, has forced us to break new grounds in structuring the material.

In the context of game theory, uncertainty first and foremost implies an awareness that there are a number of possible outcomes for each of a number of alternative strategies. The bottom line is that participants in a social exchange economy experience difficulty in securing an optimum result while no one agent controls all of the variables which influence his own result. We manage to relate uncertainty to both interdependent outcomes, interdependent decision-making and the resulting conventions and norms.

In contrast to especially mainstream economics as presented in chapters two and three, game theory stresses strategic, instead of parametric, uncertainty. However, uncertainty proved to be fundamentally different in games against nature as opposed to games featuring interdependent decision-making. In the former group of games, uncertainty relates to the set of possible outcomes. In such a situation independent decision-making in the context of a finite set of alternative states of nature leaves us with a choice among four different, but all unsatisfactory, criteria with which to resolve the problem of decision-making. The domain covering situations which occupy an intermediate position between complete ignorance and complete knowledge with regard to the probability distribution in terms of states of nature has been filled by the subjective probability approach. Subjective probabilities quantify our partial beliefs, but the related Bayesian updating restricts our attention to previously listed alternatives. Moreover, in such publications the element of interdependencies in decision-making is still lacking.

In the case of interdependent decision-making, we need to have knowledge of structural elements such as the payoff constellation and the possibility of writing and enforcing a contract. Interactions between agents may be depicted in a 2x2 diagram, representing the two independent dimensions (non-) cooperation and (non-) coordination. The various fields in such a diagram imply dissimilar problems as to the choice of a strategy.

Game theory in fact excludes such significant phenomena as surprises and structural changes from consideration. Their crucial importance to economic endeavours and thus to economics, has been strongly argued in the chapters on Austrian and Post-Keynesian economics. Nevertheless, disregarding these considerations enabled us to relate Austrian and Keynesian positions to non-cooperative coordination games and (non-) and/or cooperative Prisoners' Dilemma games respectively.

Game-theory models which describe interdependent decision-making seem to be rather vulnerable to criticism as a result of the specific assumptions which are made with regard to rationality and knowledge. We have endeavoured to list the knowledge-related concepts involved. More important, however, is the fact that we must face the importance of a common knowledge assumption: the agents' interdependency at the level of decision-making renders the very idea of calculating a best outcome a futile enterprise. Instrumental rationality cannot be deployed. Although institutions seem to enable agents to organize their behaviour along rational lines, scientists must nevertheless realise that the character of such institutions makes exact prediction highly problematic.

7: CONCLUSIONS

'We shall not cease from exploration
And the end of all our exploring
Will be to arrive where we started
And know the place for the first time.'
                                    (Eliot 1943 1983, 86, 152)

7.1 Introduction

In this thesis we have shown that economists who ignore uncertainty or relegate it to a peripheral role in the analysis are shortsighted. The attempts to introduce uncertainty into economics which have passed the review warn against unjustified self-confidence with regard to the economist's ability to analyse and predict all economic behaviour. An economist will inevitably have to discuss the agent's uncertainty sooner or later. We have also demonstrated the economic significance of both entrepreneurial behaviour and rule-following behaviour and discussed some of the consequences for economics.

The arguments led us to favour contingency approaches towards the agent's uncertainty as presented by Austrian, Post-Keynesian and some Game-Theory economists, because, at the expense of theoretical neatness, an appreciation of contingency generally enhances the realism of theories. In fact, we favour the use of a variety of approaches, because fundamentally different theories may suit different problems, while, in a given situation, deploying alternative concepts may provide additional insights.

In this closing chapter we shall first construct a taxonomy, in order to condense the different positions discussed in this research. Such a categorisation may also advance a more thoughtful use of the concept of uncertainty. Next, the argument which is the import of the thesis will be summarised and final conclusions will be drawn.

7.2 A taxonomy of uncertainty

This account of how uncertainty has been introduced into economics has mainly been presented in the form of historical overviews. However, in order to avoid duplication as far as possible, and in order to bring the comparison of the different positions adopted into relief, we propose to abandon our historical approach at this juncture.

In discussing the conclusions to be presented, we shall use the following abbreviations for brevity's sake: **MIP**, for the Mainstream opinions in the Interwar Period as discussed in chapter two; **PEU**, for the Postwar Economics of Uncertainty discussed in chapter three. PEU here omits discussion of New Classical Economics, because the latter would add next to nothing to this overview of positions on uncertainty; **ASE**, for the Austrian School of Economics, as discussed in chapter four; **PKE**, for Post-Keynesian Economics, as discussed in chapter five, and finally **EGT**, for what has been discussed in chapter six under the heading of Economic Game Theory. Each list will, however, start with the position adopted by **Knight**.

The various entries have been selected for their usefulness in elucidating the main ideas of the various schools of thought. The distinct accents placed by different authors within the same school of thought cause especial problems in the marshalling of the most crucial concepts. Therefore, we would ask the reader to regard our taxonomy as schematic rather than definitive.

Firstly:What do economists try to express when they mention the concept of uncertainty?

Knight: Uncertainty relates to the fact that certain outcomes are unmeasurable, since situations are incomparable. Furthermore, uncertainty refers to the need to act on the impulse of opinion which results from the lack of certain knowledge.

MIP: For mainstream economists in the interwar period uncertainty relates to the lack of a sufficiently detailed theory to explain and account for all contingencies. Frequency dispersions around an expectation are used to depict the workings of decision-making.

PEU: Uncertainty is related to human preferences for certain situations. It stands on a continuum with perfect certainty at one extreme and perfect ignorance on the other.

ASE: The economists in the Austrian tradition hold that uncertainty relates to the open-ended context of the man-made market economy and refers to human endeavours to bridge the gap between the future as it is envisaged and as it subsequently becomes reality.

PKE: According to Post-Keynesian economists uncertainty relates to the impossibility of knowing the future. It refers to the, subjectively-held, ranges of opinions on the consequences of present actions.

EGT: Economists who try to apply game theory relate uncertainty to the interdependency between discrete economic actors and confine it to the different constellations in which actions take place.

Secondly:In our attempt to understand what various economists are trying to express when they use a concept of uncertainty, the question arises as to the origin of uncertainty. What makes economists speak of uncertainty?

Knight: The origin of uncertainty is to be located in the tension between theory and the complex but stable reality.

MIP: Uncertainty is caused by the lack of perfect anticipation of all relevant factors determining the future. Uncertainty is endogenous and external, for it is an element of the decision-making situation and an attribute of the environment.

PEU: Uncertainty springs from the fact that we do not know which description of the world is the true one. Uncertainty is both exogenous and external.

ASE: Austrians regard our obliviousness to potentially advantageous opportunities as the main source of uncertainty. Uncertainty is exogenous and internal.

PKE: For Post-Keynesians, uncertainty is rooted in the human capacity for imagining, inventing and learning. It may present itself in the simultaneous allegiance to holding different views of future developments, but also in the volatility of opinions. Uncertainty is endogenous and internal.

EGT: According to economic game theorists, uncertainty is rooted in the fact that nobody controls all of variables which influence the result following any decision. Uncertainty is endogenous and external.

Thirdly: Do the various groups of economists regard uncertainty as essentially belonging to the province of ontology, i.e. the objects of economic research, or of epistemology, i.e. our knowledge about such objects of research?

Knight: Uncertainty belongs to ontology: it is a fact of life.

MIP: Uncertainty belongs of epistemology: situations viewed in isolation, but not in groups, are uncertain.

PEU: Uncertainty belongs to epistemology: in principle, a unique reality actually exists.

ASE: Uncertainty belongs to ontology. We cannot know the exact future developments in detail, but we know the past and the present. Imminent developments include both relatively stable features and unique qualities.

PKE: Uncertainty does not belong to the body of knowledge we have about economic practices, but should rather be considered to belong to ontology. Uncertainty influences the creation of the future, because it motivates the decisions being made.

EGT: The discussion on Economic Game Theory shows that uncertainty is considered to be an attribute of the situations discussed within economics, and thus belongs to ontology.

Fourthly: Uncertainty causes fundamental problems for the formation of expectations. What are expectations according to the various schools of thought?

Knight: Knight regards expectations as opinions about future outcomes, and thus liable to errors.

MIP: Expectations are detailed predictions of future results, comprising a probability distribution of outcomes.

PEU: Expectations are derived valuations of future results.

ASE: Expectations are essentially derived from the processed experiences, which precede the making of plans.

PKE: Expectations are understood as feasible subjective visions of the future.

EGT: Expectations are the projected results of complex interactions.

Fifthly: What are the most significant economic consequences of uncertainty?

Knight: Management problems, profits, and losses are direct consequences of uncertainty, and could not exist in the absence of uncertainty.

MIP: Profits and losses are directly linked to uncertainty.

PEU: Behaviour based on an attitude to risk may result in a redistribution of funds.

ASE: Only in the presence of uncertainty is entrepreneurial behaviour, that is all premeditated individual decision-making, possible, and this enables the entrepreneur to fill perceived gaps in market knowledge to his pecuniary advantage.

PKE: The economic consequences of uncertainty are concentrated in the expansion or contraction of the economy, and reflected in the holding or disposal of highly-liquid assets, such as money.

EGT: The consequences of uncertainty are manifest in the fact that, while the entire set of outcomes can be predicted, the actual outcome in any given case cannot be foreseen.

Sixth: On the theoretical level we may ask ourselves how the various schools of thought characterize uncertainty?

Knight: If possible at all, uncertainty may be represented by the divination of outcomes, and by the trust we invest in such guesses.

MIP: In the interwar period, mainstream economists finally decided that frequency distributions may well represent uncertainty. Reduced uncertainty is portrayed by a lower variance of the frequency distribution.

PEU: (Subjective) Expected Utility (SEU) theorists, in general, represent uncertainty by the sum of, some variant of, probability-weighted payoffs. The general equilibrium approach uses a set of mutually exclusive and exhaustive states of the world or nature in combination with human preferences for these states.

ASE: Uncertainty is indirectly represented by pattern predictions, reflecting the typical aspects of the issue at hand. In a case of low uncertainty, the unique aspects are considered to be unimportant for the projections.

PKE: Uncertainty is generally represented by the range of mutually-exclusive outcomes regarded as possible and prominent in the actors' minds Under conditions of low uncertainty, the values focused upon are close to each other.

EGT: Game theorists commonly accommodate uncertainty by establishing a matrix of numerical outcomes.

Seventh: What institutions are related to uncertainty?

Knight: The enterprise, the organised selection of personnel, and related payments.

MIP: The existence of reserves, flexible production, and a heterogeneous capital market provide some security in the face of a failure of foresight.

PEU: The institution of the perfect market enables trade on the basis of induced utilities or beliefs.

ASE: Specialisation of tasks according to the capacities for dealing with uncertainty. The role of the entrepreneur as the bearer of uncertainty, and the creation of adequate conditions are particularly stressed.

PKE: A number of diverse institutions, such as conventions, contracts, agreements and countervailing regulations, are discussed. They may help to stabilize and focus our attention to specific expectations and activities.

EGT: Various institutions such as norms, conventions and enforced rules direct decisions in a given decision-making situation.

Eighth: Given all this information of uncertainty and institutions, what do the various schools of thought advise when it comes to deciding under uncertainty?

Knight: He essentially advises the grouping of more or less similar cases, if possible, in the hope of converting uncertainties into tendencies.

MIP: The advice given is to decide on the basis of the expected value, supplemented with some evaluation of the distribution of outcomes.

PEU: One should decide by comparing neatly-specified risk-adjusted preference orderings and trade on that basis.

ASE: According to the Austrians, one should respond to uncertainty first of all by trying to perceive profitable opportunities, and otherwise by following accepted standards of behaviour.

PKE: One may try to classify different projections and choose from the various pairs of values focused upon. In situations in which uncertainty is creating a hindrance, people may take refuge in the relatively stable and flexible stores of wealth, e.g. money.

EGT: If one is following the advice offered by Game theorists, one must first appraise the situation. On the one hand, in the case of independent decision-making, one is advised to choose among a few mathematical choice criteria. On the other hand, in the case of interdependent decision-making, one may prefer to follow conventions, norms, laws, or external rules.

Ninth: Finally, we come to the connotations which respective groups of scientists have associated with uncertainty, i.e. how is uncertainty evaluated?

Knight: He seems to regard uncertainty as a paradoxical element in life, in general giving it a negative connotation, yet he did not see uncertainty as a destabilising force.

MIP: Mainstream economists writing on uncertainty in the interwar period clearly see uncertainty as a troublesome facet of life, and consequently something to be brought under control.

PEU: Mainstream economics does not change opinion: uncertainty has a negative connotation.

ASE: Economists in the Austrian school of economics are positive in their opinion about uncertainty, for it is an indication that unperceived profitable opportunities exist.

PKE: Writers of the Post-Keynesian school of thought have mixed feelings about uncertainty: on the one hand, it signals the potential for expressing creativity, but on the other it may turn out to be a destabilising force.

EGT: Economic game theorists see uncertainty as a negative fact of life, to be contained for practical reasons.

7.3 Conclusions

By means of overviews which were largely historical in character, we have made it clear that the economist is ill-advised to ignore uncertainty; he will sooner or later feel obliged to introduce the agent's uncertainty into his theories. It will be evident that uncertainty fundamentally differs from risk. Uncertainty frustrates probability-based decision-making, because uncertainty must be associated with those important and fundamental economic changes which cannot be understood in terms of *a priori* or empirically-based probabilities. Furthermore, uncertainty expresses the tension between the economist's structured theory and the compounded, complex, and largely unknown future developments. As a consequence, economists should, firstly, discuss various institutional means which influence or even direct the agents' expectations and facilitate economic actions, and secondly, be open to acknowledge boundaries of their theorising.

Uncertainty made its entrance in economic research early on in the interwar period, when Knight's *Risk, Uncertainty, and Profit* (1921) was published. Uncertainty was present in contemporary publications in the Austrian and (Post-) Keynesian schools of economics. In spite of these promising contributions to economics, the lure of theoretical precision resulted in a serious dearth of interest in non-mainstream approaches. Changes in mainstream economic thought resulted first in a side-tracking of the agent's uncertainty, next in advanced mathematical constructs to tame the problem of the agents' uncertainty and, finally, with New Classical Economics, in the rejection of the real significance for economics of the problem of the agent's uncertainty, as is reflected in both their actual modelling of the economy as consisting of ergodic processes, and in their dogmatic recommendations. In contrast, the agent's uncertainty has been taken seriously by adherents of alternatively Austrian economics, Post-Keynesian economics, and Economic Game-theory. Austrian economists hold the view that although agents do not know the future, entrepreneurial actions function as a means of enhancing their understanding of the evolving economy. As discussed in chapter four, this faith in the efficacy of human endeavours was later qualified under the influence of Post-Keynesian views. Post-Keynesians regard people's expectations as a potentially problematic factor. The opinions of the future may evolve slowly, but may also change rapidly, because we cannot know the future before it has arrived. It is nevertheless evident that we can make informed guesses as to what the future will present us with, and act on that basis. Game theorists discuss a large number of alternative constellations of interaction, and in this respect we have clarified the informative relations between (non-) coordination and (non-) cooperation type games.

On the level of the tension between theory and reality, uncertainty excludes perfect correspondence between them. Mainstream Economists in the interwar period subscribed to the belief that the models may be linked with reality by means of frequency theory. (S)EU-theorists claim that their experimental designs conditionally reflect reality, but a falsification itself does not reveal the better theory, and it is troublesome to test open-ended situations. The scientists working with Arrow-Debreu models have to face uncertainty because there are less markets in reality than the theory would predict. New Classical Economics advocates the use of structural equations, from which the influence of agents' uncertainty is excluded, resulting in at least time-independent conclusions. However, it proves troublesome to find the most fundamental "structural" equations. By using praxeology, i.e. the logic of human action, Austrian economists claim to derive universally valid knowledge. However, they feel obliged to acknowledge that coordination may not be taken for granted because the agent's judgments may be erroneous. Post-Keynesian theorists seem to be aware that models are dependent upon the factors of time, place, and the agents' expectations. Game-theorists on the one hand acknowledge the constellation-dependency of the model, but on the other, hardly resist the seductive powers of spurious precision, resulting in a tendency to concentrate on theoretically advanced solution-concepts. Generally-speaking there is no escape from the tension between theory and reality because the uncertain, active and erring agents drive the evolution of the economy. The gap between logical insights and experience cannot be bridged by logic alone. It may be advised that economists employ a variety, but not a mixture or synthesis, of models in order to trace idiosyncrasies, and provide additional insights.

Insofar as decision-making under uncertainty is concerned, the various discussions within this research indicate a clear direction for enquiry. There is a convergence on stressing the importance of: (1) the local circumstances of a decision-making situation; (2) both creative, entrepreneurial behaviour, resulting in new or changed situations, and rule-following behaviour, confirming and reproducing a situation. The first point is supported by the evidence here presented and discussed which puts the stress on: reference-points in variations on (S)EU-theory, the need to introduce history into equilibrium models, the importance of a free reign for (local) individual economic endeavours, the subjectivity of expectations, and the importance of the specific form and substance of the game. With regard to the second statement, Austrian Economics and Post-Keynesian Economics, and Economic Game-Theory seem to converge on the need to consider both entrepreneurial and rule-governed behaviour. The question of their relative importance in a given situation is more relevant than the categorical absence or presence of one or the other. However, the game-theoretical restrictions on the behavioral alternatives and the structure of the game pose a problem: there is hardly room for innovative entrepreneurial behaviour. The constellation is somehow agreed upon and activities are supposed to take place within its boundaries. We have argued in this thesis that, in many economic decision-making situations, economists should desist from pretending to know in a probabilistic sense what will result from human interactions. Decision-making alternatives are often better viewed in terms of possibilities.

Our research shows how uncertainty has often been downgraded when research priorities are couched in terms of advancing theoretical constructs and providing single-valued results, rather than with constructing theories with the prime aim of providing insights into actual economic behaviour. The significant publications presented and discussed in this thesis, together with the rise in interest among economists in general in Austrian, Post-Keynesian and Game-theoretical views and insights which became prominent in the 1970s, encourage our conviction that uncertainty is here to stay.

Rotterdam, 6 August 1993

BIBLIOGRAPHY

Adriaansen, W.L.M., and Linden, J.T.J.M. van der (eds.)(1991), *Post-Keynesian Thought in Perspective*, Deventer: Wolters-Noordhof.

Allais, M. (1979), 'The so-called Allais Paradox and Rational Decisions under Uncertainty', in Allais, M., and Hagen, O.(eds.) (1979), 437-680.

Allais, M., and Hagen, O. (eds.)(1979), *Expected Utility Hypotheses and the Allais Paradox*, Dordrecht: Reidel.

Allais, M. (1987), 'Allais Paradox', in Eatwell, J., et all (eds.)(1989a), 3-9.

Angyal, A. (1981), 'A logic of Systems', in Emery, F.E.(ed.) (1981), *Systems Thinking, 1, Selected readings*, Harmondsworth.

Appleby, L., and Starmer, C. (1987), 'Individual Choice Under Uncertainty: A review of experimental evidence, past and present', in Hey, J.D., and Lambert, P.J.(eds.) (1987), ch. 2, 25-45.

Arrow, K.J. (1951), 'Alternative Approaches to the Theory of Choice in Risk-Taking Situations', *Econometrica*, 19, 404-437.

Arrow, K.J. (1974), *The Limits of Organization*, New York: W.W. Norton, 33-34.

Arrow, K.J. (1987), 'Economic Theory and the Hypothesis of Rationality', in Eatwell, J., et all (eds.)(1989a), 25-37.

Arrow, K.J. (1987a), 'Rationality of Self and Others in an Economic System', *The Journal of Business*, 59 (1986) 4, 2, reprinted in Hogarth, R.M., and Reder, M.W.(eds.) (1987), 201-215.

Arrow, K.J., and Hurwicz, J. (1971), 'An Optimality Criterion for Decision-making under under Uncertainty, in Carter, C.F., and Ford, J.L.(eds.) (1971), *Uncertainty and Expectation in Economics*, Clifton, NJ: Kelley, 1-11.

Aumann, R.J. (1976), 'Agreeing to Disagree', *Annals of Statistics*, 4, 1236-1239.

Aumann, R.J. (1987), 'Game Theory', in Eatwell, J., et all (eds.)(1989), 1-53.

Balch, M., and Wu, S. (1974), 'Some Introductory Remarks on Behavior under Uncertainty', in Balch, M., McFadden, D., and Wu, S.(eds.) (1974), *Essay on Economic Behavior under Uncertainty*, Amsterdam: North-Holland, ch. 1, 1-22.

Barone, E. (1908), 'Il Ministro della produzione nello stato collettivista', *Giornale degli Economisti*, reprinted in Hayek, F.A. von (ed.)(1935), as 'The Ministery of Production in the Collectivist State', appendix A, 245-290.

Bateman, B.W. (1987), 'Keynes's Changing Conception of Probability', *Economics and Philosophy*, 3, 97-119.

Bateman, B.W. (1990), 'Keynes, induction and econometrics', *History of Political Economy*, 2, 2, 359-379.

Bateman, B.W. (1991), 'Das Maynard Keynes Problem', *Cambridge Journal of Economics*, 15, 101-111.

Bateman, B.W. (1991a), 'The Rules of the Road: Keynes's theoretical rationale for public policy', in Bateman, B.W., and Davis, J.B.(eds.) (1991), ch. 4, 55-68.

Bateman, B.W. (1992), 'Finding Confidence: the external influence in the creation of *The General Theory*', 1992 HES-annual conference, Conference Notes, Fairfax.

Bateman, B.W., and Davis, J.B. (eds.)(1991), *Keynes and Philosophy. Essays on the origin of Keynes's thought*, Aldershot: Edward Elgar.

Bausor, R. (1983), 'The Rational-Expectations Hypothesis and the Epistemics of Time', *Cambridge Journal of Economics*, 7, 1-10.

Begg, D.K. (1982), *The Rational Expectations Revolution in Macroeconomics: Theories & Evidence*, Baltimore: John Hopkins University Press.

Bianchi, M., and Moulin, H. (1991), 'Strategic Interactions in Economics: The Game-Theoretic Alternative', in Marchi, N.B. de, and Blaug, M.(eds.) (1991), 179-196.

Binmore, K.G. (1990), *Essays on the Foundations of Game Theory*, Oxford: Basil Blackwell.

Binmore, K.G. (1992), 'Foundations of Game Theory', in Laffont, J.-J. (1992), *Advances in Economic Theory. Sixth world congress*, Volume 1, Cambridge: Cambridge University Press, ch. 1, 1-31.

Blaug, M. (1985), *Economic Theory in Retrospect*, Cambridge: Cambridge University Press, fourth edition.

Blaug, M. (1986), *Who is Who in Economics. A biographical dictionary*, London: Wheatsheaf Books.

Boland, L.A. (1986), *Methodology and the Individual Decision Maker*, in Kirzner, I.M.(ed.) (1986), 30-38.

Brams, S.J., Schotter, A., and Schwödiauer, G. (eds.)(1979), *Applied Game Theory*, IHS-studies no.1, Physica-Verlag, Würzburg.

Brandenburger, A. (1992), 'Knowledge and Equilibrium in Games', *Journal of Economic Theory*, 6, 4, 83-101.

Brandenburger, A., and Dekel, E. (1989), 'The Role of Common Knowledge Assumptions in Game Theory', in Hahn, F.(ed.) (1989), 46-61.

Broome, J. (1991), 'Utility', *Economics and Philosophy*, 7, 1-12.

Buchanan, J. (1968), 'Knight, Frank H.' in Ellis, D.L.(ed.) (1968), *International Encyclopedia of the Social Sciences*, 8, London: MacMillan Press, 424-428.

Buiter, W.H. (1980), 'The Macroeconomics of Dr Pangloss. A critical survey of the new classical macroeconomics', *The Economic Journal*, 90, 34-50.

Caldwell, B.J. (1984), *Appraisal and Criticism in Economics. A book of readings*, London: Allen & Unwin.

Caldwell, B.J. (1988), 'Hayek's Transformation', *History of Political Economy*, 20, 4, 513-541.

Carabelli, A. (1985), 'Keynes on Cause, Chance and Possibility', in Lawson, T. and Pesaran, H.(eds.) (1985), ch. 9, 151-180.

Carabelli, A. (1988), *On Keynes's Method*, London: MacMillan Press.

Carvalho, F. (1984), 'Alternative Analyses of Short and Long Run in Post-Keynesian Economics', *Journal of Post-Keynesian Economics*, VII, 2, 214-234.

Clark, J.B. (1893), 'Insurance and Business Profit', *Quarterly Journal of Economics*, 7, 40-54.

Coase, R.H. (1988), 'The Nature of the Firm: Meaning', *Journal of Law, Economics, and Organization*, 4, 1, 19-32.

Coats, A.W. (1983), 'Half a Century of Methodological Controversy in Economics: as reflected in the writings of T.W. Hutchison', in Coats, A.W.(ed.) (1983), *Methodological Controversy in Economics: Historical Essays in Honor of T.W. Hutchison*, Greenwich, Conn.: JAI Press.

Coddington, A. (1983), *Keynesian Economics: The search for first principles*, London: Allen & Unwin.

Cournot, A.-A. (1838), *Researches into the Mathematical Principles of the Theory of Wealth*, translated by Bacon, N.T. (1897), New York: MacMillan Press.

Da Costa Werlang, S.R. (1987), 'Common Knowledge', in Eatwell, J., et all (eds.)(1989), 74-85.

Damme, E. van (1987), 'Extensive Form Games', in Eatwell, J., et all (eds.)(1989), 139-144.

Davidson, P. (1980), 'Post Keynesian Economics: Solving the crisis in economic theory', *The Public Interest*, 151-173.

Davidson, P. (1983), 'Rational Expectations: a fallacious foundation for studying crucial decision-making processes', *Journal of Post-Keynesian Economics*, 182-198.

Davidson, P. (1985), 'Sidney Weintraub- An economist of the real world', *Journal of Post-Keynesian Economics*, VII, 4, 533-539.

Davidson, P. (1988), 'A Technical Definition of Uncertainty and the Long-run Non-neutrality of Money', *Cambridge Journal of Economics*, 12, 329-337.

Davidson, P. (1990), 'Shackle and Keynes vs. Rational Expectations Theory and the Role of Time-Liquidity and Financial Markets', in Frowen, S.F.(ed.) (1990), ch. 5, 64-80.

Davis, J.B. (1989), 'Keynes on Atomism and Organism', *The Economic Journal*, 99, 1159-1172.

Debreu, G. (1959), *Theory of Value*, New York: Wiley, ch. 7, 98-102, reprinted in Diamond, P., and Rothschild, M.(eds.) (1978), ch. 11, 163-170.

Diamond, P., and Rothschild, M. (eds.)(1978), *Uncertainty in Economics. Readings and exercises*, New York: Academic Press.

Dimand, R.W. (1989), 'Review of *On Keynes's Method* by A. Carabelli', *Economic Journal*, 99, 890-891.

Dow, S.C. (1985), *Macroeconomic Thought. A methodological approach*, Oxford: Basil Blackwell, Oxford.

Dow, S.C. (1993), 'Uncertainty about Uncertainty', Conference Notes, Leeds.

Drèze, J.H. (1974), 'Axiomatic Theories of Choice, Cardinal Utility and Subjective probability, A review', in Drèze, J.H.(ed.) (1974), *Allocation under Uncertainty: Equilibrium and optimality*, 3-23, reprinted in Drèze, J.H. (1987), ch. 1, 3-22.

Drèze, J.H. (1985), '(Uncertainty and) the Firm in General Equilibrium Theory', *Economic Journal*, 95, Supplement, 1-20, reprinted in Drèze, J.H. (1987), ch. 16, 321-343.

Drèze, J.H. (1987), *Essays on Economic Decisions under Uncertainty*, Cambridge: Cambridge University Press.

Eastham, J.K. (1938), 'Commodity Stocks and Prices', *The Review of Economic Studies*, 6, 100-110.

Eatwell, J. (1982), *Whatever happened to Britain? The economics of decline*, London: G.Duckworth/B.B.C.

Eatwell, J., Milgate, M., and Newman, P. (1989), *Game Theory*, from the *New Palgrave: A Dictionary of Economics*, (1987), London: MacMillan Press.

Eatwell, J., Milgate, M., and Newman, P. (1989a), *Utility and Probability*, from the *New Palgrave: A Dictionary of Economics* (1987), London: MacMillan Press.

Ebeling, R.M. (1986), 'Towards a Hermeneutical Economics: expectations, prices, and the role of interpretation in a theory of the market process', in Kirzner, I.M.(ed.) (1986), 39-55.

Eggertsson, T. (1990), *Economic Behaviour and Institutions*, Cambridge: Cambridge University Press.

Eichner, A.S., and Kregel, J.A. (1975), 'An Essay on Post-Keynesian Theory: A new paradigm in economics', *Journal of Economic Literature*, 13, 4, 1293-1314.

Eliot, T.S. (1943), *Four Quartets*, Antwerpen: De Nederlandse Boekhandel, 1983.

Elster, J. (1983), *Sour Grapes. Studies in the subversion of rationality*, Cambridge: Cambridge University Press.

Elster, J. (ed.)(1986), *Rational Choice*, Oxford: Basil Blackwell.

Elster, J. (1989), *Salomonic Judgements. Studies in the limitations of rationality*, Cambridge: Cambridge University Press.

Emmett, R.B. (1992), 'The Therapeutic Quality of Frank H.Knight's *Risk, Uncertainty, and Profit*',unpublished ms.

Field, A.J. (1984), 'Microeconomics, Norms, and Rationality', *Economic development and structural change*, 32, 683-711.

Fishburn, P.C. (1987), 'Interdependent Preferences', in Eatwell, J., et all (eds.)(1989a), 121-127.

Fitzgibbons, A. (1988), *Keynes's Vision. A new political economy*, Oxford: Clarendon Press.

Fitzgibbons, A. (1991), 'The Significance of Keynes's Idealism', in Bateman, B.W., and Davis, J.B.(eds.) (1991), ch. 8, 126-132.

Ford, J.L. (1987), *Economic Choice under Uncertainty: A perspective theory approach*, Aldershot: Edward Elgar.

Frey, B.S. (1989), 'Institutions Matter – The comparative analysis of institutions', EEA Conference Notes, Augsburg.

Frey, B.S., and Eichenberger, R. (1989), 'Anomalies and Institutions, *Journal of Institutional and Theoretical Economics*, 145, 423-437.

Frowen, S.F. (ed.)(1990), *Unknowledge and Choice in Economics. Proceedings of a conference in honour of G.L.S. Shackle*, London: MacMillan Press.

Fudenberg, D., and Tirole, J. (1991), *Game Theory*, Cambridge, MA: Massachusetts Institute of Technology Press.

Garrison, R.W. (1986), 'From Lachmann to Lucas: on institutions, expectations, and equilibrating tendencies', in Kirzner, I.M.(ed.) (1986), 87-101.

Gauthier, D.P. (1986), *Morals by Agreement*, Oxford: Clarendon Press.

Gerrard, W.J., 'From a *Treatise on Probability* to the *General Theory*: Continuity or change in Keynes's thought?' in Gerrard, B., and Hillard, J. (eds.)(1992), *The Philosophy and Economics of J.M. Keynes*, Aldershot: Edward Elgar, 80-95.

Gerrard, B. (1993), 'Keynes on Probability, Uncertainty and Expectations: A constructive interpretation', Conference Notes, Leeds.

Gordon, S. (1974), 'Frank Knight and the Tradition of Liberalism', *Journal of Political Economy*, 82, 3, 571-577.

Gordon, W. (1984), 'The Role of Institutional Economics', *Journal of Economic Issues*, 18, 2, 369-381.

Grossman, H.I. (1980), Rational Expectations, Business Cycles, and Government Behavior, in Fischer, S.(ed.) (1980), *Rational Expectations and Economic Policy*, Chicago: University of Chicago Press, 5-22.

Hacking, I. (1975), *The Emergence of Probability. A philosophical study of early ideas about probability, induction and statistical inference*, Cambridge: Cambridge University Press.

Hacking, I. (1990), *The Taming of Chance*, Cambridge: Cambridge University Press.

Hahn, F. (1985), 'General Equilibrium Theory', in Bell, D., and Kristol, I.(eds.) (1975), *The Crisis in Economic Theory*, New York: Basic Books, ch. 8.

Hahn, F. (ed.)(1989), *The Economics of Missing Markets, Information, and Games*, Oxford: Clarendon Press.

Hahn, F. (1989a), 'Introduction', in Hahn, F.(ed.) (1989), 1-4.

Hahn, F. (1989b), 'Information Dynamics and Equilibrium', in Hahn, F.(ed.) (1989), ch. 5, 106-126.

Halpern, J.Y. (1986), 'Reasoning about Knowledge: An Overview', Proceedings of the Conference Theoretical Aspects of Reasoning about Knowledge, Californie: Alisomar.

Hamilton, W.H. (1932), 'Institutions', in Seligman, E.R.A., and Johnson, A.(eds.) (1932), *Encyclopaedia of the Social Sciences*, Volume 8, London: MacMillan Press, 84-89.

Hammond, J.D. (1991), 'Frank Knight's Antipositivism', *History of Political Economy*, 23, 3, 359-381.

Hammond, P.J. (1987), 'Uncertainty', in Eatwell, J., et all (eds.)(1989a), 280-294.

Hamouda, O.F. and Smithin, J.N. (1988), 'Some Remarks on "Uncertainty and economic analysis"', *The Economic Journal*, 98, 159-164.

Harcourt, G.C. (1986), *Controversies in Political Economy*. Selected Essays of G.C. Harcourt, editor Hamouda, O.F., Brighton: Wheatsheaf Books.

Harcourt, G.C. (1990), 'Introduction: Notes on an Economic Querist- G.L.S. Shackle', in Frowen, S.F.(ed.) (1990), xvii-xxvi.

Hardin, G. (1968), 'The Tragedy of the Commons', *Science*, 162, December 13, 1243-1248.

Hargreaves Heap, S. (1989), *Rationality in Economics*, Oxford: Basil Blackwell.

Harrod, R.F. (1951), *The Life of John Maynard Keynes*, London: MacMillan Press.

Harsanyi, J.C. (1982), *Papers in Game Theory*, Dordrecht: Reidel, reprints.

Harsanyi J.C. (1986), 'Advances in Understanding Rational Behaviour', in Butts, R.E., and Hintikka, J.(eds.) (1977), *Foundational Problems in the Social Sciences*, Dordrecht: Reidel, 315-343, reprinted in Elster, J.(ed.) (1986), ch. 3, 82-107.

Hart, A.G. (1937), 'Anticipations, Business planning, and the Cycle', *Quarterly Journal of Economics*, LI, 273-297.

Hart, A.G. (1940), *Anticipations, Uncertainty, and Dynamic Planning*, New York: A.M. Kelly, 1951.

Hartogh, G. den (1985), 'Wederkerige Verwachtingen. Konventie, norm, verplichting', Amsterdam: Juriaans, Dissertation.

Hawley, F.B. (1901), 'Enterprise and Profit', *Quarterly Journal of Economics*, 15, 75-105.

Hayek, F.A. von (ed.)(1935), *Collectivist Economic Planning. Critical studies on the possibility of socialism*, London: George Routledge & Sons ltd.

Hayek, F.A. von (1935a), 'The Nature and History of the Problem', in Hayek, F.A. von (ed.)(1935), 1-40.

Hayek, F.A. von (1935b), 'The present State of the Debate', in Hayek, F.A. von (ed.)(1935), 201-243.

Hayek, F.A. von (1937), 'Economics and Knowledge', *Economica*, IV, 33-54, reprinted in Hayek, F.A. von (1948), 33-56.

Hayek, F.A. von (1940), 'Socialist Calculation III: the competitive solution', *Economica*, VII, reprinted in Hayek, F.A. von (1948), 181-208.

Hayek, F.A. von (1943), 'The Facts of the Social Sciences', *Ethics* LIV, 1, 1-13, reprinted in Hayek, F.A. von (1948), 57-76.

Hayek, F.A. von (1945), 'The Use of Knowledge in Society', *The American Economic Review*, XXXV, 4, 519-530, reprinted in Hayek, F.A. von (1948), 77-91.

Hayek, F.A. von (1946), 'The Meaning of Competition', in Hayek, F.A. von (ed.)(1948), 92-106.

Hayek, F.A. von (1948), *Individualism and Economic Order*, Chicago: University of Chicago Press; Midway reprint, 1980.

Hayek, F.A. von (1988), *Collected Works of F.A. von Hayek*, edited by Bartley, W.W. III, Volume I: *The Fatal Conceit: the errors of socialism*, London, Routledge & Kegan Paul.

Haynes, J. (1895), 'Risk as an Economic Factor', *Quarterly Journal of Economics*, 9, 409-449.

Hey, J.D. (1979), *Uncertainty in Microeconomics*, Oxford: Martin Robertson.

Hey, J.D. (1982), 'Whither Uncertainty?', *Economic Journal*, Conference Papers, 130-139.

Hey, J.D. (1984), 'Decision under Uncertainty', in Ploeg, F. van der (ed.)(1984), ch. 17, 433-455.

Hey, J.D. (1990), 'The Possibility of Possibility', in Frowen, S.F.(ed.) (1990), ch. 10, 168-191.

Hey, J.D., and Lambert, P.J. (eds.)(1987), *Surveys in the Economics of Uncertainty*, Oxford: Basil Blackwell.

Hicks, J.R. (1931), 'The Theory of Uncertainty and Profit', *Economica*, XI, 170-189, reprinted as 'Uncertainty and Profit', in Hicks, J.R. (1982), ch. 2, 11-27.

Hicks, J.R. (1936), 'Mr. Keynes's Theory of Employment', *The Economic Journal*, XLVI (1937), 238-253.

Hicks, J.R. (1937), 'Mr Keynes and the "Classics": A suggested interpretation', *Econometrica*, V, 147-159, reprinted as 'Mr. Keynes and the Classics', in Hicks, J.R. (1982), ch. 8, 100-115.

Hicks, J.R. (1939), *Value and Capital. An Inquiry into some fundamental principles of economic theory*, Oxford: Clarendon Press, second edition, 1946.

Hicks, J.R. (1967), 'The Hayek Story', in Hicks, J.R. (1967), *Critical Essays in Monetary Theory*, Oxford: Clarendon Press, 203-215.

Hicks, J.R. (1973), 'Correspondence with J.M. Keynes', in Keynes, J.M. (1973).

Hicks, J.R. (1976), 'Time in Economics', reprinted in Hicks, J.R. (1982), ch. 21, 282-300.

Hicks, J.R. (1979), 'On Coddington's Interpretation: A reply', *Journal of Economic Literature*, XVII, 989-995.

Hicks, J.R. (1979a), 'Review of *Microfoundations*, by E.R. Weintraub', *Journal of Economic Literature*, reprinted as 'Micro and Macro', in Hicks, J.R. (1983), ch. 30, 349-352.

Hicks, J.R. (1979b), 'The Formation of an Economist', reprinted in Hicks, J.R. (1983), ch. 31, 355-364.

Hicks, J.R. (1979c), *Causality in Economics*, Oxford: Basil Blackwell.

Hicks, J.R. (1980), 'IS-LM: An Explanation', *Journal of Post-Keynesian Economics*, III, 2, 139-154.

Hicks, J.R. (1982), *Collected Essays on Economic Theory*, Volume II: *Money, Interest, and Wages*, Oxford: Basil Blackwell.

Hicks, J.R. (1982a), 'Introductory: LSE and the Robbins Circle', in Hicks, J.R. (1982), ch. 1, 3-10.

Hicks, J.R. (1982b), 'IS-LM - An Explanation', revised version of Hicks, J.R. (1980), in Hicks, J.R. (1982), ch. 23, 318-331.

Hicks, J.R. (1983), *Collected Essays on Economic Theory*, Volume III: *Classics and Moderns*, Oxford: Basil Blackwell.

Hicks, J.R. (1983a), 'A Discipline not a Science', in Hicks, J.R. (1983), ch. 32, 365-375.

High, J. (1982), 'Alertness and Judgment: comment on Kirzner', in Kirzner, I.M.(ed.) (1982), 161-168.

Hildenbrand, W. (1987), 'Cores', in Eatwell, J., et all (eds.)(1989), 108-116.

Hirshleifer, J. and Riley, J.G. (1979), 'The analytics of Uncertainty and Information − An expository survey', *Journal of Economic Literature*, XVII, 1375-1421.

Hirshleifer, J. (1982), 'Evolutionary Models in Economics and Law: cooperation versus conflict strategies', *Research in Law and Economics*, London: JAI Press, 4, 1-60.

Hodgson, G.M. (1986), 'Behind Methodological Individualism', *Cambridge Journal of Economics*, 10, 211-224.

Hodgson, G.M. (1988), *Economics and Institutions. A manifesto for a modern institutional economics*, Cambridge: Polity Press.

Hodgson, G.M. (1989), 'Evolution and Institutional Change', Newcastle upon Tyne: Newcastle upon Tyne Polytechnic, unpublished ms.

Hogarth, R.M., and Reder M.W. (eds.)(1987), *Rational Choice. The contrast between economics and psychology*, Chicago: University of Chicago Press.

Hopkins, W.S. (1933), 'Profit in American Economic Theory', *The Review of Economic Studies*, 1, 60-66.

Hutchison, T.W. (1937a), 'Note on Uncertainty and Planning', *The Review of Economic Studies*, 4, 72-74.

Hutchison, T.W. (1937b), 'Expectation and Rational Conduct', *Zeitschrift für Nationalökonomie*, 8, 636-653.

Hutchison, T.W. (1938), *The Significance and Basic Postultates of Economic Theory*, New York: A.M. Kelly, 1960.

Hutchison, T.W. (1941), 'The Significance and Basic Postultates of Economic Theory; A Reply to Professor Knight', *Journal of Political Economy*, 49, 732-750.

Hutchison, T.W. (1981), *The Politics and Philosophy of Economics. Marxians, Keynesians, and Austrians*, Oxford: Basil Blackwell.

Huussen, G.M. (1989), 'Mises and the Praxeological Point of View', *The Journal of Economic Studies*, 15, 121-133.

Huussen, G.M. (1990), 'Maakte Hayek een methodologische ommezwaai?', *Maandschrift Economie*, 54, 2, 115-127.

Jefferson, M. (1983), 'Economic Uncertainty and Business Decision-Making', in Wiseman, J.(ed.) (1983), *Beyond Positive Economics?*, London: MacMillan Press, 122-159.

Johansen, L. (1981), 'Interaction in Economic Theory', *Economie Appliquee*, 34, 2/3, 229-267.

Kahneman, D., and Tversky, A. (1979), 'Prospect Theory', *Econometrica*, 47, 263-91.

Kantor, B. (1979), 'Rational Expectations and Economic Thought', *Journal of Economic Literature*, XVII, 1422-1441.

Kapp, K.W. (1968), 'In Defense of Institutional Economics', *Swedisch Journal of Economics*, 1-18.

Keizer, W. (1989), 'Recent Reinterpretations of the Socialist Calculation Debate', *The Journal of Economic Studies*, 16, 2, 63-83.

Keynes, J.M. (1921), *A Treatise on Probability*, London: MacMillan Press, 1963.

Keynes, J.M. (1930), *Treatise on Money*, reprinted in *The Collected Writings of John Maynard Keynes*, Volume V and VI, London: MacMillan Press, 1971.

Keynes, J.M., (1933), *Essays in Biography*, reprinted in *The Collected Writings of John Maynard Keynes*, Volume X, London: MacMillan Press, 1972.

Keynes, J.M. (1936), *The General Theory of Employment, Interest and Money*, reprinted in *The Collected Writings of John Maynard Keynes*, Volume VII, London: MacMillan Press, 1973.

Keynes, J.M. (1937), 'The General Theory of Employment', *The Quarterly Journal of Economics*, reprinted in Keynes, J.M. (1973), 109-123.

Keynes, J.M. (1938), 'Letter to Shackle', April 30, Add. 7669 9/5/1 of the Shackle-papers, Cambridge: University Library.

Keynes, J.M. (1973), *The Collected Writings of John Maynard Keynes*, edited by Moggridge, D., Volume XIV: *The General Theory and After: Part II, Defence and Development*, London: MacMillan Press.

Keynes, J.M. (1979), *The Collected Writings of John Maynard Keynes*, edited by Moggridge, D., Volume XXIX: *The General Theory and After: A supplement*, London: MacMillan Press.

Keynes, M. (ed.)(1975), *Essays on John Maynard Keynes*, Cambridge: Cambridge University Press.

Kirzner, I.M. (1979), *Perception, Opportunity, and Profit. Studies in the theory of entrepreneurship*, Chicago: University of Chicago Press.

Kirzner, I.M. (1979a), 'Comment: x-inefficiency, error, and the scope for entrepreneurship', in Rizzo, M.J.(ed.) (1979), 140-152.

Kirzner, I.M. (1981), 'Mises on Entrepreneurship', *Wirtschaftspolitische Blätter*, 51-57.

Kirzner, I.M. (ed.)(1982), *Method, Process, and Austrian Economics*, Lexington, Mass: Lexington Books.

Kirzner, I.M. (1982a), 'Uncertainty, Discovery, and Human Action', in Kirzner, I.M.(ed.) (1982), 139-159.

Kirzner, I.M. (1984), 'Economic Planning and the Knowledge Problem', *Cato Journal*, 4, 2, 407-418.

Kirzner, I.M. (1985), *Discovery and the Capitalist Process*, Chicago: University of the Chicago Press.

Kirzner, I.M. (ed.)(1986), *Subjectivism, Intelligibility and Economic Understanding. Essays in honor of L.M. Lachmann on his eightieth birthday*, London: MacMillan Press.

Kirzner, I.M. (1988), 'The Economic Calculation Debate: lessons for Austrians', *Review of Austrian Economics*, 2, 1-18.

Kirzner, I.M., (1989), *Discovery, Capitalism, and Distributive Justice*, Oxford: Basil Blackwell.

Knight, F.H. (1916), 'Neglected Factors in the Problem of Normal Interest', *Quarterly Journal of Economics*, XXX, 279-310.

Knight, F.H. (1921), *Risk, Uncertainty and Profit*, Boston: Houghton Mifflin, 1948.

Knight, F.H. (1930), 'Statics and Dynamics. Some queries regarding the mechanical analogy in economics', *Zeitschrift für Nationalökonomie*, 2, 1-26, reprinted in Knight, F.H. (1935), ch. 6.

Knight, F.H. (1934), 'Profit', in Seligman, E.R.A.(ed.), *International Encyclopedia of the Social Sciences*, 480-486.

Knight, F.H. (1935), *The Ethics of Competition and Other Essays*, London: Allen & Unwin, 1936.

Knight, F.H. (1940), '"What is Thruth" in Economics?', *Journal of Political Economy*, 48, 1, 1-32.

Knight, F.H. (1941), 'A Rejoinder', *Journal of Political Economy*, 49, 750-753.

Kregel, J.A. (1976), 'Economic Methodology in the Face of Uncertainty: The modelling methods of Keynes and the Post-Keynesians', *The Economic Journal*, 86, 209-225.

Kregel, J.A. (1980), 'Markets and Institutions as Features of a Capitalist Production System', *Journal of Post-Keynesian Economics*, III, 1, 32-48.

Kreps, D.M. (1987), 'Nash Equilibrium', in Eatwell, J., et all (eds.)(1989), 167-177.

Kydland, F.E., and Prescott, E.C. (1977), 'Rules rather than Discretion', *Journal of Political Economy*, 85, 3, reprinted in Lucas, R.E., and Sargent, T.D.(eds.) (1981), 619-638.

Lachmann, L.M. (1943), 'The Role of Expectations in Economics as a Social Science', *Economica*, X, 12-23.

Lachmann, L.M. (1956), *Capital and its Structure*, Kansas City, KS: Sheed, Andrews and McMeel, second edition, 1978.

Lachmann, L.M. (1976), 'From Mises to Shackle: An Essay on Austrian Economics and the Kaleidic Society', *Journal of Economic Literature*, 14, 54-62.

Lachmann, L.M. (1977), *Capital, Expectations, and the Market Process. Essays on the theory of the market economy*, Kansas City, KS: Sheed, Andrews and McMeel.

Lachmann, L.M. (1978), *On Austriam Stocktaking: Unsettled questions and tentative answers*, in Spadaro, L.M.(ed.) (1978), *New Directions in Austrian Economics*, Kansas City, KS: Sheed & Ward, 1-18.

Lachmann, L.M. (1989), 'Letter to Shackle', December 10, Box 9/13 of the Shackle-papers, Cambridge: University Library.

Lachmann, L.M. (1990), 'G.L.S. Shackle's Place in the History of Subjectivist Thought', in Frowen, S.F.(ed.) (1990), ch. 1, 1-8.

Lange, O. (1936), 'On the Economic Theory of Socialism', in Lippincott, B.E.(ed.), *On the Economic Theory of Socialism*, New York: McGraw-Hill, 1964.

Langlois, R.N. (1986), 'Coherence and Flexibility: social institutions in a world of radical uncertainty', in Kirzner, I.M.(ed.) (1986), 171-191.

Lavington, F. (1912), 'Uncertainty in its Relation to the Net Rate of Interest', *The Economic Journal*, 22, 398-409.

Lavington, F. (1925), 'An Approach to the Theory of Business Risks', *The Economic Journal*, XXXV, 186-199.

Lavington, F. (1926), 'An Approach to the Theory of Business Risks (II)', *The Economic Journal*, 36, 192-203.

Lavoie, D. (1981), 'Introduction', *The Journal of Libertarian Studies*, 5, 1, 1-5.

Lavoie, D. (1981a), 'A Critique of the Standard Account of the Socialist Calculation Debate', *The Journal of Libertarian Studies*, 5, 1, 41-87.

Lavoie, D. (1985), *Rivalry and Central Planning. The socialist calculation debate reconsidered*, Cambridge: Cambridge University Press.

Lawson, T. (1985), 'Uncertainty and Economic Analysis', *The Economic Journal*, 95, 909-927.

Lawson, T. (1985a), 'Keynes, Prediction and Econometrics', Lawson, T. and Pesaran, H.(eds.) (1985), ch. 7, 116-133.

Lawson, T. and Pesaran, H. (eds.)(1985), *Keynes' Economics. Methodological issues*, Armonk, NY: M.E. Sharpe.

Lewis, D. (1969), *Convention*, Cambridge, MA: Harvard University Press.

Lindley, D.V. (1987), 'Thomas Bayes', in Eatwell, J., et all (eds.)(1989a), 10-11.

Little, L.T. (1938), 'Economics and Insurance', *The Review of Economic Studies*, 5, 32-52.

Littlechild, S.C. (1979), 'Comment: Radical Subjectivism or Radical Subversion', in Rizzo, M.J.(ed.) (1979), 2-49.

Loasby, B.J. (1982), 'Economics of Dispersed and Incomplete Information', in Kirzner, I.M.(ed.) (1982), 111-130.

Loasby, B.J. (1990), 'The Use of Scenarios in Business Planning', in Frowen, S.F.(ed.) (1990), 46-63.

Loomes, G. (1988), 'Different Experimental Procedures for Obtaining Valuations of Risky Actions: Implications for utility theory', *Theory and Decision*, 25, 1-13.

Loomes, G., and Sudgen, R. (1982), 'Regret Theory: An Alternative Theory of Rational Choice under Uncertainty', *The Economic Journal*, 92, 805-824.

Lucas, R.E. (1972), 'Expectations and the Neutrality of Money', *Journal of Economic Theory*, 4, 103-124, reprinted in Lucas, R.E. (1981), 66-90.

Lucas, R.E. (1977), 'Understanding Business Cycles', in Brunner, K., and Meltzer, A.H. (1977), *Stabilization of the Domestic and International Economy*, Amsterdam: North-Holland, 7-22, reprinted in Lucas, R.E. (1981), 215-239.

Lucas, R.E. (1981), *Studies in Business-Cycle Theory*, Oxford: Basil Blackwell.

Lucas, R.E. (1987), *Models of Business Cycles*, Yrjo Jahnsson Lectures, Oxford: Basil Blackwell, Paperback, 1988.

Lucas, R.E., and Rapping, L.E. (1969a), 'Real Wages, Employment, and Inflation', *Journal of Political Economy*, 77, 721-754, reprinted in Lucas, R.E. (1981), 19-58.

Lucas, R.E., and Rapping, L.E. (1969b), 'Price Expectations and the Phillips Curve', *American Economic Review*, 59, 342-350.

Lucas, R.E., and Sargent, T.D. (eds.)(1981), *Rational Expectations and Econometric Practice*, Boston: George Allen & Unwin.

Luce, R.D., and Raiffa, H. (1957), *Games and Decisions. Introduction and critical survey*, New York: John Wiley and Sons.

Machina, M.J. (1987), 'Choice under Uncertainty: Problems solved and unsolved', *Journal of Economic Perspectives*, 1, 1, 121-154.

Machina, M.J. (1989), 'Decision-Making in the Presence of Risk', in Hahn, F.(ed.) (1989), ch. 12, 278-294.

Machina, M.J. (1989a), 'Dynamic Consistency and Non-Expected Utility Models of Choice under Uncertainty', *Journal of Economic Literature*, XXVII, 1622-1668.

Machina, M.J., and Rothschild, M. (1987), 'Risk', in Eatwell, J., et all (eds.)(1989a), 227-239.

Mailath, G.J. (1992), 'Introduction: Symposium on evolutionary game theory', *Journal of Economic Theory*, 57, 259-277.

March, J.G. (1978), 'Bounded Rationality, Ambiguity, and the Engineering of Choice', *Bell Journal of Economics*, 9, 587-608, in Elster, J.(ed.) (1979), ch. 6, 142-170.

Marchi, N.B. de, and Blaug, M. (1991), *Appraising Economic Theory. Studies in the methodology of research projects*, Aldershot: Edward Elgar.

Masera, R. (1990), 'John Hicks: a personal recollection', *Open Economies Review*, 1, 291-295.

Mertens, J.-F. (1987), 'Repeated Games', in Eatwell, J., et all (eds.)(1989), 205-209.

Mertens, J.-F. (1987a), 'Supergames', in Eatwell, J., et all (eds.)(1989), 238-241.

Meyer, J.J.Ch. (1990), 'Toegepaste Logica deel II. Epistemische logica', Amsterdam: Vrije Universiteit, Syllabus.

Minsky, H.P. (1980) 'Money, Financial Markets, and the Coherence of a Market Economy', *Journal of Post-Keynesian Economics*, III, 1, 21-31.

Minsky, H.P. (1982), *Inflation, Recession, and Economic Policy*, Brighton: Wheatsheaf Books.

Minsky, H.P. (1986), *Stabilizing an Unstable Economy*, New Haven: Yale University Press.

Mises, L. von (1920), 'Die Wirtschaftsrechnung im Sozialistischen Gemeinwesen', *Archiv für Sozialwissenschaften*, 47, reprinted in Hayek, F.A. von (ed.)(1935), as 'Economic Calculation in the Socialist Commonwealth', 87-130.

Mises, L. von (1922), *Socialism. An economic and sociological analysis*, London: Jonathan Cape, translated, second edition, 1951.

Mises, L. von (1933), *Epistemological Problems of Economics*, New York: New York University Press, second translation, 1981.

Mises, L. von (1949), *Human Action. A treatise on economics*, London: William Hodge and Company, third edition, 1966.

Mises, L. von (1957), *Theory and History*, New Haven: Yale University Press.

Mises, L. von (1962), *The Ultimate Foundation of Economic Science. An Essay on Method*, Kansas City, KS: Sheed & Ward, second edition, 1978.

Mises, R. von (1928), *The Theory of Probability*, London: Allen & Unwin, second edition, 1957.

Mitchell, W.C. (1922), 'Risk, Uncertainty, and Profit. A Review', *American Economic Review*, 12, 274-275.

Moggridge, D.E. (1975), 'The Influence of Keynes on the Economics of his Time', in Keynes, M.(ed.) (1975), ch. 9, 73-81.

Morgenstern, O. (1935), 'Vollkomene Voraussight und Wirtschaftliches Gleichgewicht', *Zeitschrift für Nationalökonomie*, 6, 3, translated by Knight, F.H. as 'Perfect Foresight and Economic Equilibrium', in Schotter, A.(ed.) (1976), *Selected Economic Writings of Oskar Morgenstern*, New York: New York University Press.

Morgenstern, O. (1979), 'Some Reflections on Utility', in Allais, M., and Hagen, O.(eds.) (1979), 175-183.

Mueller, D.C. (1979), *Public Choice*, Cambridge: Cambridge University Press.

Muth, J.F. (1961), 'Rational Expectations and the Theory of Price Movements', *Econometrica*, 29, 315-335, reprinted in Lucas, R.E., and Sargent, T.D.(eds.) (1981), 3-22.

Mutsaers, B. (1992), 'Een Heel Logisch Sprookje. Over kabouters, kans en kennis', master-thesis, mimeo.

Nash, J.F. (1951), 'Non-cooperative Games', *Annals of Mathematics*, 54, 289-295.

Neale, W.C. (1987), 'Institutions', *Journal of Economic Issues*, 21, 3, 1177-1206.

Nentjes, A. (1991), 'Post-Keynesian Economics. A comment on Sawyer', in Adriaansen W.L.M., and Linden, J.T.J.M. van der (eds.)(1991), 73-77.

Neumann, J. von (1928), 'Zur Theorie der Gesellschaftsspiele', *Mathematische Annalen*, 100, 295-320.

Neumann, J. von, and Morgenstern, O. (1944), *Theory of Games and Economic Behavior*, Princeton: Princeton University Press, third edition, 1953.

O'Donnell, R.M. (1989), *Keynes: Philosophy, Economics and Politics*, London: MacMillan Press

O'Donnell, R.M. (1990), An Overview of Probability, Expectations, Uncertainty and Rationality in Keynes's Conceptual Framework, *Review of Political Economy*, 2, 2, 253-266.

O'Driscoll, G.P. (1977), *Economics as a Coordination Problem*, Kansas City, KS: Sheed Andrews & McMeel.

O'Driscoll, G.P., and Rizzo, M.J. (1985), *The Economics of Time and Ignorance*, Oxford: Basil Blackwell.

O'Driscoll, G.P., and Rizzo, M.J. (1986), 'Subjectivism, Uncertainty, and Rules', in Kirzner, I.M.(ed.) (1986), 252-267.

Olson, M. (1965), *The Logic of Collective Action*, Cambridge, MA: Harvard University Press.

Olson, M. (1982), *The Rise and Decline of Nations. Economic growth, stagflation and social rigidities*, New Haven: Yale University Press.

Orlean, A. (1987), *Heterodoxie et incertitude*, Paris: INSEE.

Paqué, K.-H. (1990), 'Pattern Predictions in Economics: Hayek's methodology of the social sciences revisited', *History of Political Economy*, 22, 2, 281-294.

Pasinetti, L.L. (1983), *Structural Change and Economic Growth. A theoretical essay on the dynamics of the wealth of nations*, Cambridge: Cambridge University Press.

Pasinetti, L.L (1991), 'At the Roots of Post-Keynesian Thought Keynes's Break with Tradition', in Adriaansen, W.L.M., and Linden, J.T.J.M. van der (eds.)(1991), 21-29.

Peeters, M. (1987), 'A Dismal Science; An essay on New Classical Economics', *De Economist*, 135, 4, 442-466.

Pellikaan, H. (1988), 'Rationele Keuze, Collective Besluitvorming en de Noodzaak van Normen', *Acta Politica*, 23, 3, 275-309.

Perlman, M. (1986), 'Perception of our discipline', *The History of Economic Thought Bulletin*, 9-28.

Perlman, M. (1990), 'The Fabric of Economics and the Golden Threads of G.L.S. Shackle', in Frowen, S.F.(ed.) (1990), ch. 2, 9-19.

Pesaran, M.H. (1984), 'The New Classical Macroeconomics: A Critical Exposition', in Ploeg, F. van der (ed.)(1984), ch. 9, 195-215.

Pesaran, M.H. (1987), *The limits to Rational Expectations*, Oxford: Basil Blackwell.

Pesaran, H., and Smith, R. (1985), 'Keynes on Econometrics', in Lawson, T., and Pesaran, H.(eds.) (1985), ch. 8, 134-150.

Ploeg, F. van der (ed.)(1984), *Mathematical Methods in Economics*, New York: John Wiley and Sons.

Poirier, D.J. (1988), 'Frequentist and Subjectivist Perspectives on the Problems of Model Building in Economics' and 'Reply', *Journal of Economic Perspectives*, 2, 1, 121-144, 166-170.

Radner, R. (1987), 'Uncertainty and General Equilibrium', in Eatwell, J., Milgate, M., and Newman, P. (1989), *General Equilibrium*, from the *New Palgrave: A Dictionary of Economics*, (1987), London: MacMillan Press, 305-323.

Radner, R. (1980), 'Collusive Behavior in Non-cooperative Epsilon-equilibria of Oligopolies with Long but Finite Lives', *Journal of Economic Theory*, 22, 136-154, reprinted in Rubinstein, A.(ed.) (1989), *Game Theory in Economics*, Aldershot: Edward Elgar, ch. 19, 373-291.

Rapoport, A. (1987), 'Prisoner's Dilemma', in Eatwell, J., et all (eds.)(1989), 199-204.

Rizzo, M.J. (ed.)(1979), *Time, Uncertainty, and Disequilibrium*, Lexington, Mass: Lexington Books.

Rizzo, M.J. (1979), 'Uncertainty, Subjectivity, and the Economic Analysis of Law', in Rizzo, M.J.(ed.) (1979), 71-90.

Robbins, L.C. (1932), *An Essay on the Nature and Significance of Economic Science*, London: MacMillan Press, second edition, 1935, 1969.

Robbins, L.C. (1979), 'On Latsis's *Method and Appraisal in Economics*: A review essay', *Journal of Economic Literature*, XVII, 996-1004.

Robinson, J. (1978), 'Keynes and Ricardo', *Journal of Post-Keynesian Economics*, 1, 1, 12-18.

Robinson, J. (1980), 'Time in Economic Theory', *Kyklos*, 33, 2, 219-229.

Rothbard, M.N. (1957), 'In defense of "Extreme Apriorism"', *Southern Economic Journal*, 23 (1), 314-320.

Rotheim, R.J. (1988), 'Keynes and the Language of Probability and Uncertainty', *Journal of Post-Keynesian Economics*, 11, 1, 82-99.

Rowley, R., and Hamouda, O.F. (1987), 'Troublesome Probability and Economics', *Journal of Post-Keynesian Economics*, 10, 1, 44-65.

Runde, J. (1993), 'Keynes after Ramsey', Conference Notes, Leeds.

Rust, J. (1988), 'Comment on Poirier: The subjective perspective of a "spiritual Bayesian"', *Journal of Economic Perspectives*, 2, 1, 145-151.

Safra, Z. (1987), 'Contingent Commodities', in Eatwell, J., et all (eds.)(1989a), 22-24.

Sargent, T.C. (1973), 'Rational Economics, the Real Rate of Interest, and the Natural Rate of Unemployment', Brookings papers on economic activity 2, 429-72, reprinted in Lucas, R.E., and Sargent, T.C.(eds.) (1981), 159-198.

Sawyer, M.C. (1991), 'Post-Keynesian Economics; the state of the art', in Adriaansen, W.L.M., and Linden, J.T.J.M. van der (eds.)(1991), 31-56.

Schelling, T.C. (1960), *The Strategy of Conflict*, Oxford University Press.

Schoemaker, P.J.H. (1982), 'The Expected Utility Model: Its variants, purposes, evidence and limitations', *Journal of Economic Literature*, 20, 529-563.

Schotter, A. (1981), *The Economic Theory of Social Institutions*, Cambridge: Cambridge Univeristy Press.

Schotter, A. (1983), 'Why Take a Game Theoretical Approach', *Economie Appliquée*, 36, 4, 673-695.

Schotter, A., and Schwödiauer, G. (1980), 'Economics an the Theory of Games: A Survey', *Journal of Economic Literature*, 18, 479-527.

Schumpeter, J.A. (1911), *The Theory of Economic Development*, Oxford: Oxford University Press, translation, 1934, 1980.

Schumpeter, J.A. (1942), *Capitalism, Socialism, and Democracy*, London: Unwin. Paperback, 7th edition, 1987.

Schumpeter, J.A. (1954), *History of Economic Analysis*, editor Schumpeter, E.B., London: Allen & Unwin. Paperback, 1986.

Schutz, A. (1932), *The Phenomenology of the Social Sciences*, Northwestern University Press, translation, 1967.

Schutz, A. (1953) 'Common-Sense and Scientific Interpretations of Human Action', *Philosophy and Phenomenological Research*, XIV, 1, 1-37, reprinted in Natanson, M.(ed.) (1963), *Philosophy of the Social Sciences*, New York: Random House, 302-348.

Selgin, G.A. (1988), 'Praxeology and Understanding: an analysis of the controversy in Austrian economics', *The Review of Austrian Economics*, 2, 19-58.

Shackle, G.L.S. (1938), *Expectations, Investment and Income*, Oxford: Clarendon Press, 1968.

Shackle, G.L.S. (1949), *Expectations in Economics*, Cambridge: Cambridge University Press, 1952.

Shackle, G.L.S. (1955), *Uncertainty in Economics, and other reflections*, Cambridge: Cambridge University Press, 1968.

Shackle, G.L.S. (1958), *Time in Economics*, Professor Dr. F. de Vries Lectures, Amsterdam: NorthHolland.

Shackle, G.L.S. (1961), *Decision, Order and Time in Human Affairs*, Cambridge: Cambridge University Press, 1969.

Shackle, G.L.S. (1966), *The Nature of Economic Thought*. Selected papers 1955-1964, Cambridge: Cambridge University Press.

Shackle, G.L.S. (1967), *The Years of High Theory. Invention and tradition in economic thought 1926-1939*, Cambridge: Cambridge University Press.

Shackle, G.L.S. (1972), *Epistemics and Economics*, Cambridge: Cambridge University Press.

Shackle, G.L.S. (1973a), 'Keynes and Today's Establishment in Economic Theory: A view', *Journal of Economic Literature*, 11, 2, 516-519, reprinted in Wood, J.C.(ed.) (1983), IV, ch. 111, 1-6.

Shackle, G.L.S. (1974), *Keynesian Kaleidics. The evolution of a general political economy*, Edinburgh: Edinburgh University Press.

Shackle, G.L.S. (1976), 'Time and Choice', Keynes lecture in economics, *Proceeding of the British Academy*, 62, 309-329, reprinted in Shackle, G.L.S. (1990b), 28-48.

Shackle, G.L.S. (1979), *Imagination and the Nature of Choice*, Edinburgh: Edinburgh University Press.

Shackle, G.L.S. (1979a), 'Imagination, Formalism, and Choice', in Rizzo, M.J.(ed.) (1979), ch. 2, 19-31.

Shackle, G.L.S. (1980), 'Evolutions of Thought in Economics', *Banca Nazionale del Lavoro Quarterly Review*, 132, 15-27, reprinted in Shackle, G.L.S. (1990b), 207-219.

Shackle, G.L.S. (1983), 'The Romantic Mountain and the Classic Lake: Alan Coddington's *Keynesian Economics*', *Journal of Post-Keynesian Economics*, 6, 2, 241-251.

Shackle, G.L.S. (1984), 'Comment on the papers by Randall Bausor and Malcolm Rutherford', *Journal of Post-Keynesian Economics*, 6, 3, 388-393.

Shackle, G.L.S. (1988), *Business, Time and Thought. Selected papers of G.L.S. Shackle*, editor Frowen, S.F., London: MacMillan Press.

Shackle, G.L.S. (1990), 'Coping with Uncertainty in Economics: G.L.S. Shackle interviewed by Peter Earl', *Review of Political Economy*, 2, 1, 105-114.

Shackle, G.L.S. (1990a), 'Speech by G.L.S. Shackle at the Conference Dinner of the George Shackle Conference', in Frowen, S.F.(ed.) (1990), 192-196.

Markets, Uncertainty and Economics

Shackle, G.L.S. (1990b), *Time, Expectations and Uncertainty in Economics*, editor Ford, J.L., Aldershot: Edward Elgar.

Shubik, A. (1987), 'Antoine Augustin Cournot', in Eatwell, J., et all (eds.)(1989), 117-128.

Simon, H.A. (1955), 'A Behavioral Model of Rational Choice', *Quartely Journal of Economics*, LXIX, 1, 99-118, reprinted in Simon, H.A. (1957), ch. 14, 241-260.

Simon, H.A. (1956), 'Rational Choice and the Structure of the Environment', *Psychological Review*, 63, 2, 129-138, reprinted in Simon, H.A. (1957), ch. 15, 261-273.

Simon, H.A. (1957) *Models of Man. Social and Rational*, New York: John Wiley and Sons, fascimile Garland, 1987.

Simon, H.A. (1976), 'From Substantive to Procedural Rationality', in Latsis, S.(ed.) (1976), *Method and Appraisal in Economics*, Cambridge: Cambridge University Press, reprinted in Hahn, F., and Hollis, M.(eds.) (1979), *Philosophy and Economic Theory*, Oxford University Press, 65-86.

Simon, H.A. (1978), 'Rationality as Process and as Product of Thought', Richard T. Ely Lecture, *American Economic Review*, 68, 2, 1-16.

Simon, H.A. (1979), 'Rational Decision Making in Business Organizations', Nobel-lecture, *American Economic Review*, 493-513.

Simon, H.A. (1987), 'Rationality in Psychology and Economics', in Hogarth, R.M., and Reder, M.W.(eds.) (1987), 25-40.

Simon, H.A. (1987a) 'Bounded Rationality', in Eatwell, J., et all (eds.)(1989a), 15-18.

Skidelsky, R. 'The Reception of the Keynesian Revolution', in Keynes, M.(ed.) (1975), ch. 11, 89-107.

Smith, V.L. (1991), 'Review Article, of Hogath, R.M., and Reder, M.W.(eds.) (1987), *Rational Choice*', *Journal of Political Economy*, 99, 4, 877-897.

Smith, V.L., McCabe, K.A., and Rassenti, S.J. (1991), 'Lakatos and Experimental Economics', in Marchi, N.B. de, and Blaug, M.(eds.) (1991), 197-226.

Snippe, J. (1987), 'Economic Rationality and the Formation of Expectations: A critical analysis', research memorandum 132, Institute of Economic Research, Faculty of Economics, University of Groningen.

Stein, J.L. (1982), *Monetarist, Keynesian & New Classical Economics*, Oxford: Basil Blackwell.

Stohs, L.M. (1980), '"Uncertainty" in Keynes's *General Theory*', *History of Political Economy*, 12, 3, 372-382.

Sudgen, R. (1987), 'New developments in the theory of choice under uncertainty', in Hey, J.D., and Lambert, P.J.(eds.) (1987), ch. 1, 1-24.

Sweezy, P.M. (1938), 'Expectations and the Scope of Economics', *The Review of Economic Studies*, 5, 234-237.

Thaler, R. (1987), 'The Psychology of Choice and the Assumptions of Economics', in Roth, A.E.(eds.) (1987), *Laboratory Experimentation in Economics*, Cambridge: Cambridge University Press, ch. 4, 99-130.

Townshend, H. (1936), 'Mr. Keynes on Investment', *The Economist*, march 21.

Townshend, H. (1937a), 'Liquidity-Premium and the Theory of Value', *The Economic Journal*, XLVII, 157-169.

Townshend, H. (1937b), 'Review of *Capital and Employment*, by R.G. Hawtrey', *The Economic Journal*, XLVII, 323-325.

Townshend, H. (1938), 'Review of *Expectation, Investment and Income*, by G.L.S. Shackle', *The Economic Journal*, XLVIII, 520-523.

Townshend, H. (1979), 'Correspondence with J.M. Keynes', in Keynes, J.M. (1979).

Tversky, A., and Kahneman, D. (1974), 'Judgement and Uncertainty: Heuristics and biases', *Science*, 185, 1124-1131, reprinted in Diamond, P., and Rothschild, M.(eds.) (1978), ch. 2, 17-34.

Tversky, A., and Kahneman, D. (1981), 'The Framing of Decisions and the Psychology of Choice', *Science*, 211, 453-458, reprinted in Elster, J.(ed.) (1986), ch. 5, 123-141.

Tversky, A., and Kahneman, D. (1982), 'Availibility: A heuristic for judging frequency and probability', in Kahneman, D., Slovic, P., and Tversky, A.(eds.) (1982) *Judgement and Uncertainty: Heuristics and biases*, Cambridge: Cambridge University Press, 163-178.

Ullmann-Margalit, E. (1978), *The Emergence of Norms*, New York: Oxford University Press.

Vanberg, V. (1986), 'Spontaneous Market Order and Social Rules. A critical examination of F.A. Hayek's theory of cultural evolution', *Economics and Philosophy*, 75-100.

Weintraub, E.R. (1975), '"Uncertainty" and the Keynesian Revolution', *History of Political Economy*, 7, 4, 530-548, reprinted in Wood, J.C.(ed.) (1983), IV, ch. 120, 152-168.

Weintraub, S. (1979), 'Generalizing Kalecki and Simplifying Macroeconomics', *Journal of Post-Keynesian Economics*, IV, 3, 101-106.

Williamson, O.E. (1975), *Markets and Hierarchies: Analysis and Antitrust Implications*, New York: Free Press.

Winslow, E.G. (1989), Organic Interdependence, Uncertainty and Economic Analysis', *The Economic Journal*, 99, 1173-1182.

Withers, H. (1927), 'Frederick Lavington (Obit.)', *The Economic Journal*, 37, 503-505.

Wood, J.C.(ed.) (1983), *John Maynard Keynes. Critical Assessment*, Volume IV, London: Croon Helm.

Wubben, E.F.M. (1992), 'The 1930s, The London School of Economics, and Keynesianism', Institute for Economic Research Discussion Paper Series, no. 9214/G, Erasmus University Rotterdam.

Wubben, E.F.M. (1993), 'Changing Winds at the L.S.E.; The rise and fall of ideas in the 1930s', *Tinbergen Institute Research Bulletin*, 5, 1, 1-8.

Zijp, R.W. van (1992), *Austrian and New Classical Business Cycle Theories*, Amsterdam: Thesis Publishers.

Zuidema, J.R. (1986), 'School of Stijl, een Vraagstuk van Indeling', in Zuidema, J.R., *Van Alle Markten Thuis*, Rotterdam: Universitaire Pers Rotterdam, 183-201.

NAME INDEX

A
Allais, M. 61, 62, 64, 208
Angyal, A. 75
Arrow, K.J. 12, 26, 55, 56, 65, 66, 73,
    165, 224, 234, 248
Aumann, R.J. 196, 197, 199, 200, 204,
    213, 220, 223, 228, 233-235

B
Balch, M. 55
Barone, E. 88, 89
Bateman, B.W. 191-193
Bausor, R. 71, 73
Begg, D.K. 70
Bell, D 63
Bernoulli, J. 205
Bianchi, M. 196, 216, 235
Binmore,K. 195, 198, 207, 211, 212,
    227, 235
Blaug, M. 11, 50, 125, 140
Boland, L.A. 98, 103
Brams, S.J. 197
Brandenburger, A. 230, 234
Broome, J. 58
Buchanan, J. 27
Buiter, W.H. 69, 71, 74

C
Caldwell, B.J. 42, 102
Carabelli, A. 188, 190
Carvalho, F. 179
Clark, J.B. 16
Coase, R.H. 39, 40
Coats, A.W. 42
Coddington, A. 126, 177
Cournot, A.-A. 28, 212

D
Da Costa Werlang 230
Damme, E. van 198
Davidson, P. 69, 73, 74, 126, 179-181,
    183
Davis, J.B. 191
Debreu, G. 12, 55, 56, 65, 66, 248
Dekel, E. 234
Dimand, R.W. 190
Dow, S.C. 126, 190
Drèze, J.H. 5, 56, 61, 66

E
Eastham, J.K. 46
Eatwell, J. 132, 183, 197
Ebeling, R.M. 119
Eggertsson, T. 216
Eichenberger, R 60
Eichner, A.S. 179, 185, 186
Eliot, T.S. 241
Elster, J. 165, 205, 223, 226
Emmett, R.B. 27

F
Field, A.J. 213, 214, 220
Fishburn, P.C. 200, 203, 206, 208
Fitzgibbons, A. 188
Ford, J.L. 56
Frey, B.S. 10, 60, 195
Fudenberg, D. 233

G
Garrison, R.W. 112, 113
Gauthier, D.P. 238
Gerrard, B. 187, 189, 193
Gordon, W. 10, 21
Grossman, H.I. 69, 70, 72

H
Hacking, I. 16, 28, 29, 54
Hahn, F. 56, 66, 234
Halpern, J.Y. 224, 229, 230, 233, 234
Hamilton, W.H. 10
Hammond, P.J. 27, 42, 55, 65
Hamouda, O.F. 15, 54, 191
Harcourt, G.C. 143, 149, 179, 183, 185
Hardin, G. 216
Hargreaves Heap, S. 219, 224-226
Harrod, R.F. 185, 187, 192
Harsanyi, J.C. 202, 212, 216, 226-228
Hart, A.G. 47-53, 55, 60
Hartogh, G. den 238
Hawley, F.B. 16, 17
Hayek, F.A. von 7, 80, 90-103, 110-112,
    122, 123, 125, 142, 143, 145
Hey, J.D. 6, 55-58, 60, 61, 64, 178, 201,
    202, 206-209
Hicks, J.R. 36-39, 47, 93, 126, 133-136,
    142-150, 193
High, J. 109
Hildenbrand, W. 200

SUMMARY / SAMENVATTING

Dit onderzoek levert een bijdrage tot vergelijking van verschillende economische scholen, middels het presenteren van een staalkaart van concepten van en meningen over economische onzekerheid, de consequenties voor de vorming van verwachtingen en het daarna komen tot besluiten. Het zal na lezing duidelijk zijn dat wetenschappers het, gewoonlijk niet of nauwelijks gemaakte, onderscheid tussen risico en onzekerheid niet kunnen veronachtzamen.

Frank Knight wordt algemeen beschouwd als de eerste econoom die het onderscheid tussen onzekerheid en risico expliciet aan de orde stelde. Hij introduceert het onderscheid in het boek *Risk, Uncertainty and Profit* (1921), waarin hij stelt dat de verklaring voor winsten en verliezen moet worden gezocht in economische onzekerheid. Hij werkt deze verklaring uit op twee nivo's: nivo één, dat van ieder die besluiten neemt. Onzekerheid veroorzaakt problemen voor besluitvorming, omdat juist belangrijke ontwikkelingen nauwelijks voorzienbaar zijn; nivo twee, dat van de (be)studerende econoom. Onzekerheid lijkt ten grondslag te liggen aan het verschil tussen de eisen en mogelijkheden van onderzoek enerzijds en de veranderlijke economische omstandigheden anderzijds. Omdat onzekerheid derhalve een fundamentele invloed uitoefent op zowel besluitvorming als op economisch onderzoek is het bestuderen van onzekerheid van groot belang.

Bezie de volgende driedeling: (1) Algemeen gesteld kunnen we zeggen dat er in een situatie van *zekerheid* slechts één uitkomst of konklusie mogelijk is. (2) In een toestand van *waarschijnlijkheid* of risico, maw. bij een kansverdeling, is er veel kennis aanwezig, namelijk over de verdeling van de mogelijke uitkomsten. (3) Knight nu stelt dat economen moeten spreken van *onzekerheid* indien er wel enige kennis is over de mogelijke uitkomsten, maar waarbij een achterliggende theorie (zoals gebruikt bij een loterij) of een verzameling relevante ervaringsgegevens (zoals de wachttijden bij een brug) ontbreekt. Onzekerheid is typisch van belang bij structurele veranderingen, omdat het dan zowel de economische besluitvormers als de hun observerende economen ontbreekt aan voldoende kennis om een besluit te onderbouwen met kansverdelingen. Het gebruik van een kansverdeling is dan niet te rechtvaardigen. Bijvoorbeeld, het al of niet ontstaan van een Europese munt of een Aziatisch handelsblok is niet in kansverdelingen te vangen. Dat kan ook worden gezegd van het einde van een hoogconjunctuur, de vraag naar vliegtuigen, het aanbod van rolschaatsen, de koers van de Japanse Yen over één jaar en de winst van een specifiek, recent gestart bedrijf. Discussies over het belang van onzekerheid en de onbruikbaarheid van een kansverdeling lijken vaak neer te komen op de vraag of dat een situatie van besluitvorming relatief uniek is, of dat deze past in wat een voortgaand stabiel patroon lijkt te zijn.

De onderzoeksvraag van het onderzoek is de volgende: hoe is onzekerheid in de economische theorievorming geïntroduceerd en wat zijn de gevolgen hiervan voor een theoretisch onderbouwde besluitvorming? Om tot een antwoord te komen is voornamelijk historisch onderzoek verricht naar de (evoluerende) meningen over onzekerheid in diverse stromingen binnen het economisch denken. Er is niet gezocht naar een bespreking van actuele meningen omtrent onzekerheid. De ontwikkeling van visies en hun opkomst en neergang lijkt leerzamer te zijn dan een verzameling van, immer voorlopige, posities op één moment. Vanwege in hoofdstuk één gegeven redenen is een inperking gemaakt tot de ontwikkelingen in deze eeuw. Empirische toetsingen lijken in deze ontwikkelingen nauwelijks van belang.

In deze geschiedschrijving van ideeën over onzekerheid is per hoofdstuk een stijl of school in het economisch denken te besproken. Achtereenvolgens komen aan de orde: de hoofdstroming van economische ideeën in het interbellum; de voornaamste micro- en macro-economische benaderingen sinds de Tweede Wereldoorlog; de Oostenrijkse School; de (Post-) Keynesiaanse stromingen; en ten slotte de Economische Speltheorie. De beschrijvingen zijn, hoewel uitgebreid, niet uitputtend te noemen. Hiervoor is een rechtvaardiging voorhanden: een dergelijk uitgebreid werk over de introductie van onzekerheid in de economische wetenschap is nog niet geschreven.

Na het inleidende eerste hoofdstuk, wordt in hoofdstuk twee de in het interbellum dominante visies op onzekerheid gepresenteerd. Hoe gingen deze economen om met het door Knight beschreven concept van onzekerheid? Tijdens het interbellum verschuift het door Knight gegeven concept van onzekerheid langzaam maar zeker naar de zijlijn, waarna het uiteindelijk uit het gezichtsveld verdwijnt en op een zijspoor terecht komt. Een benadering, waarin de beperkingen van de beoefening van economie naar voren komen, heeft dan plaats gemaakt voor een geloof in de voorspelbaarheid van toekomstige ontwikkelingen. Een tweede gesignaleerde trend is de volgende: veranderingen worden meer en meer gezien als zijnde onderworpen aan (kans-)wetten. Het dan veel gebruikte concept van onzekerheid verwijst naar het meer of minder breed zijn van kansverdelingen.

In hoofdstuk drie worden naoorlogse ontwikkelingen van de dominante benadering binnen de economie van onzekerheid beschreven, inclusief de uiteindelijke ontkenning van het belang van onzekerheid voor economisch onderzoek. Na de Tweede Wereldoorlog is onzekerheid vooral gebruikt als een wat losse term voor de ontkenning van zekerheid. Daarbij wordt in de bestudering van economische handelingen veelal aangenomen dat de wereld, in onze overpeinzingen of in werkelijkheid, bestaat uit kansverdelingen. Het micro-economisch onderzoek concentreert zich op het model van het verwachte nut. In de loop der decennia komen opeenvolgende versies hiervan onder vuur van de resultaten uit besluitvormings-experimenten. Het macro-economisch onderzoek neemt veelal het Arrow-Debreu model als uitgangspunt. De waarde van dit model is sterk verzwakt nadat bleek dat er een grote afstand bestaat tussen de alomvattende theorie met zijn vele markten en de beperkte dynamische werkelijkheid. De tendens binnen voornoemd onderzoek verschuift in de richting van meer beschrijvend onderzoek naar hoe mensen (zouden moeten) omgaan met (gebrek aan) informatie. Voordat het empirisch onderzoek fatale gevolgen kon hebben voor de onderliggende aanpak van economische problemen onder onzekerheid, werd de Nieuw Klassieke benadering populair. Hierin komt de visie naar voren dat economen al het economisch handelen mogen beschouwen als trekkingen uit gekende stabiele kansverdelingen. Aldus wordt het theoretisch uitgesloten dat innovaties, verrassingen en onverwachte veranderingen het object van onderzoek fundamenteel kunnen wijzigen, en wordt de bruikbaarheid van kansverdelingen veilig gesteld.

In hoofdstuk vier staat de Oostenrijkse School centraal. In contrast tot de meeste economen die tot dan toe zijn behandeld, hebben aanhangers van de Oostenrijkse School een uitermate positief oordeel over onzekerheid en wordt onzekerheid gezien als een overheersende factor in economisch handelen, zowel op de korte als op de lange termijn. In de theorievorming wordt sterk de nadruk gelegd op de logica van het menselijk handelen, 'praxeologie' genoemd, omdat de voorspellingen uit de economische theorie nooit exact terug te vinden zijn in een economie. Economische handelingen zijn dan niet slechts logisch gevolgtrekkingen uit berekeningen, maar het resultaat van de daaropvolgende bewuste keuzes. Het hoofdstuk begint bij Mises die reeds in de jaren twintig een, later uitgewerkte, theorie geeft van een zich voortdurend transformerende economie. Problematisch voor zijn theorie is de mogelijkheid dat verschillende mensen, met hun eigen handelingen gericht op een onzekere toekomst, elkaar al of niet bewust tegenwerken: aktiviteiten coördineren dan niet. Daarop wordt binnen deze school de nadruk verlegd naar de markt als transporteur van informatie. Het ontstaan van informatie en het decoderen van verkregen informatie is uitgewerkt: de alerte ondernemer zal de eerste zijn om signalen te combineren tot nieuwe informatie, die mogelijk een winst in zich houdt. In dit speuren is het belang van de econoom beperkt. Vanwege de veranderlijkheid van de economie is ook het decoderen van informatie in unieke en typische informatie bestudeerd. Aangezien verwachtingen niet in een causale relatie staan met de verkregen informatie is ook het voorspellen problematisch. Mede daarom worden beslissingen soms op gronden van gewoonten en normen genomen. We zien dat Oostenrijkers meer en meer ondernemersgewijs handelen bestuderen in samenhang met regelgeleid handelen.

In hoofdstuk vijf, dat gaat over (Post-)Keynesiaanse gedachten omtrent onzekerheid, is de ontwikkeling eerder andersom: de aandacht verschuift langzaam van regelgeleid handelen naar zowel regelgeleid als ondernemend handelen. Keynesianen delen het Oostenrijkse geloof in een zo zuiver mogelijke markteconomie niet. Een zekere mate van onzekerheid wordt positief gevonden omdat het de dynamiek van de economie weerspiegelt. Bij een grote onzekerheid kan het echter leiden tot een stilvallen van activiteiten. Na een bespreking van de plaats van onzekerheid in Keynes' voornaamste werk wordt de invloed hiervan op andere economen bestudeerd. Het blijkt dat al direct duidelijke interpretatie-verschillen bestaan aangaande het belang van dynamiek, onzekerheid en verwachtingsvorming. Al snel domineert de interpretatie van Hicks. Hieruit volgt een boekhoudkundige visie op onzekere ontwikkelingen, waarmee de verwachtingen van mensen misschien wel kunnen worden gestabiliseerd, maar waarbij van de dynamiek van de economie wordt geabstraheerd. Daartegenover staat de visie van Shackle over onzekerheid, verwachtingen en besluitvorming. Zijn verzet tegen kanstheorie en zijn pleidooi voor een verwachtingstheorie gebaseerd op wat mensen voor mogelijk houden, lijkt in het verlengde te liggen van de positie van Knight. Meer recent werk binnen deze stroming presenteert een verscheidenheid aan gedachten over en concepten van onzekerheid. De economie wordt gezien als een proces in de tijd, waarbij verwachtingen cruciaal zijn voor economische resultaten. Op hun beurt zijn economische, sociale, politieke en juridische instituties cruciaal voor economisch handelen.

In hoofdstuk zes wordt een stroming besproken van recente datum, de Economische Speltheorie, alhoewel ook voor deze theorie reeds aanzetten werden gegeven in de jaren dertig en veertig van deze eeuw. In deze aanpak staat de interactie tussen personen in besluitvorming en in het economisch handelen centraal. Onzekerheid is expliciet gemaakt als een verzameling van mogelijke uitkomsten. Men heeft getracht om een aantal opvallende en informatieve spelvormen door te denken. In het geval van interdependente uitkomsten onder onafhankelijke besluitvorming (bv. een spel tegen de natuur), zijn een aantal bruikbare besluitvormingscriteria ontwikkeld. In het geval dat mensen proberen te anticiperen of te reageren op elkaars besluiten lijkt het nuttig om (non-) coördinatie en (non-) coöperatie te onderscheiden als twee relevante dimensies. Bij nadere beschouwing blijkt de speltheorie sterk afhankelijk te zijn van de assumpties betreffende rationaliteit en kennis. Het onderwaarderen van conventies en normen in economisch handelen komt hierbij vanzelf naar voren.

In het concluderende slothoofdstuk is een overzicht van posities opgenomen betreffende onder andere het concept van onzekerheid, de oorzaak van onzekerheid en de gevolgen ervan. Vervolgens zijn enkele conclusies getrokken: in de bestudering van onzekerheid worden de lokale omstandigheden van een situatie van besluitvorming belangrijk gevonden; verschillende stromingen in het economisch denken groeien naar elkaar toe in het bestuderen van zowel regelgeleid als ondernemend gedrag; en de relatie tussen theorie en realiteit wordt geregeld als problematische ervaren.

De eindkonklusie is dat onzekerheid een fundamentele en functie vervult in economisch gedrag en onderzoek, hoewel veel economen het belang van onzekerheid proberen te ontkennen. Dit laatste lijkt met name aanwezig wanneer onderzoeksprioriteiten in eerste instantie liggen bij het ontwikkelen van theoretische concepten, en niet bij verschaffen van inzichten in praktisch economisch handelen onder onzekerheid.

The Tinbergen Institute is the Netherlands Research Institute and Graduate School for General and Business Economics founded by the Faculties of Economics (and Econometrics) of the Erasmus University in Rotterdam, the University of Amsterdam and the Free University in Amsterdam. The Tinbergen Institute, named after the Nobel prize laureate professor Jan Tinbergen, is responsible for the PhD-program of the three faculties mentioned. Since January 1991 also the Economic Institute of the University of Leiden participates in the Tinbergen Institute.

Copies of the books which are published in the Tinbergen Institute Research Series can be ordered through Thesis Publishers, P.O. Box 14791, 1001 LG Amsterdam, The Netherlands, phone: +3120 6255429; fax: +3120 6203395.

The following books already appeared in this series:

Subseries A. General Economics

no. 1   Otto H. Swank, "Policy Makers, Voters and Optimal Control, Estimation of the Preferences behind Monetary and Fiscal Policy in the United States".

no. 2   Jan van der Borg, "Tourism and Urban Development. The impact of tourism on urban development: towards a theory of urban tourism, and its application to the case of Venice, Italy".

no. 3   Albert Jolink, "Liberté, Egalité, Rareté. The Evolutionary Economics of Léon Walras".

no. 5   Rudi M. Verburg, "The Two Faces of Interest. The problem of order and the origins of political economy and sociology as distinctive fields of inquiry in the Scottish Enlightenment".

no. 6   Harry P. van Dalen, "Economic Policy in a Demographically Divided World".

no. 8   Marjan Hofkes, "Modelling and Computation of General Equilibrium".

no. 12   Kwame Nimako, "Economic Change and Political Conflict in Ghana 1600-1990".

no. 13   Ans Vollering, "Care Services for the Elderly in the Netherlands. The PACK-AGE model".

no. 15   Cees Gorter, "The dynamics of unemployment and vacancies on regional labour markets".

no. 16   Paul Kofman, "Managing primary commodity trade (on the use of futures markets)".

no. 18   Philip Hans Franses, "Model selection and seasonality in time series".

no. 19   Peter van Wijck, "Inkomensverdelingsbeleid in Nederland. Over individuele voorkeuren en distributieve effecten".

no. 20   Angela van Heerwaarden, "Ordering of risks. Theory and actuarial applications".

no. 21   Jeroen C.J.M. van den Bergh, "Dynamic Models for Sustainable Development".

no. 22   Huang Xin, "Statistics of Bivariate Extreme Values".

no. 23   Cees van Beers, "Exports of Developing Countries. Differences between South-South and South-North trade and their implications for economic development".